The
best preparation for

LISTENING

1
Level

The best preparation for Listening **Level 1**

Published by Nexus Co., Ltd.
5, Jimok-ro, Paju-si, Gyeonggi-do, 10880, Korea
www.nexusEDU.kr

Authors: Nexus Contents Development Team, Miran Hong
Publisher: Sangjin Lim
ISBN: 978-89-6790-702-0 54740 ㉓
      978-89-6790-701-3 (SET)
Copyright © 2014 Nexus Co., Ltd.

Printed in Korea

The
best preparation for

LISTENING

Nexus Contents Development Team · Miran Hong

1
Level

NEXUS Edu

How do we improve listening skills?

According to Asher (1974) and Hughes (1992), the four skills of language (speaking, listening, reading, and writing) are fundamentally intertwined. Then improving one language skill facilitates improvement in the other three language skills. In order to reflect this perspective during the development process of this new listening textbook, we designed tasks that give learners opportunities to relate their understanding of the sound-based messages to tasks that require speaking, reading and writing. There are several ways in which this listening series offers benefits to language learners.

Language learners need to be aware of variations in expression. We present listening information in different forms, such as in paraphrases and summaries, in order to help learners improve their awareness of how language structures are manipulated. Carefully chosen tasks encourage learners to compare, contrast, and analyze information received in different forms and to produce language appropriate to the different forms. Learners can notice the variety of language structures that reflect the way English is actually used. Sharing information in a real-life language interaction is not, after all, mostly contained in one structure.

Language learners need a variety of interesting contexts in order to make the learning experience memorable. The dialogs and passages in our listening series are in themselves interesting and offer a variety of information and ideas that add to the learner's store of general knowledge. As language learners work within these interesting contexts, they also gain awareness of differences in spoken and written discourse.

We encourage language learners to take advantage of the chances offered by this textbook to improve their listening skills in a more effective way, not only through sound-based comprehension drills, but also through our integrated skill-based tasks and structurally manipulated linguistic tasks such as summarizing and paraphrasing.

 Contents

Preface

Contents

Unit Preview

Answers

Unit Preview

Getting Ready

Students are introduced to the unit's topic. Key expressions of the unit are presented through simple exercises.

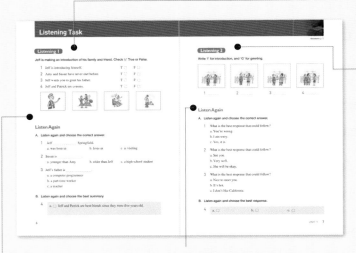

Listening Task

Listening 1 · 2

Students listen to four or five short listening scripts commonly used in everyday speech. The exercises check general comprehension of the listening material.

Listen Again

Students listen to each passage one more time.

A These multiple-choice exercises check specific level of comprehension of the listening material.

B These simple exercises require students to analyze and summarize the text-based information.

Review

Students review, by dictation,
the unit's key vocabulary and expressions.

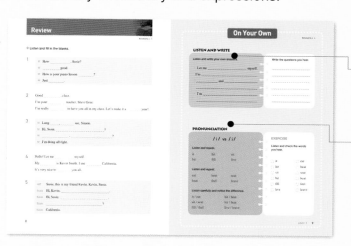

On Your Own

Listen & Write

Students identify the topic
and relate it in their own lives.

Pronunciation

Basic pronunciation rules are
reinforced for better listening
comprehension.

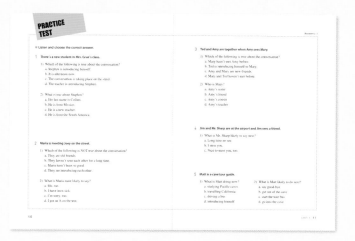

Practice Test

These multiple-choice exercises test students
on material from the entire unit.

Dictation

Students can check their
ability to write precisely what
they hear.

Answers & Translations

The answers and translations for each unit are found in this section.
Students can match their answers with the help of the answer key.

Vocabulary Test

Available via download from **www.nexusEDU.kr,**
each unit's vocabulary test enables accurate assessment of student's retention of key vocabulary.

UNIT
1

Hi! My name is Jeff Brown.

Answers p. 2

GETTING READY

1 Write 'G' for greeting, and 'I' for introduction.

Hi, my name is John Smith. _____

Hi, how are you doing? _____

How do you do, Mr. White? _____

Long time no see. _____

How have you been? _____

Let me introduce myself. _____

John, meet my friend Nancy. _____

Nice to meet you. _____

I'd like you to meet my friend, John. _____

2 Match the questions with the answers.

1. How are you? •　　• a. I'm from California.

2. Where are you from? •　　• b. Nice to meet you, too.

3. Nice to meet you. •　　• c. Fine, thanks. And you?

4. Let me introduce my friend John. •　　• d. Pretty well.

5. How's everything going? •　　• e. Hi, John. Nice to meet you.

Listening Task

Listening 1

Jeff is making an introduction of his family and friend. Check  True or False.

1	Jeff is introducing himself.	T ☐	F ☐
2	Amy and Susan have never met before.	T ☐	F ☐
3	Jeff wants you to greet his father.	T ☐	F ☐
4	Jeff and Patrick are cousins.	T ☐	F ☐

Listen Again

A. Listen again and choose the correct answer.

1 Jeff _____ Springfield.

    a. was born in   b. lives in   c. is visiting

2 Susan is _____.

    a. younger than Amy   b. older than Jeff   c. a high school student

3 Jeff's father is _____.

    a. a computer programmer

    b. a part-time worker

    c. a teacher

B. Listen again and choose the best summary.

4   a. ☐ Jeff and Patrick are best friends since they were five years old.

       b. ☐ Jeff and Patrick go to the same school since they were five.

Listening 2

Write 'I' for introduction, and 'G' for greeting.

1 _____   2 _____   3 _____   4 _____

Listen Again

A. **Listen again and choose the correct answer.**

1   What is the best response that could follow?
    a. You're wrong.
    b. I am sorry.
    c. Yes, it is.

2   What is the best response that could follow?
    a. See you.
    b. Very well.
    c. She will be okay.

3   What is the best response that could follow?
    a. Nice to meet you.
    b. It's hot.
    c. I don't like California.

B. **Listen again and choose the best response.**

4   a. ☐   b. ☐   c. ☐

Review

Answers p. 3

✳ Listen and fill in the blanks.

1

M How _____, Susie?

W _____ good.

M How is your piano lesson _____?

W Just _____.

2

Good _____, class.

I'm your _____ teacher, Sheri Grue.

I'm really _____ to have you all in my class. Let's make it a _____ year!

3

W Long _____ see, Simon.

M Hi, Susie. _____?

W _____. _____?

M I'm doing all right.

4

Hello! Let me _____ myself.

My _____ is Kevin Smith. I am _____ California.

It's very nice to _____ you all.

5

Jeff   Susie, this is my friend Kevin. Kevin, Susie.

Susie Hi, Kevin. _____.

Kevin Hi, Susie. _____.

Susie _____?

Kevin California.

On Your Own

Answers p. 4

LISTEN AND WRITE

Listen and write your own answers.

Write the questions you hear.

- Let me _____ myself.

  I'm _____

  _____ and _____

  _____

- I'm _____

  _____

_____

_____

_____

_____

_____

_____

PRONUNCIATION

/ i / vs / iː /

Listen and repeat.

it	hit	sit
bit	fill	live

Listen and repeat.

eat	heat	seat
beat	feel	leave

Listen carefully and notice the difference.

it / eat	hit / heat
sit / seat	bit / beat
fill / feel	live / leave

EXERCISE

Listen and check the words you hear.

- ☐ it
- ☐ hit
- ☐ sit
- ☐ bit
- ☐ fill
- ☐ live

- ☐ eat
- ☐ heat
- ☐ seat
- ☐ beat
- ☐ feel
- ☐ leave

✳ Listen and choose the correct answer.

1 **There's a new student in Mrs. Grue's class.**

1) Which of the following is true about the conversation?
   a. Stephen is introducing himself.
   b. It is afternoon now.
   c. The conversation is taking place on the street.
   d. The teacher is introducing Stephen.

2) What is true about Stephen?
   a. His last name is Collins.
   b. He is from Mexico.
   c. He is a new teacher.
   d. He is from the South America.

2 **Maria is meeting Joey on the street.**

1) Which of the following is NOT true about the conversation?
   a. They are old friends.
   b. They haven't seen each other for a long time.
   c. Maria hasn't been so good.
   d. They are introducing each other.

2) What is Maria most likely to say?
   a. Me, too.
   b. I have been sick.
   c. I'm sorry, too.
   d. I got an A on the test.

3   **Ted and Amy are together when Amy sees Mary.**

　1) Which of the following is true about the conversation?
　　　a. Mary hasn't met Amy before.
　　　b. Ted is introducing himself to Mary.
　　　c. Amy and Mary are new friends.
　　　d. Mary and Ted haven't met before.

　2) Who is Mary?
　　　a. Amy's sister
　　　b. Amy's friend
　　　c. Amy's cousin
　　　d. Amy's teacher

4   **Jim and Mr. Sharp are at the airport and Jim sees a friend.**

　1) What is Mr. Sharp likely to say next?
　　　a. Long time no see.
　　　b. I miss you.
　　　c. Nice to meet you, too.

5   **Matt is a cave tour guide.**

　1) What is Matt doing now?
　　　a. studying Pacific caves
　　　b. travelling California
　　　c. driving a bus
　　　d. introducing himself

　2) What is Matt likely to do next?
　　　a. say good-bye
　　　b. get out of the cave
　　　c. start the tour bus
　　　d. go into the cave

1

Ms. Grue Good morning, class. I'd like you to _____ a new _____ this morning. Stephen, will you _____?

Stephen Yes, ma'am. Hello. My name is Stephen Collins. I'm from New Mexico, _____. I'm very _____ to meet you all.

Ms. Grue Let's _____ Stephen with a big hand.

2

Joey Maria, long time _____.

Maria Yeah. So how have you been, Joey?

Joey _____! How about you?

Maria _____. Actually I've been awful.

Joey _____ to hear that. What's the _____?

3

Amy Hi, Mary!

Mary Hi, Amy!

Amy Do you two know _____?

Mary No, I don't _____ so.

Amy Well, then _____ introduce you two. Mary, this is my _____ _____ Ted Norton. Ted, this is Mary Smith. She's my cousin.

Ted It's very _____ to meet you, Mary.

Mary _____ to meet you, Ted.

4

Jim Mary? Is that really you?

Mary It certainly is!

Jim Long time no see.

_____?

Mary _____!

Jim Oh, excuse my bad manners! Mary, _____ my boss Mr. Sharp. He is _____ Germany.

Mary Nice to meet you, Mr. Sharp.

5

Good morning! _____ myself. I'm Matt. I'm your _____, today. _____ California, and I study Pacific caves. Also, I want you to _____ our driver Dan. Please _____ that we need to be quiet inside the cave. Now, _____ my light.

Do you like sports?

Answers p. 6

GETTING READY

1 Write the following words in the correct column.

science	football	math	physical education(P.E.)	walking
history	cycling	tennis	going to the gym	baseball
hiking	hockey	volleyball	social studies	

School Subjects

_____

_____

_____

_____

Team Sports

_____

_____

_____

_____

Individual Sports / Exercise

_____

_____

_____

_____

2 Match the questions with the answers.

1. Do you like sports?   •   • a. I like tennis.

2. What kind of sports do you like? •   • b. It is science.

3. How often do you play?   •   • c. Once a week.

4. What's your favorite subject?   •   • d. No, it isn't.

5. Why do you like it?   •   • e. Because I like the teacher.

6. Is math your favorite?   •   • f. Yes, I do.

Listening Task

Listen and check ☑ 'likes' or 'doesn't like'.

1	Beth	likes	doesn't like		2	Steve	likes	doesn't like
	P.E.					art		
	math					math		
	science					P.E.		
	hockey					skiing		

3	Pete	likes	doesn't like		4	Susie	likes	doesn't like
	music					P.E.		
	going to the gym					history		
	history					dance		
	English					science		

Listen Again

A. Listen again and choose the correct answer.

1 Beth likes P.E. because she _____.

   a. likes the teacher   b. is good at it   c. likes sports

2 Steve likes art because he _____.

   a. likes the teacher   b. is good at it   c. likes his classmates

3 Pete likes the subjects because _____.

   a. he can see his friends there

   b. the classes are not boring

   c. the teachers are fun

B. Listen again and choose the best summary.

4   a. ☐ Susie likes P.E. because she is good at it.

      b. ☐ Susie likes P.E. because the teacher is good-looking.

Listening 2

Listen and match sports with people.

1   2   3   4

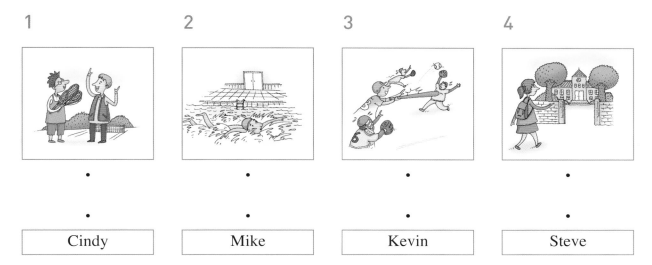

| Cindy | Mike | Kevin | Steve |

Listen Again

A.   **Listen again and choose the true statement.**

1   a. Only Steve plays tennis in his family.

     b. Steve practices tennis hard.

     c. Steve plays tennis because he is not in good shape.

2   a. Mike has a sprained ankle.

     b. Mike has a broken leg.

     c. Mike doesn't exercise at all.

3   a. Kevin doesn't want to join Jeff's baseball club.

     b. Kevin practices baseball hard.

     c. Kevin didn't see the baseball game last night.

B.   **Listen again and choose the correct sentence.**

4   a. ☐   b. ☐

Review

Answers p. 7

✲ **Listen and fill in the blanks.**

1

John What __________ do you like best?

Jane I like __________.

John Me too. I like the __________. Are you __________ at it?

Jane No, I'm not. But I __________ hard.

2

I am too _________. I'm out of shape. So I've started exercising. I __________ in the morning, _________ in the afternoon and _________ to the gym in the evening. It's hard but I feel better about myself. People around me like the change, especially my ______________.

3

Peter What's your ___________ sport?

Susan I like __________. How about you?

Peter I _________ play any sports. I just ________ sometimes.

4

Amy was fat and didn't do any ____________ but now she loves going to the ____________. She exercises there ____________ or four ____________ a week. That is a lot. Maybe that is how she lost ____________ weight.

5

Jeff Wow! You got an A in __________.

Pat Yes. Math is my _________ subject.

Jeff You like math best, don't you?

Pat No, I like ___________ best, but I like our math ___________ best.

On Your Own

Answers p. 8

LISTEN AND WRITE

Listen and write your own answers.

- My _____ subject is _____.
- My _____ subject is _____.
- My _____ teacher is _____.
- I like _____.
- I _____.

Write the questions you hear.

_____

_____

_____

_____

_____

PRONUNCIATION

/ u / vs / uː /

Listen and repeat.

full   pull   look
hood   should

Listen and repeat.

fool   pool   Luke
who'd   shoed

Listen carefully and notice the difference.

full / fool   pull / pool
look / Luke   hood / who'd
should / shoed

EXERCISE

Listen and check the words you hear.

- ☐ full   ☐ fool
- ☐ pull   ☐ pool
- ☐ look   ☐ Luke
- ☐ hood   ☐ who'd
- ☐ should   ☐ shoed

✳ Listen and choose the correct answer.

1   **Brad is talking to Mary about his favorite subject.**

   1) What subject does Brad like best?
      a. math   b. science   c. social studies   d. English

   2) Why does he like the subject?
      a. He likes the teacher.
      b. He is good at it.
      c. The girl he likes is in the class.
      d. There are a lot of secrets.

2   **Susan is talking about her favorite exercise.**

   1) What kind of exercise does Susan like?
      a. swimming   b. walking   c. soccer   d. aerobics

   2) What is NOT a reason Susan likes the exercise?
      a. She can do it with other people.
      b. She likes fresh air.
      c. She can do it anywhere.
      d. She likes to exercise outdoors.

3   **Ben is talking to Jane about what he does after school.**

   1) What kind of sports does Ben play after school?
      a. ice hockey   b. volleyball   c. soccer   d. baseball

   2) What is NOT true about the conversation?
      a. Ben loves sports.
      b. Ben plays ice hockey every day.
      c. Ben goes cycling sometimes.
      d. Ben always exercises after school.

4 **Scott is talking to Annette in the classroom.**

1) What is the girl going to do?
   a. play tennis
   b. swim
   c. meet friends
   d. go to the library

2) What is true about the conversation?
   a. The boy is going to the library.
   b. The girl is going to play tennis.
   c. They will go swimming together.
   d. The girl goes swimming at least once a week.

5 **Andrew and Lesley are talking during a class.**

1) In which class are the boy and the girl talking?
   a. P.E.
   b. math
   c. history
   d. English

2) Which one of the following is NOT true?
   a. The boy likes P.E. because he likes exercise.
   b. The girl likes her history teacher.
   c. The boy is not interested in history.
   d. The boy doesn't like doing homework.

1

Mary   What is your _____ subject, Brad?

Brad   It's science. I love it.

Mary   Because you are _____.
Right?

Brad   No. I am good at _____, but not
at _____.

Mary   Then why do you like science so
much?

Brad   Well, this is a _____ between
you and me. It's because Laura is in
the class. That's why.

Mary   Ah, now _____.

2

I like _____ exercise. I love _____
_____ but I don't like water. I like to
_____ alone. I don't like team
sports. I like this exercise because I can
do it _____. I don't need
anything. I need just _____.
My favorite exercise is _____.

3

Jane   What do you do _____ school,
Ben? You always _____ home.

Ben   I play ice hockey.

Jane   Do you play it _____?

Ben   No, just _____.

Jane   Then what do you do the other days?

Ben   I go cycling.

Jane   You really like _____.

4

Scott   Annette! Are you going to the
_____?

Annette   No, I'm _____.
Do you want to come with me?

Scott   Well, not now. _____
do you go swimming?

Annette   _____, or whenever I
_____.

Scott   I guess it is refreshing.

Annette   Definitely. Do you like swimming,
too?

Scott   _____. But I enjoy
playing tennis.

Annette   Me, too! We should play _____
sometime. I have to go now. Bye!

Scott   See you soon!

5

Andrew   I _____ this class. It's _____,
isn't it?

Lesley   Sometimes, but I like the teacher.

Andrew   Oh, I see. That's why you always
do your _____.

Lesley   Yes. What about you? Which class
do you like _____?

Andrew   I'm _____ but the
teacher gives too much homework.

Lesley   What about P.E.? We don't have
any homework.

Andrew   _____. I think I like
P. E. class best.

UNIT
3

She is tall and thin.

Answers p. 10

GETTING READY

1   What do the following words describe? Write them under the correct title.

long	in her teens	dark	curly	tall	athletic
thin	young	heavy	bald	blond	straight
slim	middle-aged	in his early forties			

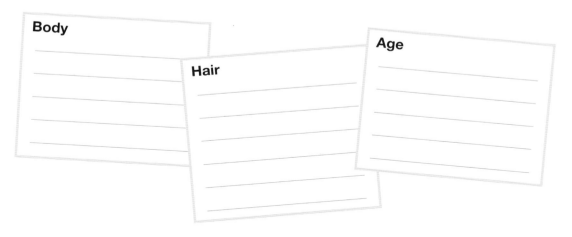

Body

Hair

Age

2   Match the questions with the answers.

1. Is he tall?   •   •   a. No, he doesn't.

2. How tall is he?   •   •   b. Yes, he is.

3. What does she look like? •   •   c. He is six feet tall.

4. Does he have a beard? •   •   d. No, she isn't.

5. Is she wearing glasses? •   •   e. She has dark brown hair.

Listening Task

What are the following descriptions about? Put a check in the right place.

	Hair	Age	Body
1			
2			
3			
4			
5			

Listen Again

A. Listen again and choose the true statement.

1 a. He looks older than he really is.
    b. He is in his thirties.
    c. He is very kind.

2 a. She has brown hair.
    b. Her hair is short and curly.
    c. She has shiny hair.

3 a. He is tall and heavy.
    b. He is a football player.
    c. He has dark skin.

4 a. She has dark hair.
    b. She sometimes keeps her hair long.
    c. Her hair is curly.

B. Listen again and choose the best summary.

5   a. ☐ He is a middle-aged man but he looks younger.
      b. ☐ He is a grandfather and he looks very old.

Listening 2

Who are they talking about? Listen and choose the correct picture.

1   a.    b.

2   a.   b.

3   a.    b.

4   a.    b.

Listen Again

A. Listen again and choose the correct answer.

1   What is Jeff likely to say?

   a. You got it.   b. That's okay.   c. She doesn't know.

2   What is the man likely to say?

   a. No, that isn't true.   b. No, he doesn't.   c. No, I don't.

3   What is the woman likely to say?

   a. No, he isn't.

   b. He doesn't know.

   c. He's wearing a blue shirt.

B. Listen again and choose the best response.

4   a. ☐   b. ☐   c. ☐

Review

Answers p. 12

✳ Listen and fill in the blanks.

1

W _____ does your brother look like?

Is he as _____ as you?

M No, he is not _____. He's thin, _____ and handsome.

2

My little sister is very _____. She has _____ hair and big _____ eyes.

She will be three _____ old next month.

3

M Is this your mother?

W No, she's my aunt. My mom has short _____ hair, and she doesn't

_____ glasses.

M Is she the _____ in the long brown coat?

W That's right.

4

Many people think Mr. Smith is _____ even though he is not that old.

He is only in his _____ forties, but people think he's over _____.

He has _____ hair, and he is a little _____. Maybe that's why.

5

W Sharapova is great! Look at her playing.

M She is very _____. I guess she's over six _____.

W Yes. She is in her _____, and she is the world champion.

M Is she that _____?

W Yes. And she is very _____, isn't she?

LISTEN AND WRITE

Listen and write your own answers.

- I'm _____
- I'm _____ old.
- I _____ than _____
- Yes, I have _____
  No, I don't have _____
- Yes, I _____
  No, I don't _____

Write the questions you hear.

_____

_____

_____

_____

_____

_____

_____

PRONUNCIATION

/ r / vs / l /

Listen and repeat.

right	read	wrong	rate
rock	ray	fry	correct

Listen and repeat.

light	lead	long	late
lock	lay	fly	collect

Listen carefully and notice the difference.

right / light	read / lead
wrong / long	rate / late
rock / lock	ray / lay
fry / fly	correct / collect

EXERCISE

Listen and check the words you hear.

- ☐ right   ☐ light
- ☐ read   ☐ lead
- ☐ wrong   ☐ long
- ☐ rate   ☐ late
- ☐ rock   ☐ lock
- ☐ ray   ☐ lay
- ☐ fry   ☐ fly
- ☐ correct   ☐ collect

✲ Listen and choose the correct answer.

1　**An eight-year-old boy is talking about a girl.**

1) What is NOT mentioned about the girl?
　　a. hair　　　　　b. skin　　　　　c. height　　　　d. eyes

2) What is true about the girl?
　　a. She has black hair.
　　b. She has freckles.
　　c. She has brown eyes.
　　d. She has dark skin.

2　**A mother is reporting about her missing son to a police officer.**

1) The boy is _____.
　　a. short　　　　　b. thin　　　　　c. nine　　　　　d. at home

2) Which of the following is NOT true about the boy?
　　a. His hair is black.
　　b. He is tall.
　　c. He is wearing a red T-shirt.
　　d. He is wearing glasses.

3　**A woman is talking about her friend.**

1) Who is Jane?

a.　　　　　　　b.　　　　　　　c.　　　　　　　d.

4 **A man is trying to find his wife at a beach resort.**

1) The man says his wife is _____.
   a. short
   b. tall
   c. fat
   d. old

2) What is the man likely to do next?
   a. eat dinner
   b. go to the swimming pool
   c. go home
   d. drink soda pop

5 **Sarah and Mike are looking through Mike's photo album.**

1) What is NOT true about the conversation?
   a. Mike was cute and fat when he was a baby.
   b. Mike's grandfather is a movie star.
   c. Mike's grandfather was handsome when he was young.
   d. Mike used to play with his neighbor when he was young.

Answers p. 14

1

I like Jenny. She is very _____. Her _____ are like an ocean. Her long _____ hair moves like grass in the wind. Her skin is _____ and _____. She smiles like an angel. She has some _____ on her face and I love them too. I always look at her but she never looks at me.

2

W Excuse me, officer. Please find my son. He's _____ all day.

M Calm down and tell me. What does he _____?

W He's _____ for _____.

M How old is he?

W Nine.

M What about his _____?

W He has short _____ hair.

M Anything else? Is he wearing _____ or something?

W Not glasses, but he's _____ a red T-shirt and white shorts.

3

My friend Jane is _____, not very tall, not very _____. She's a little _____, but not _____. She has _____ eyes and short brown hair. She likes casual wear so maybe she will be wearing _____ and a shirt.

4

M Can you help me find my wife? I really need to find her _____.

W Sure. What does she look like?

M Well, she's kind of _____, and she's _____.

W Do you remember _____ she is wearing?

M She is wearing a _____ and a red one-piece swim suit.

W I think I saw her at the swimming pool.

5

W Who's this cute _____ baby?

M Doesn't he look like me?

W Not at all! Who's this little, _____ girl wearing _____?

M She was my next door neighbor when I was young. We _____ play all the time.

W I see. What about this tall, _____ man? Is he your dad?

M No, my grandpa _____.

W Really? He _____ a movie star.

UNIT
4

What time do you get up?

Answers p. 15

GETTING READY

1 The following is about John's typical day. Write the time in the blanks.

1. John gets up at _____.

2. He drinks coffee at _____.

3. He exercises from _____ to _____.

4. He leaves home for work at _____.

5. He works from _____ to _____.

6. He comes home at _____.

7. He goes to bed at _____.

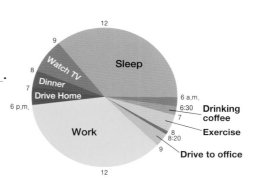

2 Match the questions with the answers.

1. What time do you get up?   •   • a. Six.

2. What do you do after school?   •   • b. My mom does.

3. How do you go to school?   •   • c. No, I don't.

4. How many classes do you have?   •   • d. By bicycle.

5. Do you have a lot of homework?   •   • e. I play baseball.

6. Who wakes you up in the morning?   •   • f. At 7:30.

Listening Task

Listening 1

Jeff is talking about his daily schedule. Listen and write the correct time.

Monday Schedule

1 _____	Get up
2 _____	Get on the school bus
3 _____	School starts
_____	Have lunch
4 _____	Come home from school
Have free time until _____	
_____	Go to bed

Listen Again

A. Listen again and choose the correct answer.

1 How does he wake up in the morning?

    a. His mother wakes him up.

    b. The alarm clock wakes him up.

    c. He wakes up by himself.

2 What does he do first?

    a. take a shower   b. have breakfast   c. read a newspaper

3 What does he do right after lunch?

    a. play baseball   b. go to class   c. play basketball

B. Listen again and choose the best summary.

4   a. ☐ He comes back home at 3:30 and goes to bed at 6 o'clock.

    b. ☐ He comes back home at 3:30 and has free time until 6 o'clock.

Listening 2

People are talking with their doctor. What are their problems?

1
    a. He gets up at 7:30.
    b. He drinks coffee in the morning.

2
    a. She works too much.
    b. She calls too much.

3
    a. She never has any fun.
    b. She sleeps too much.

4
    a. She stays up too late.
    b. She doesn't like her mom.

Listen Again

A. Listen again and choose the correct answer.

1 He gets up at _____.
   a. 6:00   b. 6:30   c. 7:30

2 She starts her daily work at _____.
   a. 8:00   b. 8:30   c. 9:00

3 She usually _____.
   a. has some fun   b. does what most mothers do   c. goes outside

B. Listen again and choose the correct sentence.

4   a. ☐   b. ☐

Answers p. 17

✳ Listen and fill in the blanks.

1

W What time do you _____ in the morning?

M At _____ .

W What do you _____ then?

M I usually _____ a shower.

2

Mom, I'm tired. I have five _____ a day. I do my _____ after school.
I _____ care of our cat Lucy. And sometimes I _____ you with
housework. It's my only free time. Please let me take rest until _____ .

3

M _____ are you at work?

W From _____ in the morning till _____ in the afternoon.

M When do you _____?

W At _____

4

My sister is an early bird. She _____ her day at 5. She sleeps 5 _____
a day and does a lot of work _____ the _____ . She comes back home
around _____ p.m.

5

W Where is Amy?

M She is out. She _____ our dog Max in the _____ .

W When does she _____ back?

M In _____ minutes. She has a piano lesson at _____ .

Answers p. 17

LISTEN AND WRITE

Listen and write your own answers.

- I get up at _____
- I go to school _____
- I go to school _____
- From _____
- I come home _____
- I _____

Write the questions you hear.

_____

_____

_____

_____

_____

PRONUNCIATION

/ s / vs / z /

Listen and repeat.

sing	sip	seal
soon	send	Sue

Listen and repeat.

zing	zip	zeal
zoom	zen	zoo

Listen carefully and notice the difference.

sing / zing	sip / zip
seal / zeal	soon / zoom
send / zen	Sue / zoo

EXERCISE

Listen and check the words you hear.

☐ sing	☐ zing
☐ sip	☐ zip
☐ seal	☐ zeal
☐ soon	☐ zoom
☐ send	☐ zen
☐ Sue	☐ zoo

✳ Listen and choose the correct answer.

1 **A reporter is interviewing Mr. Coleman, CEO of a big restaurant chain.**

1) What is true about Mr. Coleman?
    a. He gets up very early.
    b. He walks for exercise.
    c. He goes to bed after midnight.
    d. He starts his day before noon.

2) What time does he probably drink his first coffee of the day?
    a. at 7:30 a.m.
    b. at 2:00 a.m.
    c. at 1:00 a.m.
    d. at 1:00 p.m.

2 **This is about Bill's job.**

1) What do you think he does?
    a. a doctor
    b. a reporter
    c. a pilot
    d. a policeman

2) What is true about Bill's day?
    a. He goes to bed at the same time every day.
    b. He is always at work during the day.
    c. He sometimes shows up on TV.
    d. He is busy only at night.

3   Pat is asking about Jeff's schedule.

1) What time are they going to meet?
   a. at 4:30 p.m.   b. at 5:30 p.m.
   c. at 6:00 p.m.   d. at 6:30 p.m.

2) Which of the following is true?
   a. Jeff has a busy schedule today.
   b. The piano lesson takes 30 minutes.
   c. Jeff is going to see Pat after the piano lesson.
   d. They will probably play computer games.

4   Sophie wakes up in the afternoon.

1) What happened to Sophie?
   a. She dreamt that she woke up late and missed all her final exams.
   b. She woke up late and realized that she had missed the exams.
   c. She woke up in the afternoon and thought that she had missed all her final exams.
   d. She was very upset because she failed this semester.

2) What time did Sophie plan to finish revising math, science and English?
   a. 5:30   b. 7:00   c. 7:30   d. 8:00

5   Sarah and Sophie are talking on the phone.

1) Where will Sophie and Sarah go tomorrow?
   a. school   b. football club   c. shopping mall   d. home

2) What time are Sarah and Sophie going shopping tomorrow?
   a. 3:30   b. 12:00   c. 5:30   d. 7:00

Dictation

Listen and fill in the blanks.

1

M1 How do you _____ your day?

M2 I have a cup of coffee.

M1 _____ what do you do?

M2 I _____ and read the newspaper.

M1 You do a lot of things in the morning. What time do you _____?

M2 _____ 12:30.

M1 You mean in the morning?

M2 No, in the afternoon. I come home from work after _____. I go to bed at 2:00 in the morning.

2

Bill is _____ all the time. When there are big and small things _____ around town, he is there. There are good and bad _____ all the time. They happen every day and night. Sometimes he _____ at 1:00 a.m., and sometimes at 2:00 p.m. In _____ he writes reports and _____ on TV.

3

Pat Hi, Jeff! I need to see you today. _____ this afternoon?

Jeff I have a _____ at 4:30. That's it.

Pat When does it _____?

Jeff At 5:30. It _____ just one hour.

Pat Can I drop by your house _____ then?

Jeff Sure. Bye. Hey, Pat! _____ the board game with you.

4

Ah~ that was a good sleep. Oh my goodness, it's _____? What am I going to do? I _____ all the final exams! I was _____ wake up at 5:30, revise math, science and English for two hours, eat my _____, and leave home at 8 o'clock. I don't believe this! Sophie, you stupid! Wait, _____? Ah~ it's summer vacation. That _____ was for yesterday. Phew!

5

Sophie Hi, is Sarah there?

Sarah Hi, Sophie! It's me.

Sophie About _____ tomorrow—what time is _____?

Sarah _____ in the afternoon.

Sophie Well, I have to pick my little brother up at 3:30 and then take him to his football club at 5:30. Six o'clock is _____, isn't it?

Sarah Yeah, I think so. Shall we make it _____?

Sophie Good. _____ then.

What's the weather like?

Answers p. 20

1 Write the name of the month, temperature, and the weather word under the correct picture.

dry	sunny	windy	snowy
95°F (36°C)	32°F (0°C)	70°F (22°C)	20°F (-7°C)
January	April	August	October

*F: Fahrenheit C: Celsius

_____   _____   _____   _____

_____   _____   _____   _____

_____   _____   _____   _____

2 Match the questions with the answers.

1. What's the weather like in Tokyo? •   • a. It's thirty-five degrees.

2. What's the temperature? •   • b. No, it isn't.

3. Is it raining yet? •   • c. Yes, we do.

4. Do you have a lot of snow in winter? •   • d. It's freezing in Tokyo.

5. How's the weather in Seoul? •   • e. It's nice and warm.

6. Is there lightning and thunder? •   • f. Yes, there is.

Listening Task

Listen about the weather and number the pictures.

  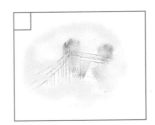 

Listen Again

A. Listen again and choose the false statement.

1   a. It is humid outside.

    b. It is cool outside.

    c. They have the air-conditioner on.

2   a. It is usually foggy in London.

    b. It is cold in London.

    c. The man is talking with his Aunt on the phone.

3   a. Amy is away from home.

    b. Amy is not ready for cold weather.

    c. There is a lot of snow in Washington D.C.

B. Listen again and choose the best summary.

4   a. ☐ It's getting chilly and it's going to rain. It's colder than other years.

    b. ☐ The day is getting dark and it's going to rain. It's cold as usual.

Listening 2

Listen to weather reports and choose the correct answer.

1 What is the weather like today?
   a. It's sunny.   b. It's cold.   c. It's windy.

2 How's the weather today?
   a. It's stormy.   b. It's snowing.   c. It's very cold.

3 What's the weather like today?
   a. very foggy   b. very hot   c. very humid

4 How's the weather today?
   a. sunny but cold   b. hot and rainy   c. cloudy and windy

Listen Again

A. Listen again and choose the correct answer.

1 The weather will be _____ tomorrow.
   a. the same   b. better   c. worse

2 The weather tomorrow will be _____.
   a. better   b. nice and sunny   c. even colder

3 The weather will be _____ tomorrow.
   a. still foggy   b. sunny   c. rainy

B. Listen again and choose the correct sentence.

4   a. ☐   b. ☐

Review

Answers p. 22

✳ **Listen and fill in the blanks.**

1

M What is the _____ like today?

W It is hot and _____ .

M What's the _____ ?

W It is 96 _____ Fahrenheit.

2   It is warm and partly _____ nationwide. The _____ are in the _____ seventies, and the _____ are in the _____ fifties. The temperature will drop to the high _____ into the night and it will get _____ tomorrow.

3

M _____ is the weather there in London?

W The weatherman says it's _____ .

M _____ warm there?

W No, it's pretty _____ .

4   Dear Diary,

Maybe we have to cancel our trip next _____ . The weather _____ says it will be _____ . They said it's going to be stormy from _____ through _____ . I really hope the _____ gets better because I really want to go.

5

M Brr... It's _____ .

W Is it still _____ ?

M No, it's not. But the _____ is getting stronger.

W Maybe we should make sure all the windows are shut.

On Your Own

Answers p. 22

LISTEN AND WRITE

Listen and write your own answers.

- Today is _____.
- I think it's about _____.
- Yes, _____.
- No, _____.
- I favorite season is _____.
- Because _____.

Write the questions you hear.

_____

_____

_____

_____

_____

_____

PRONUNCIATION

/ v / vs / b /

Listen and repeat.

van	very	vote
calve	dove	jive

Listen and repeat.

ban	berry	boat
cab	dub	jibe

Listen carefully and notice the difference.

van / ban	very / berry
vote / boat	calve / cab
dove / dub	jive / jibe

EXERCISE

Listen and check the words you hear.

☐ van	☐ ban
☐ very	☐ berry
☐ vote	☐ boat
☐ calve	☐ cab
☐ dove	☐ dub
☐ jive	☐ jibe

✳ Listen and choose the correct answer.

1 This is a weekly weather forecast.

1) How does the weather change? [Listen twice.]
   a. cloudy   →   stormy   →   sunny
   b. cloudy   →   sunny   →   stormy
   c. sunny   →   cloudy   →   rainy
   d. rainy   →   stormy   →   sunny

2) When will they see the blue sky?
   a. on Monday   b. on Tuesday   c. on Thursday   d. on Friday

2 Two people are talking about the seasons.

1) What season is it now?
   a. spring   b. summer   c. autumn   d. winter

2) What was the weather like in the summer?
   a. hot and dry   b. warm and humid
   c. hot and humid   d. cool and dry

3 Two people are talking about weather.

1) What is the weather like today?
   a. snowy   b. stormy   c. rainy   d. cold

2) Which of the following is NOT true about the conversation?
   a. The weather will be worse tomorrow.
   b. It will be rainy tomorrow.
   c. The weather is very unusual this year.
   d. It was warm in the spring.

4 **The following is an e-mail message.**

  1) Who wrote this mail to whom?
     a. Regina wrote it to Jane.
     b. Jane wrote it to Sarah.
     c. Jane wrote it to Regina.
     d. Regina wrote it to Sarah.

  2) How's the weather in Rome in December?
     a. It snows much.
     b. It usually rains.
     c. It's cold.
     d. It's cloudy.

5 **Tom is talking to his mom.**

  1) What is the best response that could follow?
     a. That's a great news.
     b. I don't like hot weather.
     c. I like rainy day.
     d. Today's weather is nice.

  2) What is the conversation about?
     a. Today's temperature
     b. Saturday's temperature
     c. Today's and Saturday's weather
     d. Saturday's picnic

1

The weather will be very _____ this week. On Monday it will be _____ and _____. Tuesday through Thursday it will be _____ and very _____. There will even be thunderstorms and lightning. The _____ weather will clear up from Thursday evening, and on Friday morning we'll see _____ blue skies all over the nation. The weekend will be sunny and clear.

2

M Look at the color of the trees. I like this _____. It's cool and dry. It's _____.

W Same here. The summer was too _____ and _____. I could hardly breathe in the summer.

M That's true. But this season is too short. The leaves are already starting to fall. I don't like _____ either.

3

W I am all _____. I am really tired of this _____.

M Me, too. There is too much rain this summer.

W The weather is crazy this year. It was very _____ in the spring.

M Yes, it even _____.

W How about tomorrow? Did you hear the _____ for tomorrow?

M Yes. It will be worse tomorrow. There will be _____.

4

Hi, Regina!

I'm now in the Vatican City in Rome. It's a _____ city but I'm not happy. Can you guess why? It's not _____! The weather forecast said it won't snow all December. People here tell me that it's the _____. It's raining every day. I will write again soon. _____ to Sarah for me!

Love,
Jane

5

Tom Mom, I feel hot. Can you get me a glass of water?

Mom What's the weather like _____?

Tom It's _____. It's 33 _____ today. Didn't you listen to the weather forecast?

Mom No. Do you know what the weather will be like this _____? I'm going on a _____.

Tom On Saturday, it'll be _____ and about 22 degrees.

Where is my shirt?

Answers p. 24

1   Find the items in the picture and write the number in the blank.

It is on the table.   _____

It is by the door.   _____

It is behind the sofa.   _____

It is in the middle of the room.   _____

It is next to the sofa.   _____

2   Match the questions with the answers.

1. Where is the bookshelf?   •   •   a. Yes, there is.

2. Is there a table in the room?   •   •   b. There are three.

3. How many cupboards are there?   •   •   c. I see them in the corner.

4. Where do you see the plants?   •   •   d. Yes, it is.

5. Is the stove opposite the window? •   •   e. It's next to the sofa.

Listening 1

Sue is moving in. She's telling a helper where to put the items. Put the numbers.

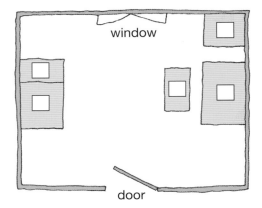

Listen Again

A. Listen again and choose the true statement.

1   a. The sofa is in front of the window.

    b. The sofa is beside the window.

    c. The sofa is on the right side of the room.

2   a. The nightstand isn't close to the sofa.

    b. The nightstand is in the right corner.

    c. The sofa is in the left corner.

3   a. The bookshelf is next to the sofa.

    b. The bookshelf and the sofa are facing each other.

    c. The bookshelf is in the right side of the room.

B. Listen again and choose the best summary.

4   a. ☐ The TV is going to be facing the sofa.

    b. ☐ The TV and the sofa are going to be on the same side of the room.

Jeff and Mrs. Brown are looking for something. Circle the thing in each picture.

1

2

3

4

Listen Again

A. Listen again and choose the correct answer.

1 Jeff found it _____ .
   a. in the box   b. behind the box   c. next to the box

2 It was on the _____ shelf from the top.
   a. second   b. third   c. fourth

3 Jeff found it _____ the sugar bowl.
   a. in front of   b. inside   c. behind

B. Listen again and choose the correct sentence.

4   a. ☐   b. ☐

Review

Answers p. 26

✳ Listen and fill in the blanks.

1

W _____ are my glasses?

M I saw them _____ the table _____ the living room.

W No... They're not there. Oh, here they are. They're _____ the table.

2 Let me tell you _____ the room looks like. The door is on the _____,

and the window is on the _____ . There is a small table _____ the door,

and there's a telephone _____ the table. There is a sofa _____ the

window.

3

W Have you seen my MP3 player _____?

M It was _____ the books on your desk.

W Yes, it's here, _____ the dictionary.

4 I often forget my car _____ when I go to work in morning.

I leave them somewhere _____ my room, usually _____ the desk.

My wife Karen always gets them for me.

5

M I remember I put it right here _____ the wall. And it's nowhere.

W Have you looked _____ the sofa?

M No. Yes, I _____ it. Thanks.

Answers p. 26

LISTEN AND WRITE

Listen and write your own answers.

- My bag is _____
- My books are _____
- There are _____

  _____
- Yes, there are _____

  _____

Write the questions you hear.

_____

_____

_____

_____

_____

PRONUNCIATION

/ f / vs / p /

Listen and repeat.

| fee | fine | feel |
| fast | fat | wife |

Listen and repeat.

| pea | pine | peel |
| past | pat | wipe |

Listen carefully and notice the difference.

fee / pea	fine / pine
feel / peel	fast / past
fat / pat	wife / wipe

EXERCISE

Listen and check the words you hear.

☐ fee	☐ pea
☐ fine	☐ pine
☐ feel	☐ peel
☐ fast	☐ past
☐ fat	☐ pat
☐ wife	☐ wipe

✳ Listen and choose the correct answer.

1   **Jenny is describing her kitchen.**

1) Choose the correct picture.

a.

b.

c.

d.

2   **People are looking for their cat.**

1) Choose the best summary.

a. ☐ Their cat was sleeping in the living room then by the front door and now she might be sleeping under the basement stairs.

b. ☐ Their cat is missing. She always sleeps under the basement stairs because she likes dark places.

3 **Jeff is looking for something.**

1) Where is it? Choose the correct picture.

a.    b.    c.

2) Where will he probably go after the conversation?

a. library   b. restaurant   c. gym   d. store

4 **Sophie is describing her bedroom.**

1) Choose the correct picture.

a.   b.    c.

5 **A husband and his wife are talking in the morning.**

1) What's NOT true about the conversation?
   a. The wife is looking for the keys.
   b. The husband doesn't remember where he put his keys.
   c. The wife is telling him where to check.
   d. The husband often loses his keys.

2) Where were the keys?
   a. under the coffee table   b. on the sofa
   c. beside the phone   d. in his pocket

Answers p. 28

1

This is my kitchen. In my kitchen there is a round table _____ . There are three chairs around it. _____ one of the chairs my cat Lucy is sleeping. On another chair is my apron. _____ the table is a wastepaper basket. There is some wastepaper on the floor _____ it. _____ the wastepaper basket are my old slippers. My kitchen is really _____ .

2

M _____ Lucy? I haven't seen her all day.

W I saw her sleeping _____ , _____ the sofa this morning.

M She is not there.

W She was on the mat _____ .

M When was that?

W Just a _____ .

M No, she's gone.

W Check _____ the basement stairs. She likes dark places.

3

M Mom, can you help me find my library card?

W Oh, you _____ it again. It must be _____ of your desk.

M It's not there.

W Then it may be _____ around the _____ .

M _____ , Mom. It is under a book on the bookshelf.

4

In my bedroom, there is a bed _____ the left side wall. The fan is _____ . My desk is next to the window on the _____ of the room. On the right side of the desk, there is a bookcase. Oh, I forgot to tell you about my best friend— my computer! _____ the desk.

5

M Honey, have you seen my keys?

W You _____ them again? I think I saw them in the _____ .

M I already looked there, but I couldn't find them.

W Aren't they _____ ?

M No.

W Check if they are _____ the phone. You picked up the phone when you came back home last night, didn't you?

M Ah, _____ !

UNIT 7

How much is it?

Answers p. 28

GETTING READY

1 Find the missing words from the box and write them in the blanks.

| tax | price tag | household | out of season | used | new arrival |

1. How much is it? The _____ is missing.

2. It's not new. It's _____.

3. Shampoo, toothbrush, and towels are all _____ goods.

4. It's not on sale because it's a _____.

5. It's spring. Christmas items are _____.

6. With _____ your final total is $57.80.

2 Match the questions with the answers.

1. May I help you? •   • a. It's on sale.

2. How much is it? •   • b. Sorry, but I can't.

3. How come this is so cheap? •   • c. Yes, please.

4. Do you have a cheaper one? •   • d. Of course we do.

5. Can you come down a little? •   • e. Yes, I'm looking for a hat.

6. Can I ring them up for you? •   • f. It's $35.90.

Listening Task

Listening 1

Listen and match the items with the correct price tags.

1 　　2 　　3 　　4

a. 　　b. 　　c. 　　d.

Listen Again

A. Listen again and choose the correct answer.

1 Why does Mrs. White say she doesn't like the item?

　a. She doesn't like the price.

　b. She doesn't like the design.

　c. She doesn't like the color.

2 Why does Mrs. White say she doesn't like the item?

　a. They're too small.　　b. They're too big.　　c. They're too expensive.

3 Why does Mrs. White say she doesn't like the item?

　a. It looks cheap.　　b. It is heavy.　　c. She doesn't like gold.

B. Listen again and choose the best summary.

4　a. ☐ The lady will buy the pin because she likes its price and size.

　b. ☐ The lady is buying a pin because her daughter is shy.

Listening 2

Are they going to buy the item, or not? Put a check .

1   Yes _____   No _____

2   Yes _____   No _____

3   Yes _____   No _____

4   Yes _____   No _____

Listen Again

A.   Listen again and choose the false statement.

1   a. She paid tax.

b. She bought soap.

c. She didn't know there was tax for household goods.

2   a. The jacket is a new arrival.

b. The store isn't having a sale.

c. Only old items are on sale.

3   a. The shirt is for the past season.

b. He was in the store before.

c. The shirt is cheap because it has a problem.

B.   Listen again and choose the correct sentence.

4   a. ☐   b. ☐

Review

Answers p. 30

✳ **Listen and fill in the blanks.**

1

W   How _____ is the hat?

M   It's $ _____ .

W   I can't believe it. It's too _____ .

M   It's the hottest item this _____ . Everybody is wearing _____ .

2

This sweater is my favorite clothing item. It's 100% lamb's wool. It's light,

_____ and beautiful. It was $140.60. It's _____ and it was not _____

_____ because it was a _____ but after all it was worth it. I love it!

3

M   Look! I got these brand-new sunglasses. Guess the _____ .

W $_____ .

M   Cheaper.

W   Then $_____ .

M   Still cheaper. I got them for only $_____ .

W   I can't believe it!

M   Me, neither. I got them from on-line auction for used goods. But it was new.

It even had the _____ on it. I was lucky!

4

W   Okay, let me _____ them up for you. It _____ to $296.65, with

_____ .

M   Do you take _____ ?

W   Yes, we take VISA, American Express, and Master Card.

M   Here you are.

Answers p. 31

LISTEN AND WRITE

Listen and write your own answers.

Write the questions you hear.

- Yes, I bought _____.

  No, I didn't _____ this week.

- It was _____.

- I like to buy _____.

- I like to shop _____.

_____

_____

_____

_____

_____

PRONUNCIATION

/ ai /

Listen and repeat.

I	ice	die
my	fight	like
tie	mind	sign
bye	buy	by

Read the sentences below and circle the words that have the 'ai' sound in them.

1. I like my tie.
2. I am finding the guy who liked my idea.

Now listen and check the answer.

✳ Listen and choose the correct answer.

1   **A man is in a store.**

1) The man is shopping for a _____ .
a. pair of shoes   b. briefcase   c. suitcase

2) What is true about the conversation?
a. The man has to pay tax.
b. The man thinks the item is cheap.
c. The man is not going to buy the item.
d. The man is going to pay less than $90.

2   **The customer can't hear very well.**

1) Choose the correct price.
a. $580.89   b. $518.89   c. $158.90

3   **Jeff is in a store.**

1) What is Jeff shopping for?
a. a present for his girl friend
b. a present for his mother
c. a present for his teacher
d. a present for himself

2) What is Jeff NOT likely to say?
a. Can you come down a little?
b. I'll take it.
c. I'll ring them up for you.
d. My mom will like it.

4   **Sarah is talking to the shopkeeper.**

   1) How much is the original price of the bag?
       a. $20
       b. $25
       c. $30
       d. $40

   2) Why did the shopkeeper give Sarah a discount?
       a. Sarah was a student.
       b. Sarah was a good shopper.
       c. Sarah didn't have enough money to pay for the bag.
       d. Sarah wanted to buy a present for her mom.

5   **Patrick is telling his sister about what he bought today.**

   1) What are the items Patrick bought?
       a.   b.   c.

   2) How much did Patrick pay for the items?
       a. $15
       b. $20
       c. $30
       d. $50

Answers p. 32

1

W How may I help you, sir?

M _____ a briefcase.

W Here we have a _____ of them.

M Hmm... How much is this one?

W It's $89.90.

M I want something a little _____. Can you _____ a little?

W No, sir. It's already on sale.

M All right. I'll take it.

W So, your final total is $93.80.

M Wasn't it _____ something?

W There is tax, sir.

M Oh, I see.

2

W What can I do for you?

M I really like this pair of pants. What's the _____? There's no _____.

W _____.

M $158.89?

W No, _____.

3

Clerk What can I do for you?

Jeff I'm looking for a _____ for my mom.

Clerk How much can you _____?

Jeff Around $_____.

Clerk How about some accessories, like _____ or hats?

Jeff Show me some belts please.

Clerk Here you are. This one is $_____ and it's very pretty.

4

Clerk May I help you?

Sarah Well, I'm _____ for a present for my mom.

Clerk How about this _____? It is _____, but not that expensive.

Sarah How much is it?

Clerk $40. Isn't it _____?

Sarah Yeah, but _____.

Clerk I'll give you a _____. How about $30?

Sarah It's very kind of you, but I've got only $25 now.

Clerk Deal.

Sarah Thank you so much.

5

Sophie, guess what I _____ for you today. You'll like it. On my way home, I saw an old lady _____ summer hats. The hats were hand-made. I asked how much they were, and the old lady said, "$____ each." I had $____ in my pocket, so I _____ two, the green one and the red one. Look, aren't they beautiful?

UNIT 8

Don't cross the road!

Answers p. 33

GETTING READY

1 Find the missing words in the box and write them in the blanks.

driver's license	handicapped	ticket	school zone
crosswalk	jaywalking	fasten	

1. Slow down! It is a _____. There are lots of children around.

2. I parked my car in a _____ parking area.

3. I got a _____ for speeding.

4. You always have to _____ your seat belt.

5. You need to carry your _____ when driving.

6. Always cross the road on the _____.

7. _____ is dangerous.

2 Match two expressions that have the same meaning.

1. Turn right.   •   • a. You should fasten your seat belt.

2. Stop.   •   • b. You cannot park here.

3. Buckle up.   •   • c. You may not cross the street here.

4. Don't cross the street here.   •   • d. You can make a right turn here.

5. No parking!   •   • e. You have to stop here completely.

6. Do not enter.   •   • f. You may not enter here.

Listening Task

Listening 1

Listen and check ☑ True or False.

		T	F
1	They are going to cross the street.	☐	☐
2	The woman is driving.	☐	☐
3	The dialogue is between a woman and the police officer.	☐	☐
4	They are talking inside a subway.	☐	☐

Listen Again

A. Listen again and choose the correct answer.

1 What is the best response that could follow?

   a. You are okay.

   b. You still shouldn't jaywalk.

   c. You can cross the street here.

2 What is the best response that could follow?

   a. Oh, no!

   b. I got it.

   c. Hooray!

3 What is the best response that could follow?

   a. Of course not.

   b. No, not at all.

   c. Oh, please, officer.

B. Listen again and choose the best response.

4   a. ☐   b. ☐   c. ☐

Listening 2

Listen and number the signs.

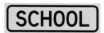

SCHOOL

HANDICAPPED
PARKING
STATE PERMIT REQUIRED

_____   _____   _____   _____

Listen Again

A. Listen again and choose the correct answer.

1 What is the speed limit in the school zone?
   a. 40 mph   b. 30 mph   c. 20 mph

2 She paid a _____ fine because she parked in the _____ parking area.
   a. large, free   b. heavy, handicapped   c. big, special

3 He entered a _____ road and had an accident.
   a. small   b. busy   c. one-way

B. Listen again and choose the correct sentence.

4   a. ☐   b. ☐

Review

Answers p. 34

✳ Listen and fill in the blanks.

1

W   What is the _____ on the highway?

M   It's _____ mph.

W   That's fast. Be sure to _____ your seat belt.

2   My dad had a car _____ the other day. He was on the way home from

work. He _____ a small road and _____ into a truck. Luckily he was

not hurt but it was very dangerous. Be careful not to _____ the sign.

3

M   You are _____.

W   I am not.

M   Don't you see the _____ over there? It's a school _____.

W   Oh, I didn't know that.

4   Last night, I _____ my car on the street for a moment to buy something. When

I went back to my car, it was _____. People told me it was _____

away. Don't ever park your car on the _____.

5

M   You can't _____ the street here.

W   It is not _____ right now.

M   But you must not _____ anyway. Look! There is a _____

over there.

On Your Own

Answers p. 35

LISTEN AND WRITE

Listen and write your own answers.

- Yes, I _____

  No, I _____
- Yes, I always _____
- No, I often forget _____
- It's _____

Write the questions you hear.

_____

_____

_____

_____

_____

PRONUNCIATION

/ au /

Listen and repeat.

out	cow	how
now	about	brown
cloud	down	house
mouth	sound	town

Read the sentences below and circle the words that have the 'au' sound in them.

1. How about the brown house in downtown?

2. How many cows can you count outside?

Now listen and check the answer.

✳ **Listen and choose the correct answer.**

1   **Brian is talking with a police officer.**

1) What is NOT true about the conversation?
   a. Brian ran a red light.
   b. Brian was speeding.
   c. Brian was driving his father's car.
   d. The policeman will take him to the police station.

2) Brian has to go to the police station because _____.
   a. he drove his father's car
   b. he didn't have a driver's license
   c. he drove drunk
   d. he ran a red light

2   **The following is about a road.**

1) What is the best expression that could follow?
   a. slow down
   b. don't jaywalk here
   c. don't run
   d. hurry up

2) The road is dangerous because there are _____.
   a. many cars
   b. many overpasses
   c. many crosswalks
   d. many trees

3   **The following is a conversation between Mrs. Brown and Jeff.**

1) What is true about the conversation?
   a. Jeff was driving his mother's car.
   b. Jeff was speeding on the highway.
   c. Jeff will pay the fine.
   d. Jeff will get allowance next month.

2) Jeff was driving at _____ mph and the fine is _____ dollars.
   a. 50, 40   b. 40, 40   c. 40, 50   d. 50, 50

4   **Three people are talking.**

1) Where is the conversation taking place?
   a. on a street   b. on a car   c. in Peter's house   d. in the man's house

2) Choose the correct summary of the conversation.
   a. ☐   Peter was playing on the street and a driver nearly ran him over, so the driver came to the house to warn Peter and his mom.
   b. ☐   A driver came to Peter's house to ask if Peter was playing on the street.

5   **The following is a conversation between a police officer and a lady.**

1) Where is the conversation taking place?
   a. on the street   b. in a parking lot
   c. at the police station   d. at the driver exam center

2) Why was she fined by the police officer?
   a. She lied to the officer.
   b. She didn't pay for her sticker.
   c. She parked in a space for the handicapped.
   d. She was waiting for her handicapped husband.

Dictation

Listen and fill in the blanks.

Answers p. 37

1

Police Officer	You _____ a red light.
Brian	I didn't, sir.
Police Officer	Yes, you did. I was watching you. I need to see your _____, please.
Brian	Maybe I was nervous driving. This is actually my _____ _____ driving.
Police Officer	I am sorry, but I have to give you a _____.
Brian	I don't have a license. This is _____.
Police Officer	I have to take you to the _____ then.

2

It is a _____ street. It's _____. There are many cars. There are many people _____ by. There is an overpass over there. There is a _____ over here.

3

W	What is this? It's a 50 dollar-_____ from the police station.
M	I am sorry, Mom. I _____ your car and got a ticket.
W	What did you do?
M	I was _____.
W	How _____ were you driving?
M	It was just _____ mph, but it was a school zone.
W	You won't get any allowance next month.
M	Sure.

4

Mom	Peter, don't play _____. Okay?
Peter	Okay, okay. Don't worry, Mom. I won't.
Man	Is this your son?
Mom	Yes, he is. What's the _____?
Man	I nearly _____ your son. He was playing on the street with other kids.
Mom	I'm so sorry. I told him not to play near the street. Thank you for telling me what _____.
Man	Listen, young man, it's very _____ to play near the street, okay?

5

M	Excuse me, lady, this space is for the _____.
W	Well, it's my husband's car, and he is handicapped.
M	But I can't find any _____ for the handicapped on your car.
W	Oh, maybe he forgot to _____.
M	You better tell me the truth.
W	Alright, I'm sorry. I couldn't find a _____ anywhere, so I came here. I promise I won't do this again.
M	I understand, but you have to pay the _____ of $100.
W	$100!

68

UNIT 9

What do you do?

Answers p. 37

GETTING READY

1 Fill in the blanks with the letters of the words in the box below.

a. dentist	b. nurse	c. flight attendant	d. chef
e. hairdresser	f. tour guide	g. librarian	

1. This person serves passengers on a flight. _____

2. This person makes food in a restaurant. _____

3. This person takes care of your teeth. _____

4. This person guides tourists around. _____

5. This person cuts your hair. _____

6. This person helps doctors. _____

7. This person helps you find books. _____

2 Match the questions with the answers.

1. What do you do? •   • a. I run a restaurant.

2. What is your job like? •   • b. From 9 a.m. to 1 p.m.

3. How do you like your job? •   • c. I don't like it very much.

4. What are the working hours? •   • d. Pretty well.

5. How's your job going? •   • e. It's boring.

Listening Task

Listening 1

People are talking about their jobs. Which jobs are they talking about?

1 a. pilot   b. flight attendant   c. travel agent

2 a. doctor   b. farmer   c. nurse

3 a. waiter   b. chef   c. shop clerk

4 a. police officer   b. sports player   c. doctor

Listen Again

A. Listen again and choose the correct answer.

1 What is NOT the reason she likes her job?

   a. She meets many people.

   b. She can travel a lot.

   c. She can make a lot of money.

2 What is his job NOT like?

   a. He looks after sick people.

   b. He helps doctors.

   c. He works only at night.

3 The problem is _____.

   a. he doesn't make much money

   b. he doesn't have his own restaurant

   c. he is getting fat

B. Listen again and choose the best summary.

4 a. ☐ Her husband has a tough job and she is proud of him but her husband's job is dangerous.

   b. ☐ Her husband is though. She is proud of her husband because his job is dangerous.

Listening 2

Listen and choose the correct word to fill in the blank.

1 Mr. Peterson is a _____.
   a. mail carrier   b. factory worker   c. bus driver

2 The girl wants to be a _____.
   a. nurse   b. preschool teacher   c. baby-sitter

3 Pat is working _____.
   a. in a restaurant   b. full-time   c. as a manager

4 Cindy is a _____.
   a. waitress   b. hairdresser   c. flight attendant

Listen Again

A. Listen again and choose the correct answer.

1 What is the best response that could follow?
   a. Three times a day.   b. Nine hours.   c. Long ago.

2 What is the best response that could follow?
   a. Once a week.   b. Seven hours a day.   c. $300 a week.

3 What is the best response that could follow?
   a. Sorry to hear that.   b. That's okay.   c. No problem.

B. Listen again and choose the best response.

4   a. ☐   b. ☐   c. ☐

Review

Answers p. 39

✳ Listen and fill in the blanks.

1

W   What do you _____?

M   I am a _____.

W   How do you like your _____?

M   Well, it's okay. I don't like working _____, but at least I can help people.

2   Looking _____ a clerk for a shoe _____. Working _____ are from 11 a.m. to 8 p.m. Starting salary is $7 an _____. Needs to speak some Spanish.

3

W   Where do you _____?

M   I work at a gas station.

W   _____ do you work?

M   _____ a day.

4   Today was my first day of _____. I think I did pretty well. I like my _____ and my new _____. And I get $ _____ a month so the pay is good, too. I think I was lucky getting this _____.

5

M   I've got a new part-time job, Susan.

W   What is it _____?

M   I work _____ hours a day, and get 7 dollars an _____.

W   That's not bad.

M   No. The problem is working hours. I have to work _____ at night.

On Your Own

Answers p. 40

LISTEN AND WRITE

Listen and write your own answers.

- Yes, I _____

  No, I don't _____

- It's _____

  _____

- I want _____

- Because I _____

Write the questions you hear.

_____

_____

_____

_____

_____

_____

PRONUNCIATION

/ ei /

Listen and repeat.

A	day	Jay	lay
may	say	cake	gave
main	pain	they	wait

Read the sentences below and circle the words that have the "ei" sound in them.

1. Jay may bake a cake one day.
2. Wait. Don't say they gave us pain.
3. May made a cake for David's birthday.

Now listen and check the answer.

✳ Listen and choose the correct answer.

1   **A man is talking about his job.**

1) What is the man's job?
   a. plumber
   b. mechanic
   c. taxi driver
   d. dentist

2) What is NOT true about the conversation?
   a. It is cold now.
   b. He is busy at work.
   c. He fixes ten cars a day.
   d. There are many car accidents these days.

2   **A man is talking about his job.**

1) What is the man's job?
   a. nurse
   b. dentist
   c. teacher
   d. engineer

2) What is true about the man?
   a. He likes sweets.
   b. He likes working indoors.
   c. He doesn't like children.
   d. He enjoys helping people.

3   **A woman is talking about her job.**

  1) The woman works as a _____ .
      a. waitress
      b. cashier
      c. teacher
      d. manager

  2) What is NOT true about the woman?
      a. She works part-time.
      b. She goes to school in the evening.
      c. She works in a restaurant.
      d. She wants to be a teacher.

4   **Emily and her father are talking.**

  1) What do you think Emily's dad does?
      a. doctor
      b. dentist
      c. librarian
      d. businessman

5   **Two boys are talking.**

  1) Which one is true about Philip?
      a. He doesn't want to be a writer.
      b. He might be a biology teacher.
      c. He wants to be a doctor.
      d. His father wants him to be a doctor.

Listen and fill in the blanks.

Answers p. 41

1

W _____?

M Pretty _____. The roads are very slippery these days. And there are many car accidents.

W How many cars do you fix _____?

M I _____ about ten cars a day.

W Wow, _____.

2

People _____ when they have _____ with their teeth. These days there are more children coming to _____. They eat too many sweets, don't they? Anyway I like _____ because I can help other people. The problem is that I work indoors. I can't get fresh air very much. That's the _____ part of _____.

3

M _____ for a living?

W I work as a _____ at a supermarket.

M _____ do you work a day?

W Five hours.

M So you are a _____.

W Yes, I go to school in the evening. I am studying _____.

4

Emily Dad, what do you do every day?

Dad _____.

Emily What is your job?

Dad Well, _____.

Emily Really?

Dad Yes. _____ other people to find the books they want to read.

5

Philip Peter, _____ do you _____?

Peter Well, I'm interested in biology, so maybe I'll be a biology _____. What about you, Philip?

Philip _____. But I'm _____ English, particularly writing.

Peter That's true. Hey, you can be a _____!

Philip Sounds good but my father wants me _____.

Peter A doctor?

How can I get there?

Answers p. 42

1 Look at the map and fill in the blanks with the words in the box.

parking lot   post office   City Hall   drugstore   cinema   police station

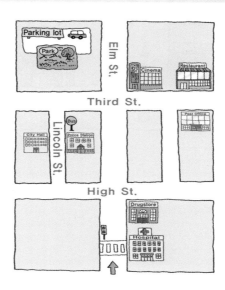

1. The _____ is across from the restaurant.

2. The _____ is past the traffic light.

3. The _____ is behind the park.

4. The _____ is across from the police station.

5. The _____ is next to the hospital.

6. The _____ is on the corner of Third and Elm St.

7. The _____ is on Lincoln St. near the bus stop.

Listening Task

People are giving directions. Listen and number the place on the map.

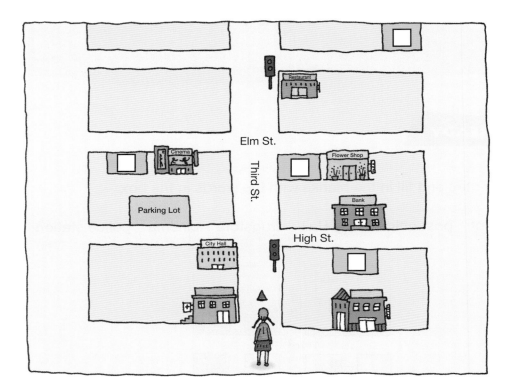

Listen Again

Listen again and circle the correct words. (Don't look at the map above.)

1   She has to go straight (two / three) more blocks.

2   She has to turn (right / left).

3   It's (past / next to) the cinema.

4   She has to turn (right / left) at the (first / second) traffic light.

Listening 2

People are asking for and giving directions. Listen and choose the correct map.

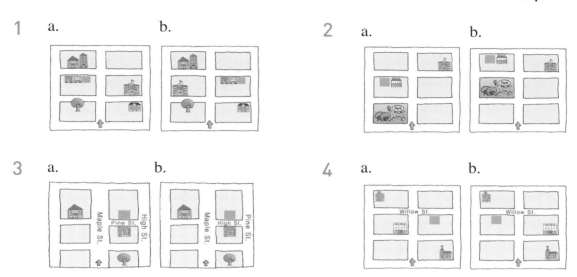

1 a.   b.   2 a.   b.

3 a.   b.   4 a.   b.

Listen Again

Listen again and circle the correct words. (Don't look at the map above.)

1   City Hall is (two / three) blocks away.
    You have to turn (right / left).
    It's (fourth / third) building on your (right / left).

2   The movie theater is three blocks (up / down) the road.
    It's (next to / past) the restaurant on your (right / left).

3   The drugstore is on (Hill / High) Street.
    It's (facing / behind) the hotel. It's between Maple and (Spruce / Pine).

4   The toy store is up (one / two) more block(s).
    You have to turn (right / left) on Willow Street.
    It's (far / not far) from the corner.

Review

Answers p. 43

✳ Listen and fill in the blanks.

1

M _____ me. How can I _____ to the nearest subway station?

W Go down two more _____ and turn right. It's around the _____.

M Thanks.

2 First, walk _____ this road.

Turn _____ at the third _____ light.

Then, go one _____ block and you're on High Street.

It's _____ the cinema and the drugstore.

3

M Where can I _____ some light bulbs?

W There's a hardware store _____ Maple Ave.

M Where _____ Maple Ave?

W It's right _____ the fire station. You _____ it.

4 We've moved. Our new address is 256 Spruce Street. It's on the other _____ of

the river. At the end of the bridge, turn _____, and _____ the second right.

It's the _____ building on your right. Hope to see you there!

5

M Mom, I can't find it. Is it _____ the bookstore or _____ the

drugstore?

W Neither. It is _____ the hotel, _____ the parking lot.

M Oh, I have been on the _____ street. The hotel is on Maple Street, right?

W Right.

On Your Own

Answers p. 43

LISTEN AND WRITE

Listen and write your own answers.

- My school is _____

  _____

- It's _____

- Yes, there is _____

- No, there isn't _____

Write the questions you hear.

_____

_____

_____

_____

_____

PRONUNCIATION

/ ou /

Listen and repeat.

go   Joe   low   know
no   sew   bone   gold
only phone over

Read the sentences below and circle the words that have the "ou" sound in them.

1. No, only Joe knows where both of the gold phones are.

2. Tony and Moe don't own the oak tree by my home.

Now listen and check the answer.

✳ Listen and choose the correct answer.

1 **Two people are asking for and giving directions.**

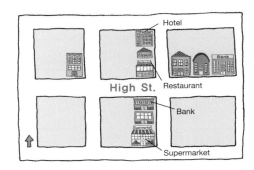

1) Which place is the man looking for? Find the place on the map.

    a. bank   b. supermarket   c. hotel   d. restaurant

2 **The following are some directions.**

1) Which map is marked right?

a.

b.

3   **The following are some directions.**

1) Find the right map.

a.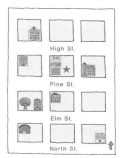

b.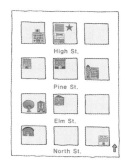

4   **Maria is asking to a gentleman something.**

1) Which one is NOT true?

a. The post office is a block away from the subway station.

b. The subway station is not far away from the post office.

c. The post office is two blocks away from where they are.

d. The post office is close to the police station.

5   **Sarah is waiting for Jenny at home.**

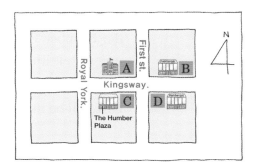

1) Which one is Sarah's house?

a. A   b. B   c. C   d. D

Dictation

Answers p. 45

1

M _____?

W Walk up High Street and _____ the second left.
It's the third building _____.

M Second left on High. Third on the right.

W No, not on the _____, on the _____.

M Oh, thanks.

W _____.

2

First, get out of the hotel. _____ and walk until you see the church. There's a bridge. _____ the bridge and _____ for a few minutes. You'll _____ a tall _____ at the intersection.
It is the small building _____ it.

3

M Where is the restaurant?

W Do you know where City Hall is?

M Yes, _____ North Street.

W Let's start from City Hall. _____ the street _____.

M Yes, three blocks from the City Hall.

W It is High Street. Turn left on High and go two more blocks.

M Yes.

W _____. It's just _____, next to the shoe store.

4

W Excuse me, could you tell me _____ _____ the nearest subway station?

M Sure. _____ two blocks.

W Yes.

M _____, there is a big post office. There, turn left.

W Post office, _____.

M Then _____ and you'll see the subway station. You can't miss it.

W _____.

M You're welcome.

5

Jenny Hi, Sarah. It's Jenny.

Sarah Hi, _____?

Jenny I'm lost. I'm at Royal York and Kingsway. _____ to your house _____?

Sarah O.K. Do you see the Humber Plaza?

Jenny Yeah, _____.

Sarah All right. Cross the street and get to the Humber Plaza. _____ one block along Kingsway Road. My house is on the corner.

Jenny O.K. I'll be there soon!

UNIT 11

I'd like a steak.

Answers p. 46

GETTING READY

1 List the words in the correct box.

rice   beef   cake   chicken   cookie   coffee   fish   milk   juice
ice cream   pie   cereal   carrots   tea   onion   peas

Grain
_____
_____
_____

Meat and Fish
_____
_____
_____

Drinks
_____
_____

Vegetables
_____
_____
_____

Desserts
_____
_____
_____

2 Match the questions with the answers.

1. Would you like something to drink?   •   • a. I'd like a steak.

2. What would you like, sir?   •   • b. Yes. I'd like a meatball spaghetti.

3. May I take your order?   •   • c. No, I don't. I'm tired of them.

4. Do you feel like a sandwich?   •   • d. Yes, orange juice please.

5. How about some pizza?   •   • e. Sounds great.

Listening Task

Listening 1

Listen and choose the meal they are talking about.

1 a. breakfast   b. lunch   c. dinner

2 a. breakfast   b. lunch   c. dinner

3 a. breakfast   b. lunch   c. dinner

4 a. breakfast   b. lunch   c. dinner

Listen Again

A. Listen again and choose the correct answer.

1 What is true about the conversation?

a. He has eaten a lot of sandwiches.

b. He didn't eat anything for breakfast.

c. They will eat sandwich.

2 What are they probably going to eat?

a. pizza   b. seafood   c. steak

3 What is NOT true about the conversation?

a. The Chinese restaurant is new.

b. The Chinese restaurant is in downtown.

c. The food is good but the service is not.

B. Listen again and choose the best summary.

4 a. ☐ They will eat some seafood because she had a long week and wants to eat good food.

b. ☐ She doesn't want to eat fast food because her favorite food is lobster.

Listening 2

Listen and choose which food they will eat.

 a. b.   2 a. b.

3 a.   b.   4 a .   b.

Listen Again

A. Listen and choose the correct answer.

1   What is the best response that could follow?
   a. To go.   b. It's not for me.   c. I don't want to go.

2   What is the best response that could follow?
   a. No, thanks.   b. French dressing, please.   c. Yes, please.

3   What is the person NOT likely to say?
   a. Coke, please.   b. No, I don't.   c. Just water, please.

B.   Listen again and choose the best response.

4   a. ☐   b. ☐   c. ☐

Review

Answers p. 48

✳ Listen and fill in the blanks.

1

W   May I _____ your _____ ?

M   Yes, I'd _____ a Sweet Cajun Shrimp.

W   Which _____ would you like?

M   Clam chowder, please.

2   This place is just great. The _____ is good, and the _____ is even better. I especially like the _____ . The cheese cake is just wonderful. You've got to _____ it.

3

W   Let's have _____ together.

M   Sounds good. _____ do you want to go?

W   _____ the Spaghetti Palace?

M   I'm _____ of spaghetti. Let's have _____ for a change.

4   My favorite _____ is ice cream. My mom is worried because I eat too much _____ . But I can't help it. Chocolate ice cream from Toska Rabbins is _____ in the world.

5

W   Let's eat _____ this evening. I had a _____ week and I'd like to eat something _____ .

M   Where would you like to go?

W   How about some _____ ?

M   Okay.

On Your Own

Answers p. 48

LISTEN AND WRITE

Listen and write your own answers.

- I usually have _____

  _____

- I'd like _____

- _____

- I will eat _____

  _____

Write the questions you hear.

_____

_____

_____

_____

_____

PRONUNCIATION

/ oi /

Listen and repeat.

boy	joy
enjoy	Roy
toy	oil
boil	coil
coin	join
noise	point

Read the sentences below and circle the words that have the "oi" sound in them.

1. Roy is the boy with that noisy toy.
2. The boys have a few coins to buy coils and oil.

Now listen and check the answer.

✳ Listen and choose the correct answer.

1 **What are they ordering?**
   Check ☑ M(man) or W(woman) on the menu.

2 **People are ordering food in a restaurant.**

   1) They are going to eat _____.
      a. steak   b. burger   c. salad   d. sandwich

   2) What is true about the conversation?
      a. They are ordering the same food.
      b. They have been there many times.
      c. They are in a Chinese restaurant.
      d. The sandwich has chicken in it.

3   **A mother and her son are talking.**

1) What are they probably going to eat?
    a. spaghetti   b. chicken barbecue   c. pork ribs   d. grilled beef

2) What is true about the conversation?
    a. The boy never liked spaghetti before.
    b. They are talking about lunch.
    c. They'll probably eat out later this week.
    d. They'll not eat at home this evening.

4   **Patrick and his mom are ordering in a restaurant.**

1) Match the food with the person who ordered it.

                    • baked potato
    Mom   •   • a glass of wine
                    • chocolate fudge cake
    Patrick •   • water with ice
                    • seafood spaghetti
                    • beef steak

5   **Sarah and Jim are talking.**

1) What are they mainly talking about?
    a. Japanese sushi
    b. Korean sushi
    c. Differences between Japanese and Korean sushi
    d. What to eat for lunch

2) What will probably happen next?
    a. They will go to a Japanese restaurant.
    b. They will study in the library.
    c. They will go swimming.
    d. They will eat in a Korean restaurant.

Answers p. 50

1

Waiter	Good evening! _____?
Man	I'd like a T-bone steak.
Waiter	How would you like _____, sir?
Man	Medium rare. And I'll have the salad with _____, please.
Waiter	And you, ma'am?
Woman	Roast beef and onion soup, please.
Waiter	Would you like _____?
Man	Coffee, please.
Woman	_____ orange juice.
Waiter	Okay. _____ will be ready in ten minutes.

2

Woman	What's on the menu?
Man	There's _____. What is the club sandwich?
Woman	Let me ask. Uh, excuse me. What's the club _____ like?
Waiter	It is made with grilled beef and _____ sauce. _____.
Woman	I'd like to try it. How about you?
Man	I'll have that too.

3

M	Mom, I'm hungry. _____?
W	Spaghetti. It's your favorite, isn't it?
M	No, not any more. _____ spaghetti. Let's _____, please.
W	What do you want to eat?
M	_____ barbecue at Bill's Barbecue.
W	Okay. But no more _____ this week.
M	Hooray!

4

Waiter	Good evening, are you ready to order?
Mom	Yes, I _____ the seafood spaghetti, please, with a glass of white wine.
Waiter	Yes, ma'am. And you, young man?
Patrick	I'll _____ the beef steak, cooked medium, with baked _____.
Waiter	And would you like anything to _____?
Patrick	Just water with ice, please.
Waiter	Anything for _____?
Patrick & mom	Chocolate fudge cake with fresh _____!

5

W	Have you ever _____ Korean sushi, Jim?
M	What's that? Isn't sushi Japanese?
W	Yeah, with raw fish. Korean sushi is _____.
M	Oh!
W	It's rice with ham, egg, cheese and lots of vegetables all rolled up in seaweed.
M	It sounds really _____ and yummy!
W	It is. I love Korean sushi.
M	Well, why don't we _____ _____? I'm getting hungry.
W	Great!

Can I speak to Amy, please?

Answers p. 50

GETTING READY

1 Choose two expressions for each situation.

a. Can I speak to Nancy, please?　　b. Who's calling?

c. I'm sorry but he's on another line.　　d. This is she.

e. You must have the wrong number.　　f. Sorry but he's not in.

g. I think you dialed the wrong number.　　h. Is John in?

i. Just a second. I'll get him for you.　　j. Do you want to leave a message?

k. Speaking.　　l. Who is this please?

m. May I take a message?　　n. Hold on.

1. To ask about caller's name

2. To say the person cannot come to the phone

3. To ask what the caller wants to say

4. To say the caller has reached a wrong place

5. To say who the caller wants to talk to

6. To say the receiver is the one who the caller wants

7. To tell the caller to wait

Listening Task

Listening 1

Which is the caller's message and which is the receiver's?
Write C (caller) or R (receiver).

1 _____   2 _____

3 _____   4 _____

Listen Again

A. Listen again and choose the true statement.

1 a. Sue will call again.

   b. Sue wants Amy to call her.

   c. Sue can't take the phone call after 7.

2 a. She wants Ms. Grue to call her back.

   b. She will call again tonight.

   c. Her son is sick.

3 a. The caller's name is Jane.

   b. The caller may leave his or her phone number.

   c. The caller should call again later.

B. Listen again and choose the best summary.

4 a. ☐ Power Auto's business hours are from 9 to 8 Monday through Friday.

   b. ☐ Power Auto's people work Monday through Saturday and they like to have their customers' call.

Listening 2

Four people are making phone calls. Check ✓ who is the caller.

1   Mr. Brown ☐   Mr. Smith ☐

2   Brian ☐   Jane ☐

3   Jane ☐   Tim ☐

4   Amy ☐   Sarah ☐

Listen Again

A. Listen again and choose the true statement.

1   a. Mr. Smith is out.

     b. Mr. Smith can't come to the phone.

     c. Mr. Smith will be on the phone soon.

2   a. Brian has reached Jane.

     b. Brian will call back.

     c. Brian will wait for Jane's call.

3   a. Tim has reached Jane.

     b. Tim and Jane will meet today.

     c. Tim left a message.

B.   Listen again and choose the correct sentence.

4   a. ☐   b. ☐

✳ Listen and fill in the blanks.

1

W Hello, could I _____ to Mr. Brown, please?

M I'm sorry, but he's on another line. May I take a _____?

W No, thanks. I'll _____ later.

2 Hi, you have reached Jane's. I'm not home right now. Please _____ a message and I'll get back to you as soon as _____ . Thanks.

3

W Hello, is Mary _____?

M I'm _____ but she's _____. Would you like to _____ a message?

W Just _____ her Jane called.

M Okay, I'll do that.

4 Hi, Susan. This is Joe. I'm _____ our date on Friday. I may work late that night. Will you _____ a _____? You can me reach me at home any time after _____ p.m. this evening.

5

W Is this 314-_____?

M No, you dialed the _____ number. It's _____-_____.

W Oh, I'm sorry.

M No problem.

Answers p. 52

LISTEN AND WRITE

Listen and write your own answers.

- It's _____

- _____

- _____

- Hi,_____

- _____

- You can reach me _____

_____

Write the questions you hear.

_____

_____

_____

_____

_____

_____

PRONUNCIATION

Single-syllable words

Single-syllable words are words that need to be pronounced without any breaks.

Listen and repeat.

a	the	is
are	am	you
eat	rode	look
five	Scott	rich
black	train	night
place	string	strike

EXERCISE

The sentences below have only single-syllable words.

Listen first and repeat.

1. Rich rode the train all night and all day for five days.

2. You and your black bike will do well in the race.

3. He was struck by a huge spring, but he is fine now.

PRACTICE TEST

✳ **Listen and choose the correct answer.**

1 **Someone is leaving a message for Mr. Wilson. Choose the right memo.**

a.
Tim Baker
Call as soon as
possible
405-5356

b.
Mr. Wilson
called
Call him back
405-0356

c.
Tim Baker
Call him back
as soon as possible
405-0356

2 **The following is a message for Debbie.**

1) What is true about the message?
   a. Debbie and Sue are sisters.
   b. Debbie and Sue are living in the same town.
   c. Debbie is expected to call back after she gets the message.
   d. Debbie is living in Ohio.

2) When are they probably going to see each other?
   a. this week   b. next month   c. next week   d. tomorrow

3 **The following is a phone conversation.**

1) Choose a group of right words to fill in the blanks.

   _____ called _____ , but she is _____ , so he _____ the line.

   a. Susan- Charles - busy - holds
   b. Charles - Susan - on another line - holds
   c. Charles - Susan - out - holds
   d. Charles - Susan - busy - holds

2) Charles is Susan's _____ .
   a. boyfriend   b. neighbor   c. cousin   d. classmate

98

4 **Tom is calling Jenny.**

1) Which one summarizes the dialogue best?
   a. Tom is calling Jenny, but Jenny's not home.
   b. Jenny isn't home, so Tom wants to talk to her mom.
   c. Jenny isn't home, so Tom wants Jenny to call him back.
   d. Jenny is leaving her number because Tom isn't home.

2) What's Tom's phone number?
   a. 237-8076
   b. 273-8079
   c. 237-1876
   d. 273-1870

5 **The following is a message for Lesley.**

1) Why did Mrs. Brown call Lesley?
   a. She wants Lesley to help James with essay writing.
   b. She wants to meet and discuss something with Lesley.
   c. She wants information on how to improve writing skills.
   d. She wants to know where Lesley can teach James.

1

M Hello, may I _____ Mr. Wilson, please?

W Sorry, but he's out to lunch right now. _____?

M Yes, please. This is Tim Baker from Boston. I'd like him to call me back as soon as he returns.

W Does he have your _____?

M I think so, but just in case, it's 405-0356.

W _____. All right.

M Thank you.

2

Hi, Debbie. This is Sue. How are you doing? It's been years since I've _____. My family is going to take a trip to Ohio next week. My _____ and _____ are having a tennis match there. I may be _____ you then. I'll call you when I get to town. _____. Bye!

3

M Hello? _____ Susan, please?

W May I ask _____?

M This is Charles Hunt, Susan's classmate.

W She's on another _____. Would you hold or do you want to leave a _____?

M I'll hold.

W Sure. Susan... There's a phone call for you.

W2 Hello?

M It's me Charles, Susan.

W2 Oh, Charles! _____?

4

M Hello! _____?

W She's not here. Who's calling?

M _____ Tom. I'm her classmate.

W Would you like to leave a message?

M Could you tell her to call me back?

W No problem. Does she know your _____?

M I think so, but just in case, it's 237-_____.

W 237-1876. Okay, I'll make sure she gets it.

M _____. Bye!

W Bye!

5

Hi, Lesley. _____ Mrs. Brown. My son James is in Grade 9 and he needs some help with writing essays. He wants to develop his _____. I wonder if you give him writing lessons at _____ once a week. If you could _____ when you get this, that'd be great. My phone number is 416-989-_____. Thank you. Bye!

What do you do in your free time?

Answers p. 55

GETTING READY

1 Put a check(✓) on activities you do more than once a month.

go to the movies _____   eat out _____

go to a concert _____   chat online _____

go shopping _____   ride a bike _____

go fishing _____   play computer games _____

go to a park _____   surf the Internet _____

2 Match the questions with the answers.

1. What's your favorite pastime? •   • a. No, not really. Why?

2. What are you doing this weekend? •   • b. I'd like to play tennis.

3. Are you busy this Saturday? •   • c. Yes, I'd love to.

4. Do you feel like going to the movies? •   • d. That's a good idea.

5. What would you like to do? •   • e. It's playing computer games.

6. Why don't we rent a video and watch it? •   • f. I'm visiting my aunt.

Listening Task

People are talking about their pastimes. Listen and number the pictures.

Listen Again

A. Listen again and choose the correct answer.

1 Which of the following is NOT true?

   a. She doesn't like to watch people.

   b. She goes shopping because she has many things to buy.

   c. She sometimes eats there.

2 Which of the following is true?

   a. He rides a bike with his children.

   b. He and his wife enjoy the same pastime.

   c. He goes to the park because there are many people.

3 Which of the following is true?

   a. He doesn't have stress at all.

   b. He doesn't go out in order to save money.

   c. He likes to be alone.

B. Listen again and choose the best summary.

4   a. ☐ The speaker likes to go out with her friends on weekends because she never has fun on weekdays.

   b. ☐ The speaker likes to chat, dance, play games, and go to movies on weekdays.

What is the second speaker going to do on the weekend? Choose the correct picture.

1 a.   b.   2 a.   b.

3 a.   b.   4 a.   b.

Listen Again

A. Listen again and choose the correct answer.

1 What is true about Joe?

    a. He doesn't like sports.

    b. He doesn't like to be with the noisy crowd.

    c. He likes TV very much.

2 What is true about Jan?

    a. Jan has never played tennis.

    b. Jan won't play tennis this weekend.

    c. Jan's friend is very good at tennis.

3 What is true about Angie?

    a. Angie likes movies better than concerts.

    b. Angie doesn't like concerts.

    c. Angie has another plan.

B. Listen again and choose the correct sentence.

4

    a. ☐   b. ☐

Review

Answers p. 57

✳ Listen and fill in the blanks.

1

W   What is your favorite _____?

M   I _____ computer games. How about you?

W   I go _____ with my friends. There's a new ice rink in town.

2   I don't understand people going out for _____. I need to _____ on weekends. I can _____ sports and movies on TV. I can buy things on the _____.

3

M   What _____ you _____ this weekend?

W   I am going to _____ with my family. It's my mom's birthday.

M   I'm playing board games with Tim, so _____ if you have time.

4   My favorite _____ is watching _____. Today, I got a new DVD. I'm going to ask my best friend if she is _____ this _____ evening. I am sure that she will enjoy _____ it with me.

5

M   Do you _____ playing tennis with me?

W   That would be _____. But I'm not good at it. I haven't played it for _____.

M   Don't _____. I'm not very good either.

LISTEN AND WRITE

Listen and write your own answers.

- I _____

- I'm going to _____

- Yes, I _____

  No, I don't like _____

- Yes, I love _____

  No, I _____

Write the questions you hear.

_____

_____

_____

_____

_____

_____

PRONUNCIATION

/ t / vs / d /

Listen and repeat.

| tad | ten | time |
| town | trip | try |

Listen and repeat.

| dad | den | dime |
| down | drip | dry |

Listen carefully and notice the difference.

tad / dad	ten / den
time / dime	town / down
trip / drip	try / dry

EXERCISE

Listen and check the words you hear.

☐ tad	☐ dad
☐ ten	☐ den
☐ time	☐ dime
☐ town	☐ down
☐ trip	☐ drip
☐ try	☐ dry

✳ Listen and choose the correct answer.

1   **People are talking about weekend activities.**

1) The man is _____ the woman's invitation.
a. accepting   b. declining

2) What are they talking about? Find the missing words in the following sentences.

The woman is inviting the man to _____, but he wants to _____ at home. He finds the woman's idea to be _____.

a. go to a park - sleep - fun
b. go to a park - play computer games - boring
c. a mountain - play computer games - boring

2   **The following is about John.**

1) John's favorite pastime is _____.
a. playing football
b. reading
c. running
d. playing computer games

2) What is NOT true about John?
a. He is a little shy.
b. He is energetic.
c. He likes to exercise.
d. He has no stress.

3   **Amy is talking with her friend about their weekend activity.**

   1) They will go _____ this Saturday.
      a. dancing   b. skating
      c. shopping   d. eating

   2) What is NOT true about the conversation?
      a. They will meet in the morning.
      b. There is a big sale in the mall.
      c. They will probably go there by bus.
      d. They will probably buy some clothes.

4   **A boy is talking about his pastime.**

   1) Choose the best summary.
      a. ☐   His favorite pastime is helping disabled children.
      b. ☐   He volunteers to help disabled children because he is bored.

5   **Sue plans to have a party.**

   1) What is Sue asking Monica?
      a. To go to a theater together.
      b. To bring some DVDs.
      c. To sleep over in her house with other friends.
      d. To recommend a good movie to watch.

   2) When are Monica and Sue going to meet?
      a. Friday night
      b. Friday afternoon
      c. Friday morning
      d. Today

1

W   What are you _____ this _____?

M   I'm going to play computer games.

W   Why don't you _____ some fresh air?

M   Any good ideas?

W   Sure. _____ watch birds in the park.

M   Watching birds? What a _____ thing to do!

W   It's better than _____.

M   I don't think so. Computer games are _____.

2

John is full of energy. He _____ to fight stress. But he is a little shy. He _____ people around when he exercises. He usually exercises alone.

3

Amy   _____ this Saturday?

Jenny   Yes. I have _____.

Amy   Would you like to _____ with me? There is a big sale for summer clothes in the mall.

Jenny   I'd love to. _____ shall we meet?

Amy   How about 11 _____?

Jenny   Sounds great. I'll ask my mom to give us _____.

Amy   Sounds good!

4

Believe or not, my _____ pastime is volunteering to help disabled children. I eat, read and _____ with them every Saturday. I enjoy _____ with them and I also learn a lot from them. Volunteering is _____ to spend some _____ on weekends.

5

Sue   Hi, Monica! _____ this Friday night?

Monica   _____. Why?

Sue   I'm having a slumber party. _____?

Monica   I'd love to. Who else is coming?

Sue   Andrea, Patricia, and Sarah. I'll borrow some DVDs.

Monica   _____?

Sue   Do you have any _____?

Monica   Not really. We can go together and _____.

Sue   Wonderful. Let's meet _____ on Friday.

Monica   Sure.

Can you describe it?

Answers p. 59

GETTING READY

1 Group the words into four categories, and write the numbers in the blanks.

sneakers	plastic	black	striped	jacket
checked	letters	leather	hat	wood
wallet	sunglasses	backpack	suitcase	umbrella
pink	tan			

items

design / pattern

material

color

2 Match the questions with the answers.

1. What does it look like? •   • a. Yes. It's a pink wool sweater.

2. Can you describe it? •   • b. It's about two kilograms.

3. What color is it? •   • c. It's square.

4. What shape is it? •   • d. It's just three days old.

5. How heavy is it? •   • e. It's plastic.

6. How old is it? •   • f. It looks big and expensive.

7. What is it made of? •   • g. It's black and white.

Listening Task

People are describing their bags. Listen and number the pictures.

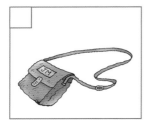   

Listen Again

A. Listen again and choose the correct answer.

1   What is true about the bag?

   a. It's new.   b. It's too big.   c. It's made of leather.

2   What is NOT true about the bag?

   a. It's made of leather.

   b. It's heavy.

   c. It's pretty.

3   What is true about the bag?

   a. It's heavy.

   b. It's strong.

   c. It's good for a long trip.

B. Listen again and choose the best summary.

4
   a. ☐ It has black wheels and a handle.

   b. ☐ It's a black suitcase that holds a lot but it's not too big.

Listening 2

What are they looking for? Choose the right picture.

1   a.   b.   2   a.    b.

3   a.   b.   4   a.    b.

Listen Again

A. Listen again and choose the correct answer.

1   What is he likely to say?

   a. Is it in a case?

   b. Which would you like?

   c. You can come and check.

2   What is he NOT likely to say?

   a. there aren't.

   b. I don't think we have them.

   c. we have it.

3   What is she NOT likely to say?

   a. all your cards and IDs are safe.

   b. how would you like it?

   c. come and get it anytime between 10 a.m. and 4 p.m.

B. Listen again and choose the best response.

4   a. ☐   b. ☐   c. ☐

Answers p. 61

✳ **Listen and fill in the blanks.**

1

W I'm _____ for my hat.

M What _____ it look _____?

W It's brown with a _____ design. It is a little old.

2

Hello, I'm _____ about my umbrella.

It is blue and has a wooden _____.

There are my initials on the handle.

3

M Can you _____ your bag?

W It is gray with brown _____.

M Is it made of leather?

W No, it's _____.

4

They are _____. They are _____ and very _____.

I really need to _____ them. They are my _____ pair of _____.

5

M Gee, I can't _____ it anywhere.

W What are you _____?

M My sweat shirt.

W Is it white with some _____ on it?

M That's right.

W It is in the laundry basket. I haven't washed it yet.

On Your Own

Answers p. 61

LISTEN AND WRITE

Listen and write your own answers.

- I'm wearing _____

_____

- My shoes are _____

_____

- My bag is _____

Write the questions you hear.

_____

_____

_____

_____

PRONUNCIATION

/ k / vs / g /

Listen and repeat.

came	cap	card
come	cold	crab

Listen and repeat.

game	gap	guard
gum	gold	grab

Listen carefully and notice the difference.

came / game	cap / gap
card / guard	come / gum
cold / gold	crab / grab

EXERCISE

Listen and check the words you hear.

☐ came	☐ game
☐ cap	☐ gap
☐ card	☐ guard
☐ come	☐ gum
☐ cold	☐ gold
☐ crab	☐ grab

PRACTICE TEST

✳ Listen and choose the correct answer.

1 **A woman is describing her lost jacket.**

1) Which one is her jacket? Choose the right picture.

a.   b.   c.   d.

2 **A student lost something in the dormitory.**

1) What is he looking for?

a. socks　　　　b. gloves　　　　c. pants　　　　d. sneakers

2) What is true about the notice?
a. They have white stripes.
b. The stripes are on the front.
c. He wore them for only two months.
d. They're covered with leather.

3 **Susan is at the dry cleaner's.**

1) Which clothing item are they talking about?
a. shirt　　　　　　　　b. jacket
c. blouse　　　　　　　d. dress

2) What does Susan's clothing item look like?
a. It is green.　　b. It is striped.　　c. It is checked.

4   **Sarah is looking for something.**

1) What is Sarah looking for?

a.

b.

c.

d.

2) Which is NOT true about the item Sarah is looking for?
    a. made of leather   b. black
    c. old   d. size 6

5   **Paul is describing something that he needs to camp out.**

1) What's it?
    a. sleeping bag   b. mattress
    c. tent   d. parasol

2) What is NOT true about the item?
    a. It's red.
    b. It's heavy and old.
    c. It's for four people.
    d. It's for camping out.

1

M _____ your jacket?

W It is black with _____ buttons.

M _____ ?

W It is leather, very fine leather.

M What _____ is it?

W It's size 6.

M _____ ?

W It is brand new. Oh, one more thing. There are two pockets on the front. Oh, _____ . I must have it back.

2

Looking for _____ .

Lost in the library. Size 8.

White with _____ on the side.

Leather cover. Almost new; only two _____ .

Please call anytime at 012-675-_____ .

3

W Excuse me. I think you gave me the _____ blouse.

M Why do you say that?

W _____ . It is tan. Besides it is not striped. It is with the _____ design.

M Aren't you Sarah Brown?

W No, _____ Brown.

M Oh, I am sorry. _____ .

4

M _____ ?

W I'm looking for a pair of sandals.

M Okay. _____ ?

W Yes. They are _____ with high heels.

M What size?

W _____ .

M Anything else?

W They look _____ .

M Are these leather ones?

W No.

M Then I don't think we have your _____ . I'm sorry.

5

It's waterproof, so you _____ worry about rain. It comes in many _____ . Mine is for four people but it's light and _____ . What color? It's red and I bought it last month so it's _____ . You need it for _____ .

What is wrong with you?

Answers p. 63

GETTING READY

1   Fill in the blanks with the word in the box.

fever	sore	runny	sneeze	cast
toothache	stomachache	itch	headache	watery

1. My head hurts. I have a bad _____ all morning.

2. I have a broken arm. My arm is in a _____ .

3. I have a skin problem. I have a terrible _____ all over my body.

4. I ate too much. I have a _____ .

5. I have to go to the dentist. I have a _____ .

6. I have the flu. I have a _____ throat, a _____ nose, and a high _____ .

7. I have an allergy in the spring. I have _____ eyes. When I _____ , people say, "Bless you."

2   Match the questions with the answers.

1. What's wrong with your leg?   •   • a. I think I should.

2. What happened to your eyes?   •   • b. Not very well.

3. How are you feeling?   •   • c. I broke it last month.

4. What's the problem?   •   • d. I think I have the flu.

5. Why don't you go to the doctor? •   • e. I have an allergy.

Listening Task

Listening 1

What are the problems? Number the pictures.

Listen Again

A. Listen again and choose the correct answer.

1 How did he get the problem?

a. He tripped while playing football.

b. He fell off while cycling.

c. He fell down while climbing.

2 How did he get the problem?

a. He slept with windows open.

b. He walked in the rain.

c. He didn't wear a coat.

3 How did he get the problem?

a. He ate too much chocolate.

b. He ate too much turkey.

c. He drank too much soda.

B. Listen again and choose the best summary.

4   a. ☐ She's itching all over her body and she needs something from the woods.

     b. ☐ She's itching all over her body and the problem is she can't sleep at all.

118

People are talking about their health problems. Number the pictures.

Listen Again

A. Listen again and choose the correct answer.

1 What is the person probably going to do?
   a. go to the eye doctor
   b. go to the dentist
   c. go to the drugstore

2 What is true about the conversation?
   a. She sprained her arm.
   b. It is getting worse.
   c. She will have the cast taken off in a month.

3 What is NOT true about Nancy?
   a. She is taking lots of medicine.
   b. She can't speak because her throat hurts.
   c. She can't go to see her friend.

B. Listen again and choose the correct sentence.

4   a. ☐   b. ☐

Review

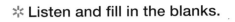

Answers p. 65

✳ Listen and fill in the blanks.

1

W What's _____ with your _____?

M I bumped into a tree in the dark the _____ day.

W Is it getting _____?

M I _____ so.

2 Do you have itchy watery _____? Do you _____ all the time? If you have an allergy, this _____ is just for you. Just _____ it three times a day and you will feel better.

3

W My tooth _____ so much.

M Maybe you have a cavity. _____ you go to the dentist?

W I think I _____.

4 Mary is not feeling _____. She has a _____ throat, a _____ nose, and a high _____. She needs to see a _____ right now. I think she got a _____ when she went to dance _____.

5

M Do you still have the _____?

W Yes, it is very _____.

M Aren't you _____ any medicine?

W No, I don't like medicine.

M You are brave.

On Your Own

Answers p. 65

LISTEN AND WRITE

Listen and write your own answers.

- I feel _____
- I _____
- Yes, I _____
- No, I don't _____
- Yes, _____
- No, _____

Write the questions you hear.

_____

_____

_____

_____

_____

_____

PRONUNCIATION

/ p / vs / b /

Listen and repeat.

pan	pack	pie
pig	tap	mop

Listen and repeat.

ban	back	buy
big	tab	mob

Listen carefully and notice the difference.

pan / ban	pack / back
pie / buy	pig / big
tap / tab	mop / mob

EXERCISE

Listen and check the words you hear.

☐ pan   ☐ ban

☐ pack   ☐ back

☐ pie   ☐ buy

☐ pig   ☐ big

☐ tap   ☐ tab

☐ mop   ☐ mob

✳ Listen and choose the correct answer.

1 Mr. Brown is talking with his doctor.

1) Mr. Brown has a _____ problem.

   a. sleeping   b. personal   c. speaking   d. hearing

2) What is NOT true about Mr. Brown?

   a. He doesn't have much energy.   b. He isn't worried about anything.

   c. He has a problem with his eyes.   d. He is very tired.

2 Two friends are talking about John.

1) John is absent from school because of _____.

   a. his leg   b. his arm   c. his ankle   d. his eyes

2) Which of the following is true?

   a. He is getting better.

   b. It is the first time he is absent from school.

   c. It happened three weeks ago.

   d. He was bitten by a dog.

3 The following is from Jeff's diary.

1) Jeff ruined his test because _____.

   a. he is not good at math   b. the test was hard

   c. he has the flu   d. he didn't know the answers

2) What is NOT true about his body condition?

   a. He has a fever.   b. He sneezes a lot.

   c. His eyes are watery.   d. He has a sore throat.

4   **Tom meets Helen by chance.**

1) What's Helen's problem now?
   a. She doesn't want to tell Tom her problem.
   b. She feels bad because she failed the test.
   c. She wants to cry but she can't.
   d. She failed the test because she didn't study hard.

5   **Jenny is talking to her mom.**

1) What is NOT true about Jenny?
   a. She has a sore throat.
   b. She has a cold.
   c. She has a fever.
   d. She has a headache.

2) What is Jenny's mom probably going to do next?
   a. She'll call the doctor's office.
   b. She'll call the attendance desk at school.
   c. She'll go to see the doctor.
   d. She'll get some tea.

1

W _____, Mr. Brown?

M I am so tired these days. I am out of energy.

W Do you _____ and _____ well?

M No, _____ like eating. And I can't sleep very well either.

W Are you worried about anything?

M No, _____.

W Okay, let me _____ your eyes first.

2

W John is absent from school again.

M Yes, he _____ now.

W What happened to him?

M He was _____ a dog on the leg and it is not _____.

W Oh, _____. When did it happen?

M Three days ago.

3

I _____ really _____ today and I've ruined my math test. The test was not hard. I knew all the answers. But I got six questions wrong. I _____ think clearly. It's _____. I keep sneezing. My eyes are watery. _____ and my head hurts.

4

Tom   Hey, Helen, _____?

Helen I feel like crying.

Tom   Oh no, _____?

Helen I didn't pass the literacy test.

Tom   What happened to you? Didn't you _____ the exam?

Helen Yes, I did. But I had a _____ _____ during the exam.

Tom   Really? And how is your headache now?

Helen _____ but I feel bad anyway.

5

Mom   Wake up, Jenny! You'll _____ again!

Jenny (Groan) Mom, I think _____ _____. Can you call the school and tell them that I'm sick?

Mom   You caught a cold again?

Jenny (Coughs) I think I have a fever and a really _____.

Mom   Okay. You need to rest. _____ _____. Do you want some tea?

Jenny No, thanks. Do you think I need _____?

Mom   You should take some _____ first.

How was the date?

Answers p. 68

GETTING READY

1 List the words under the correct title.

great	terrible	boring	fun	exciting
unhappy	lucky	sad	wonderful	disappointing

Good experience

_____
_____
_____
_____

Bad experience

_____
_____
_____
_____

2 Match the questions with the answers.

1. How was your weekend? •   • a. Yes, I did.

2. How did you like the movie? •   • b. I went to the beach.

3. Did you have fun at the party? •   • c. I was at home.

4. What did you do with John? •   • d. It was great. I got some good rest.

5. Where did you go? •   • e. It was fun. I liked the actor.

6. Where were you? •   • f. We danced.

Listening Task

Listening 1

Choose the picture that matches the story.

1 a.  b.

2 a.   b.

3 a.  b.

4 a.  b.

Listen Again

A. Listen again and choose the correct answer.

1   What did he like best about the trip?

   a. food   b. museums   c. people

2   What is NOT true about her weekend?

   a. She did lots of housework.

   b. She did the work with her family.

   c. She did have much rest.

3   What is NOT true?

   a. He got up too late in the morning.

   b. He had no breakfast.

   c. He got sick because he studied too hard.

B. Listen again and choose the best summary.

4   a. ☐ He enjoyed a date with a girl. They are going to meet again and walk on the clouds.

   b. ☐ He had a date with a girl and they had fun together. They are going to meet again.

Listening 2

Listen and choose the correct word to fill in the blank.

1 Amy felt _____.
   a. excited   b. sad   c. disappointed

2 Pat is _____.
   a. horrified   b. sleepy   c. very well

3 Jeff had a _____ test.
   a. math   b. English   c. science

4 Susan couldn't make it to a _____.
   a. class   b. rehearsal   c. party

Listen Again

A. Listen again and choose the correct answer.

1 What is NOT true about Jane?
   a. She was sad.   b. She cried.   c. She was ready to leave.

2 What is true about Pat?
   a. He doesn't like horror movies.
   b. Somebody chased him at night.
   c. He didn't sleep very well last night.

3 What happened to Jeff?
   a. He dropped out of school.
   b. He had a fight with his friend.
   c. He made mistakes on the test.

B. Listen again and choose the correct sentence.

4   a. ☐   b. ☐

Review

Answers p. 70

❋ **Listen and fill in the blanks.**

1

M _____ was your date? Tell me, please.

W It was _____ . He is handsome and very nice. But we are so _____ .
I don't want to go out with him _____ .

M Oh...

2 I had a _____ with Brian last night. We went to see a _____ . It was
_____ . But Brian didn't _____ to like it. He yawned all the time.

3

W _____ you _____ a nice weekend?

M Yes, how about you?

W I had the most _____ weekend in my life. I was home alone and
nothing _____ .

4 The concert was _____ . I enjoyed it a lot. But on the _____ home we got
caught in a _____ jam. We got home too _____ and I was very _____ .

5

W You have a D in math! What's _____ with you?

M I made terrible _____ on the test.

W _____ ?

M I was not _____ .

On Your Own

Answers p. 70

LISTEN AND WRITE

Listen and write your own answers.

- It _____

  _____

- _____

- _____

- _____

Write the questions you hear.

_____

_____

_____

_____

_____

PRONUNCIATION

/ ð / vs / θ /

Listen and repeat.

| they | that | then |
| there | this | father |

Listen and repeat.

| thank | thousand | thirsty |
| theme | theater | math |

Listen carefully and notice the difference.

they / thank   that / thousand

then / thirsty   there / theme

this / theater   father / math

EXERCISE

Listen carefully and fill in the blanks.

1. My _____ is going to a movie _____.

2. _____ is nobody _____.

3. A _____ people already saw _____ movie.

4. _____ is my favorite subject.

5. Can I get something to drink? I'm really _____.

✳ Listen and choose the correct answer.

1 Two boys are talking.

1) How was Bill's weekend?
   a. terrible
   b. wonderful
   c. boring
   d. busy

2) What is true about the conversation?
   a. Bill won first place on the TV quiz show.
   b. The prize was only game CDs.
   c. They're going to play the game today.

2 The following is from Jeff's diary.

1) How is Jeff feeling now?
   a. terrific
   b. unhappy
   c. wonderful
   d. excited

2) Circle the correct words.

Jeff was playing (baseball / basketball) today.

He broke his neighbor's (door / window).

Now he has to clean the (garage / bathroom) for (one / two) week(s).

3   **Amy is talking with her friend.**

1) How was her camping trip?
   a. fun   b. scary
   c. exciting   d. wonderful

2) Why was the trip sleepless?
   a. They had fun telling jokes all night.
   b. They played games all night.
   c. They heard animal sounds all night.
   d. They saw some animals.

4   **Sophie meets her mom.**

1) Where is the conversation probably taking place?
   a. restaurant   b. airport   c. their home   d. airplane

2) Which might NOT be true for the situation?
   a. Sophie's just come back from her trip.
   b. Sophie enjoyed the food in Mexico.
   c. Sophie enjoyed long-distance flights.
   d. Sophie had great experience during the trip.

5   **The following is what Jim wrote in his diary.**

1) Put what happened to Jim in the order.
   He missed the bus.   (_____)
   He couldn't get into his house.   (_____)
   He had a nightmare.   (_____)

2) How is Jim least likely to be feeling?
   a. tired   b. sad   c. unhappy   d. great

Listen and fill in the blanks.

Answers p. 72

1

Jason   How was your weekend, Bill?

Bill   _____!

Jason   How come?

Bill   I won the first place on the _____
quiz show.

Jason   Wow! _____ the prize?

Bill   Three hot game CDs and 50 _____.

Jason   Great! _____ the games
with you today?

Bill   Sure.

2

Today, _____.
I hit a ball and it broke my neighbor's
_____. My neighbor Mr. Grumble
was _____ and he called _____.
My mom told me to pay for the broken
window. I said _____ have any
money. Then she said I could clean the
_____ for a week. I had no
_____.

3

M   Hi, Amy! _____ trip?

W   It was totally sleepless.

M   You had _____ all
night, didn't you?

W   No. _____ games
and telling jokes. Then we heard some
_____. The animals howled
all night. It was so _____.

4

Sophie   Hi, mom!

Mom   Hi, sweetie! _____
from your trip?

Sophie   Actually, I am. I _____
_____ for 11 hours and I couldn't
_____ at all.

Mom   Too bad. Did you have _____
in Mexico?

Sophie   Yeah, _____.
I learned so many things.

Mom   I'm glad _____ that. Let's go
home.

Sophie   Yeah, I'm _____.

Mom   How was the food there?

Sophie   Spicy and hot. But _____.

5

Dear Diary,

I had the most _____ ever.
I woke up from _____.
I missed the bus, so I was late for _____.
You think _____? It
got even _____. I came home and
realized I had forgotten my _____.
I had to wait _____ until my
mom _____ her office. I'm
just glad _____ is over now.

수준별 맞춤

Vocabulary 시리즈

The VOCA+BULARY
완전 개정판 1~7

This Is Vocabulary
초급, 중급, 고급,
어원편

Grammar 시리즈

Grammar 공감
Level 1~3

After School Grammar
Level 1~3

Grammar Bridge
Level 1~3

중학영문법 뽀개기
Level 1~3

The Grammar with Workbook
Starter
Level 1~2

OK Grammar
Level 1~4

The Grammar
Starter
Level 1~3

This Is Grammar
초급 1·2
중급 1·2
고급 1·2

The More The Better

The
best preparation for

LISTENING

Answers

Nexus Contents Development Team · Miran Hong

Integrated Approach to Listening Comprehension

The more language structures are presented,
the better language awareness is improved.

www.nexusbook.com / www.nexusEDU.kr
MP3 Free Download

1
Level

NEXUS Edu

The
best preparation for

LISTENING

Answers

Nexus Contents Development Team · Miran Hong

1
Level

NEXUS Edu

UNIT 1
Hi! My name is Jeff Brown.

1. Hi, my name is Jeffrey Brown, but everyone calls me Jeff. I was born in Michigan but now I live in Springfield, Ohio. I am in the ninth grade.

2. Let me introduce my family and friend. These are my sisters Amy and Susan. Amy is in the 10th grade and Susan is in college. Susan doesn't live with us. She lives in the dorm at school.

3. Now, meet my parents. My father is a computer programmer, and my mother is a music teacher. She works only part time.

4. Lastly, this is my best friend Patrick. We have been friends since we were five. He lives in my neighborhood. We go to the same school.

Getting Ready   p. 5

1.	I	G	G	G	G
	I	I	G	I	

2. 1. c   2. a   3. b   4. e   5. d

1. 인사하는 표현에는 'G', 소개하는 표현에는 'I'라고 쓰시오.

안녕, 내 이름은 John Smith야.	I
안녕, 어떻게 지내니?	G
처음 뵙겠습니다, White 씨.	G
오랜만이야.	G
그동안 어떻게 지냈니?	G
내 소개를 할게.	I
John, 내 친구 Nancy를 소개할게.	I
만나서 반가워.	G
내 친구 John을 소개할게.	I

2. 질문을 답과 연결시키시오.

1. 잘 지내니?   c. 잘 지내, 고마워. 너는?
2. 너는 어디에서 왔니?   a. 나는 캘리포니아 출신이야.
3. 만나서 반가워.   b. 나도 만나서 반가워.
4. 내 친구 John을 소개할게.   e. 안녕, John. 만나서 반가워.
5. 어떻게 지내니?   d. 아주 잘 지내.

해석

1. 안녕, 내 이름은 Jeffrey Brown이야. 하지만 모두 나를 Jeff라고 불러. 나는 미시간 주에서 태어났는데, 지금은 오하이오 주에 있는 스프링필드에 살아. 나는 9학년이야.

2. 우리 가족과 친구를 소개할게. 이쪽은 우리 누나 Amy와 Susan이야. Amy는 10학년이고, Susan은 대학생이야. Susan은 우리와 함께 살지 않아. 그녀는 학교 기숙사에 살아.

3. 이제, 부모님을 소개할게. 아빠는 컴퓨터 프로그래머시고, 엄마는 음악 선생님이셔. 엄마는 파트타임으로만 일을 하셔.

4. 마지막으로, 나의 가장 친한 친구 Patrick이야. 우린 다섯 살 때부터 친구였어. 얘는 우리 동네에 살아. 우리는 같은 학교에 다녀.

Listening Task   p. 6~7

Listening 1		1. T	2. F	3. F	4. F
Listen Again	A	1. b	2. b	3. a	
	B	4. a			
Listening 2		1. G	2. G	3. I	4. I
Listen Again	A	1. c	2. b	3. a	
	B	4. c			

Listening 1   p. 6

Jeff가 그의 가족과 친구를 소개하고 있다. True(참) 또는 False(거짓)에 표시하시오.

1. Jeff는 자기소개를 하고 있다. （T）
2. Amy와 Susan은 전에 만난 적이 없다. （F）
3. Jeff는 당신이 자신의 아버지와 인사하기를 바란다. （F）
4. Jeff와 Patrick은 사촌이다. （F）

Listen Again   p. 6

A. 다시 듣고 알맞은 답을 고르시오.

1. Jeff는 스프링필드에(서) _____.
   a. 태어났다   ★b. 살고 있다   c. 방문한다

2. Susan은 _____.
   a. Amy보다 어리다
   ★b. Jeff보다 나이가 많다
   c. 고등학생이다

3. Jeff의 아버지는 _____이다.
   ★a. 컴퓨터 프로그래머   b. 시간제 근로자   c. 교사

B. 다시 듣고 가장 적절하게 요약한 것을 고르시오.

4. a. ★ Jeff와 Patrick은 다섯 살 때부터 가장 친한 친구이다.
   b. ☐ Jeff와 Patrick은 다섯 살 때부터 같은 학교에 다닌다.

Listing 2

듣고, 소개하는 대화이면 'I'를 인사하는 대화이면 'G'를 적으시오.

1. __G__   2. __G__   3. __I__   4. __I__

스크립트

1.

Cindy Hi, Jeff! Am I late?
Jeff   No, not at all. How are you doing, Cindy?
Cindy Fine, thanks. And you?
Jeff   Great! It's a nice party, isn't it?
Cindy _____Yes, it is._____

2.

Jeff   Long time no see, Mary.
Mary   Yeah. So how have you been?
Jeff   Pretty well. How about you?
Mary   Just fine. How is your sister Amy?
Jeff   _____Very well._____

3.

Jeff   Hi! My name is Jeff Brown.
Kevin Hi, Kevin Smith.
Jeff   Are you new here?
Kevin Yes, I am. I've just moved from California.
Jeff   _____Nice to meet you._____

4.

Jeff   Cindy, this is Kevin, new from California.
       Kevin, Cindy.
Cindy Hi, Kevin. Nice to meet you.
Kevin It's great to meet you, Cindy.
Cindy Welcome to Springfield!
Kevin _____Thank you._____

해석

1. Cindy 안녕, Jeff! 내가 늦었니?
   Jeff 아니야, 전혀. 잘 지내니, Cindy?
   Cindy 잘 지내, 고마워. 너는?
   Jeff 아주 잘 지내! 멋진 파티야, 안 그러니?
   Cindy _____응, 그래._____

2. Jeff 오랜만이야, Mary.
   Mary 그래. 그동안 어떻게 지냈니?
   Jeff 아주 잘 지냈어. 너는 어때?
   Mary 잘 지내. 너의 누나 Amy는 잘 지내니?
   Jeff _____아주 잘 지내._____

3. Jeff 안녕! 내 이름은 Jeff Brown이야.
   Kevin 안녕, 나는 Kevin Smith야.
   Jeff 여기 처음이니?
   Kevin 응. 나는 캘리포니아에서 막 이사 왔어.
   Jeff _____만나서 반가워._____

4. Jeff   Cindy, 얘는 캘리포니아에서 새로 온 Kevin이야. Kevin, Cindy야.
   Cindy 안녕, Kevin. 만나서 반가워.
   Kevin 만나게 되어 너무 반가워, Cindy.
   Cindy 스프링필드에 온 걸 환영해!
   Kevin _____고마워._____

Listen Again

A. 다시 듣고 알맞은 답을 고르시오.

1. 이어질 응답으로 가장 적절한 것은?
   a. 넌 틀렸어.   b. 미안해.   ★c. 응, 그래.

2. 이어질 응답으로 가장 적절한 것은?
   a. 또 보자.   ★b. 아주 잘 지내.   c. 그녀는 괜찮을 거야.

3. 이어질 응답으로 가장 적절한 것은?
   ★a. 만나서 반가워.   b. 덥다.   c. 난 캘리포니아가 싫어.

B. 다시 듣고 가장 어울리는 응답을 고르시오.

4. a. ☐ 천만에.   b. ☐ 나도 그래.   c. ★ 고마워.

스크립트

a. You're welcome.   b. Me, too.   c. Thank you.

Review

1. are you, Pretty, going, fine
2. morning, homeroom, happy, big
3. time no, How are you doing, I'm fine, How about you
4. introduce, name, from, meet
5. Nice to meet you, Glad to meet you, Where are you from

※ 듣고 빈칸을 채우시오.

해석

1. M 잘 지내니, Susie?
   W 잘 지내.
   M 피아노 레슨은 잘 되어 가니?
   W 아주 잘 되고 있어.

2. 안녕하세요, 여러분.
   나는 여러분의 담임 선생님인 Sheri Grue입니다.
   여러분 모두를 만나게 되어서 아주 기뻐요. 멋진 한 해를 만들어 봐요!

3. W 오랜만이다, Simon.
   M 안녕, Susie. 어떻게 지내니?
   W 잘 지내. 너는?
   M 나도 잘 지내.

4. 안녕! 내 소개를 할게.

내 이름은 Kevin Smith야. 나는 캘리포니아 출신이야. 모두들 만나서 반가워.

5. **Jeff** Susie, 내 친구 Kevin이야. Kevin, Susie야.
   Susie 안녕, Kevin. 만나서 반가워.
   Kevin 안녕, Susie. 만나서 반가워.
   Susie 너는 어디에서 왔니?
   Kevin 캘리포니아에서.

On Your Own p. 9

LISTEN & WRITE

들리는 질문을 써 보세요.

스크립트

| Introduce yourself. | 자신을 소개해 보세요. |
| How are you doing? | 요즘 어떻게 지내세요? |

PRONUNCIATION

/ i / vs. / iː /

☞ 듣고 따라해 보시오.
   그것, 때리다, 앉다, 조각, 채우다, 살다

☞ 듣고 따라해 보시오.
   먹다, 열, 좌석, 치다, 느끼다, 떠나다

☞ 잘 들어보고 차이점을 발견해 보시오.
   그것 / 먹다, 때리다 / 열, 앉다 / 좌석, 조각 / 치다
   채우다 / 느끼다, 살다 / 떠나다

듣고 들리는 단어를 체크하시오

스크립트 eat, heat, sit, beat, feel, live

그것	☐	먹다	★
치다	☐	열	★
앉다	★	좌석	☐
조각	☐	치다	★
채우다	☐	느끼다	★
살다	★	떠나다	☐

Practice Test p. 10~11

1. 1) a 2) a   2. 1) d 2) b   3. 1) d 2) c
4. 1) c   5. 1) d 2) d

✻ 듣고 알맞은 답을 고르시오.

1. Grue 선생님 반에 전학생이 왔다.

스크립트

W Good morning, class. I'd like you to meet a new friend this morning. Stephen, will you introduce yourself?
M Yes, ma'am. Hello. My name is Stephen Collins. I'm from New Mexico, south of here. I'm very glad to meet you all.
W Let's welcome Stephen with a big hand.

해석
W 안녕하세요, 여러분. 오늘 아침에는 새로운 친구를 소개할게요. Stephen, 네 소개를 하겠니?
M 네, 선생님. 안녕. 내 이름은 Stephen Collins야. 나는 이곳의 남쪽에 있는 뉴멕시코 주에서 왔어. 너희 모두를 만나게 되어 매우 기뻐.
W 열렬한 박수로 Stephen을 환영합시다.

1) 다음 중 대화 내용과 일치하는 것은?
   ★a. Stephen이 자신을 소개하고 있다.
   b. 지금은 오후이다.
   c. 대화는 길거리에서 일어나고 있다.
   d. 선생님이 Stephen을 소개하고 있다.

2) Stephen에 대한 내용과 일치하는 것은?
   ★a. 그의 성은 Collins이다.   b. 그는 멕시코에서 왔다.
   c. 그는 새로 온 선생님이다.   d. 그는 남아메리카에서 왔다.

2. 길거리에서 Maria가 Joey를 만나고 있다.
스크립트

Joey	Maria, long time no see.
Maria	Yeah. So how have you been, Joey?
Joey	Great! How about you?
Maria	Not so good. Actually, I've been awful.
Joey	Sorry to hear that. What's the problem?
Maria	I have been sick.

해석
Joey Maria, 오랜만이야.
Maria 그래. 그동안 어떻게 지냈니, Joey?
Joey 아주 잘 지냈어! 너는 어때?
Maria 그렇게 좋진 않았어. 사실, 끔찍했어.
Joey 정말 유감이다. 무슨 일인데?
Maria 나 아팠어.

1) 대화 내용에 대해 다음 중 일치하지 않는 것은?
   a. 그들은 오래된 친구이다.
   b. 그들은 오랫동안 서로 보지 못했다.
   c. Maria는 잘 지내지 못했다.
   ★d. 그들은 서로 소개를 하고 있다.

2) Maria가 할 말로 가장 적당한 것은 무엇인가?
- a. 나도 그래.　　★b. 나 아팠어.
- c. 나도 미안해.　　d. 시험에서 A를 받았어.

3. Ted와 Amy가 함께 있는데 Amy가 Mary를 만난다.

스크립트

Amy	Hi, Mary!
Mary	Hi, Amy!
Amy	Do you two know each other?
Mary	No, I don't think so.
Amy	Well, then let me introduce you two. Mary, this is my new friend Ted Norton. Ted, this is Mary Smith. She's my cousin.
Ted	It's very nice to meet you, Mary.
Mary	Glad to meet you, Ted.

해석

Amy	안녕, Mary!
Mary	안녕, Amy!
Amy	너희 둘 아는 사이야?
Mary	아니, 아닌 것 같은데.
Amy	음, 그럼 내가 너희들을 소개시켜 줄게. Mary, 내 새 친구 Ted Norton이야. Ted, Mary Smith야. 내 사촌이야.
Ted	만나서 정말 반가워, Mary.
Mary	만나서 반가워, Ted.

1) 다음 중 대화 내용과 일치하는 것은?
- a. Mary는 전에 Amy를 만난 적이 없다.
- b. Ted는 Mary에게 자기를 소개하고 있다.
- c. Amy와 Mary는 새로 사귄 친구이다.
- ★d. Mary와 Ted는 전에 서로 만난 적이 없다.

2) Mary는 누구인가?
- a. Amy의 여동생　　b. Amy의 친구
- ★c. Amy의 사촌　　d. Amy의 선생님

4. Jim과 Sharp 씨는 공항에 있으며 Jim은 친구를 만난다.

스크립트

Jim	Mary? Is that really you?
Mary	It certainly is!
Jim	Long time no see. How have you been?
Mary	Just great!
Jim	Oh, excuse my bad manners! Mary, meet my boss Mr. Sharp. He is from Germany.
Mary	Nice to meet you, Mr. Sharp.
Mr. Sharp	Nice to meet you, too.

해석

Jim	Mary? 너 맞니?
Mary	물론이지!
Jim	정말 오랜만이네. 어떻게 지냈어?
Mary	잘 지냈지!
Jim	아, 내 무례를 용서해. Mary, 내 상사이신 Sharp 씨를 소개할게. 독일에서 오셨어.
Mary	만나서 반갑습니다. Sharp 씨.
Mr.Sharp	저도 만나서 반갑습니다.

1) Sharp 씨가 다음에 할 말은 무엇입니까?
- a. 오랜만입니다.
- b.당신이 그립습니다.
- ★c. 저도 만나서 반갑습니다.

5. Matt는 동굴 관광 안내원이다.

스크립트

Good morning! Let me introduce myself. I'm Matt. I'm your guide, today. I'm from California, and I study Pacific caves. Also, I want you to meet our driver Dan. Please remember that we need to be quiet inside the cave. Now, follow my light.

해석

반갑습니다. 제 소개를 하겠습니다. 이름은 Matt이며 오늘 여러분을 안내할 사람입니다. 저는 캘리포니아 출신이며, 태평양의 동굴들을 연구하고 있습니다. 아울러 우리의 운전사 Dan을 소개하겠습니다. 동굴 안에서 조용히 하는 것을 기억하세요. 이제, 제 불빛을 따라 오십시오.

1) Matt는 지금 무엇을 하고 있습니까?
- a. 태평양의 동굴들을 연구하고 있다.
- b. 캘리포니아를 여행하고 있다.
- c. 버스를 운전하고 있다.
- ★d. 자신을 소개하고 있다.

2) Matt가 다음에 할 일은 무엇입니까?
- a. 작별 인사를 한다.　　b. 동굴을 나온다.
- c. 관광 버스를 출발시킨다.　★d. 동굴 안으로 들어간다.

Dictation　　　　　　　　　　p. 12

1. meet, friend, introduce yourself, south of here, glad, welcome
2. no see, Great, Not so good, Sorry, problem
3. each other, think, let me, new friend, nice, Gald
4. How have you been, Just great, meet, from
5. Let me introduce, guide, I'm from, meet, remember, follow

UNIT 2
Do you like sports?

Getting Ready

1.

School Subjects 교과목	Team Sports 단체 스포츠	Individual Sports/ Exercise 개인 스포츠 / 운동
science	football	walking
math	tennis	cycling
P.E.	baseball	going to the gym
history	volleyball	hiking
social studies	hockey	

2. 1. f   2. a   3. c   4. b   5. e   6 .d

1. 아래의 단어를 알맞은 칸에 적으시오.

과학	미식축구	수학	체육	걷기
역사	자전거 타기	테니스	체육관 가기	야구
등산	하키	배구	사회	

2. 질문을 답과 연결시키시오.
1. 스포츠를 좋아하니?   f. 응, 좋아해.
2. 어떤 종류의 스포츠를 좋아하니?   a. 나는 테니스를 좋아해.
3. 얼마나 자주 경기를 하니?   c. 일주일에 한 번.
4. 네가 가장 좋아하는 과목이 뭐니? b. 과학이야.
5. 왜 그걸 좋아하니?   e. 선생님을 좋아하거든.
6. 수학을 제일 좋아하니?   d. 아니, 그렇지 않아.

Listening Task

Listening 1
1. Beth   - likes : P.E., hockey
           - doesn't like : math, science
2. Steve - likes : art, skiing
           - doesn't like : math, P.E.
3. Pete   - likes : music, going to the gym, English
           - doesn't like : history
4. Susie - likes : P.E., dance
           - doesn't like : history, science
Listen Again   A   1. a   2. b   3. a
               B   4. b
Listening 2   1. Steve   2. Mike
                            3. Kevin   4. Cindy
Listen Again   A   1. b   2. a   3. b
               B   4. b

Listening I

듣고 '좋아한다'나 '싫어한다'에 표시하시오.

스크립트

1. I'm Beth. I like P.E. best. The teacher is fun. But I hate math and science. They are too boring. And sports? I play hockey.

2. I'm Steve. My favorite subject is art. Why? Because it's my best subject. Actually I like drawing, you know. But I don't like math and P.E. They are my worst subjects. As for sports... I like skiing, yeah, skiing.

3. I'm Pete. What subjects do I like? Well, I love music class best, and English too. All my friends are there. But I don't like art and history classes. I don't like the group. And for exercise I go to the gym.

4. I'm Susie. Oh, I love P.E. I love the teacher. He is so handsome. The subjects I don't like... Uh... History and science. History and science give me a headache. They are too hard. And sports... Well, I don't play any sports. But I dance.

해석
1. 나는 Beth야. 나는 체육을 가장 좋아해. 선생님이 재미있으셔. 그러나 수학과 과학을 싫어해. 너무 지루해. 스포츠? 나는 하키를 해.

2. 나는 Steve야. 가장 좋아하는 과목은 미술이야. 왜냐고? 내가 가장 잘하는 과목이기 때문이야. 사실 나는 그림 그리는 걸 좋아해. 그러나 수학과 체육을 싫어해. 내가 제일 못하는 과목이야. 스포츠로는... 스키, 그래, 스키를 좋아해.

3. 나는 Pete야. 내가 어떤 과목을 좋아하냐고? 음, 음악 수업을 가장 좋아하고, 영어도 좋아해. 내 친구들이 모두 거기에 있어. 그러나 미술과 역사 수업을 좋아하지 않아. 거기 있는 애들이 싫어. 그리고 운동으로는 체육관에 가.

4. 나는 Susie야. 오, 나는 체육을 좋아해. 선생님이 좋아. 아주 잘생겼어. 싫어하는 과목은... 역사와 과학이야. 역사와 과학은 머리가 아파. 너무 어려워. 그리고 스포츠는... 음, 나는 어떤 스포츠도 하지 않아. 그러나 나는 춤을 춰.

Listen Again

A. 다시 듣고 알맞은 답을 고르시오.
1. Beth는 _____ 때문에 체육을 좋아한다.
   ★a. 선생님이 좋기   b. 그 과목을 잘 하기   c. 운동을 좋아하기

2. Steve는 _____ 때문에 미술을 좋아한다.
   a. 선생님이 좋기   ★b. 그 과목을 잘 하기   c. 급우들이 좋기

3. Pete는 _____ 때문에 그 과목을 좋아한다.
  ★a. 거기에서 그의 친구들을 만날 수 있기
  b. 수업이 지루하지 않기
  c. 선생님들이 재미있기

B. 다시 듣고 가장 적절하게 요약한 것을 고르시오.

4. a. ☐ Susie는 잘하는 과목이라서 체육을 좋아한다.
  b. ★ Susie는 선생님이 잘생겨서 체육을 좋아한다.

Listening 2
p. 15

듣고 스포츠와 사람을 연결하시오.

스크립트

1.
Jeff   Look at all these rackets! Are they all yours, Steve?
Steve No. My whole family plays tennis.
Jeff   You must be very good at it.
Steve No, not really. But I work hard.
Jeff   That's why you're in great shape.

2.
Susan Mike, do you still jog every morning?
Mike   I want to, but I can't. I have sprained my ankle.
Susan So you're not exercising at all?
Mike   I swim instead.

3.
Kevin The Pirates were great last night, weren't they?
Jeff   By the way, how often do you practice baseball, Kevin?
Kevin Three times a week.
Jeff   That's a lot. Why don't you join my baseball club?
Kevin Sounds great. Thanks for inviting me, Jeff!

4.
Jeff   What do you do for exercise, Cindy?
Cindy Exercise? You know me. I don't exercise at all. I hate it.
Jeff   So you don't exercise at all?
Cindy I walk. I walk to school. That's it.

해석
1. Jeff   이 라켓들을 봐! 이것들 모두 너의 것이니, Steve?
   Steve 아니야. 우리 가족 모두 테니스를 쳐.
   Jeff   너 테니스 잘 하겠다.
   Steve 아니야, 그렇게 잘하지는 않아. 하지만 열심히는 해.
   Jeff   그래서 네가 몸매가 좋구나.

2. Susan Mike, 아직도 매일 아침 조깅을 하니?
   Mike   그러고는 싶은데, 그러지 못해. 발목을 삐었어.
   Susan 그러면 전혀 운동을 하지 않니?
   Mike   대신에 수영을 해.

3. Kevin 어젯밤 Pirates팀은 훌륭했어, 그렇지 않니?
   Jeff   그건 그렇고, Kevin, 너는 얼마나 자주 야구 연습을 하니?
   Kevin 일주일에 세 번.
   Jeff   많이 하는구나. 우리 야구 클럽에 가입하는 거 어때?
   Kevin 그거 좋겠다. 초대해 줘서 고마워, Jeff!

4. Jeff   너는 무슨 운동을 하니, Cindy?
   Cindy 운동? 알잖아. 나는 운동을 전혀 안 해. 난 운동이 싫어.
   Jeff   그래서 운동을 전혀 안 하니?
   Cindy 걷기를 해. 학교에 걸어 다니잖아. 그게 다야.

Listen Again
p. 15

A. 다시 듣고 맞는 것을 고르시오.

1. a. 가족 중 Steve만 테니스를 한다.
  ★b. Steve는 테니스를 열심히 연습한다.
  c. Steve는 몸매가 안 좋아서 테니스를 한다.

2.★a. Mike는 발목이 삐었다.
  b. Mike는 다리가 부러졌다.
  c. Mike는 운동을 전혀 하지 않는다.

3. a. Kevin은 Jeff의 야구 클럽에 가입하고 싶어 하지 않는다.
  ★b. Kevin은 야구를 열심히 연습한다.
  c. Kevin은 어젯밤 야구 경기를 보지 않았다.

B. 다시 듣고 맞는 문장을 고르시오.

4. a. ☐ Cindy는 운동으로 걷기를 너무 좋아하기 때문에 학교에 걸어간다.
  b. ★ Cindy는 운동을 싫어하기 때문에 거의 하지 않는다.

스크립트

a. Cindy walks to school because she loves walking for exercise.
b. Cindy hardly exercises because she hates it.

Review
p. 16

1. subject, math, teacher, good, work
2. fat, jog, swim, go, girlfriend
3. favorite, football, don't, walk
4. exercise, gym, three, times, a lot of
5. math, best, science, teacher

※ 듣고 빈칸을 채우시오.

해석
1. John 어떤 과목을 가장 좋아하니?
   Jane 수학을 좋아해.

7

John 나도 그래. 나는 선생님이 좋아. 너는 수학을 잘하니?

Jane 아니. 하지만 열심히 해.

2. 나는 너무 뚱뚱해. 건강도 안 좋아. 그래서 운동을 시작했어. 아침에는 조깅을 하고, 오후에는 수영을 하고, 저녁에는 체육관에 가. 힘들긴 하지만 자신감이 생겨. 주위 사람들, 특히 내 여자 친구가 내가 변한 걸 좋아해.

3. Peter 가장 좋아하는 운동이 무엇이니?

Susan 미식축구를 좋아해. 너는 어때?

Peter 나는 운동은 하지 않아. 그냥 가끔 걸어.

4. Amy는 뚱뚱했고 운동을 하지 않았지만, 이제는 체육관에 가는 것을 좋아한다. 그곳에서 일주일에 세 번 또는 네 번 운동한다. 많은 양이다. 몸무게가 많이 줄어든 이유는 그 때문일 것이다.

5. Jeff 와! 너 수학에서 A를 받았구나!

Pat 응. 수학은 내가 제일 잘 하는 과목이야.

Jeff 너는 수학을 제일 좋아해, 그렇지 않니?

Pat 아니, 과학이 제일 좋긴 한데, 수학 선생님을 제일 좋아해.

On Your Own
p. 17

LISTEN & WRITE

들리는 질문을 써 보세요.

스크립트

> What is your favorite subject?
> What is your worst subject?
> Who's your favorite teacher?
> What kind of sports do you like?
> How often do you play it?

해석
당신이 가장 좋아하는 과목은 무엇입니까?
당신이 가장 못하는 과목은 무엇입니까?
당신이 가장 좋아하는 선생님은 누구입니까?
무슨 운동을 가장 좋아합니까?
얼마나 자주 그 운동을 합니까?

PRONUNCIATION

/ u / vs / uː /

☞ 듣고 따라해 보시오.
가득한, 당기다, 보다, 두건, 해야 한다

☞ 듣고 따라해 보시오.
바보, 수영장, 누가복음, who'd, shoed

☞ 잘 들어보고 차이점을 발견해 보시오.
가득한 / 바보, 당기다 / 수영장, 보다 / 누가복음,
두건 / who'd, 해야 한다 / shoed

듣고 들리는 단어를 체크하시오.

스크립트 full, pool, Luke , hood, shoed

가득한	★	바보	☐
당기다	☐	수영장	★
보다	☐	누가복음	★
두건	★	who'd	☐
해야 한다	☐	shoed	★

Practice Test
p. 18~19

1. 1) b 2) c   2. 1) b 2) a   3. 1) a 2) b
4. 1) b 2) d   5. 1) c 2) a

※ 듣고 알맞은 답을 고르시오.

1. Brad는 Mary에게 자신이 가장 좋아하는 과목을 이야기하고 있다.

스크립트

Mary What is your favorite subject, Brad?

Brad It's science. I love it.

Mary Because you are good at it. Right?

Brad No. I am good at math, but not at science.

Mary Then why do you like science so much?

Brad Well, this is a secret between you and me. It's because Laura is in the class. That's why.

Mary Ah, now I see.

해석

Mary 가장 좋아하는 과목이 무엇이니, Brad?

Brad 과학. 나는 과학을 좋아해.

Mary 네가 잘하기 때문이구나. 맞지?

Brad 아니야. 수학을 잘 하지만, 과학은 아니야.

Mary 그러면 왜 과학을 그렇게 좋아하니?

Brad 음, 이건 너와 나 사이의 비밀이야. 같이 과학 수업을 듣는 Laura 때문이야. 그게 이유야.

Mary 오, 이제 알겠어.

1) Brad가 가장 좋아하는 과목은 무엇인가?
   a. 수학   ★b. 과학   c. 사회   d. 영어

2) 그 과목을 왜 좋아하는가?
   a. 선생님을 좋아한다.
   b. 그 과목을 잘 한다.
   ★c. 좋아하는 여자 아이가 그 반에 있다.
   d. 비밀이 많이 있다.

2. Susan은 자신이 가장 좋아하는 운동에 대해 말하고 있다.

스크립트

I like outdoor exercise. I love fresh air but I don't like water. I like to exercise alone. I don't like team sports. I like this exercise because I can do it anytime anywhere. I don't need anything. I need just a pair of shoes. My favorite exercise is _____ walking _____ .

해석

나는 실외 운동을 좋아한다. 신선한 공기를 좋아하지만 물은 싫어한다. 혼자 운동하는 것을 좋아한다. 단체 스포츠를 싫어한다. 언제 어디서나 할 수 있기 때문에 나는 이 운동을 좋아한다. 아무 것도 필요하지 않다. 단지 신발 한 켤레만 있으면 된다. 내가 가장 좋아하는 운동은 _____ 걷기 _____ (이)다.

1) Susan이 좋아하는 운동은 무엇인가?
   a. 수영   ★b. 걷기   c. 축구   d. 에어로빅

2) Susan이 이 운동을 좋아하는 이유가 <u>아닌</u> 것은?
   ★a. 다른 사람들과 함께 할 수 있다.
   b. 신선한 공기를 좋아한다.
   c. 어디서나 할 수 있다.
   d. 실외 운동을 좋아한다.

3. Ben은 방과 후에 뭘 하는지에 대해 Jane에게 말하고 있다.

스크립트

Jane   What do you do after school, Ben? You always hurry home.
Ben   I play ice hockey.
Jane   Do you play it every day?
Ben   No, just three times a week.
Jane   Then what do you do the other days?
Ben   I go cycling.
Jane   You really like sports.

해석

Jane   학교 끝나고 뭘 하니, Ben? 항상 서둘러 집에 가던데.
Ben   아이스하키를 해.
Jane   매일 해?
Ben   아니, 일주일에 세 번만 해.
Jane   그러면 다른 날에는 뭐 해?
Ben   자전거를 타.
Jane   운동을 정말 좋아하는구나.

1) Ben은 방과 후에 어떤 운동을 하는가?
   ★a. 아이스하키   b. 배구
   c. 축구   d. 야구

2) 대화 내용과 일치하지 않는 것은?
   a. Ben은 운동을 좋아한다.
   ★b. Ben은 매일 아이스하키를 한다.
   c. Ben은 가끔씩 자전거를 탄다.
   d. Ben은 항상 학교가 끝난 후에 운동을 한다.

4. 교실에게 Scott가 Annette에게 이야기하고 있다.

스크립트

Scott   Annette! Are you going to the library?
Annette   No, I'm going swimming. Do you want to come with me?
Scott   Well, not now. How often do you go swimming?
Annette   Once a week, or whenever I feel down.
Scott   I guess it is refreshing.
Annette   Definitely. Do you like swimming, too?
Scott   Not really. But I enjoy playing tennis.
Annette   Me, too! We should play together sometime. I have to go now. Bye!
Scott   See you soon!

해석

Scott   Annette! 도서관에 갈 거야?
Annette   아니, 수영하러 갈 거야. 같이 갈래?
Scott   음, 지금 말고. 수영장에 얼마나 자주 가?
Annette   일주일에 한 번, 아니면 언제든 기분이 안 좋을 때.
Scott   수영을 하면 기분이 좋아지나 보구나.
Annette   물론. 너도 수영 좋아해?
Scott   별로. 하지만 난 테니스 치는 걸 좋아해.
Annette   나도 좋아하는데! 언제 한번 같이 치자. 나 이제 가야 해. 안녕!
Scott   나중에 봐!

1) 여학생이 하려고 하는 것은 무엇인가?
   a. 테니스 치기   ★b. 수영   c. 친구 만나기   d. 도서관에 가기

2) 대화 내용과 일치하는 것은?
   a. 남학생은 도서관에 갈 것이다.
   b. 여학생은 테니스를 칠 것이다.
   c. 그들은 함께 수영하러 갈 것이다.
   ★d. 여학생은 적어도 일주일에 한 번은 수영하러 간다.

5. Andrew와 Lesley가 수업 중에 이야기를 하고 있다.

Andrew	I hate this class. It's boring, isn't it?
Lesley	Sometimes, but I like the teacher.
Andrew	Oh, I see. That's why you always do your history homework.
Lesley	Yes. What about you? Which class do you like best?
Andrew	I'm good at math but the teacher gives too much homework.
Lesley	What about P.E.? We don't have any homework.
Andrew	You're right. I think I like P.E. class best.

해석

Andrew	이 수업 정말 싫어. 정말 따분하지 않아?
Lesley	가끔씩, 그렇지만 난 저 선생님이 좋아.
Andrew	오, 알았다. 그래서 네가 항상 역사 숙제를 해오는 구나.
Lesley	그래. 너는? 넌 어떤 수업을 가장 좋아해?
Andrew	나는 수학을 잘하지만 선생님께서 숙제를 너무 많이 내 주셔.
Lesley	체육은 어때? 숙제가 전혀 없잖아.
Andrew	맞아. 내 생각에 난 체육을 가장 좋아하는 것 같아.

1) 어떤 수업 중에 소년과 소녀가 이야기를 하고 있는가?
   a. 체육   b. 수학   ★c. 역사   d. 영어

2) 다음 중 사실이 <u>아닌</u> 것은 무엇인가?
   ★a. 소년은 운동을 좋아하기 때문에 체육 수업을 좋아한다.
   b. 소녀는 역사 선생님을 좋아한다.
   c. 소년은 역사에 관심이 없다.
   d. 소년은 숙제하는 것을 좋아하지 않는다.

Dictation   p. 20

1. favorite, good at it, math, science, secret, I see
2. outdoor, fresh air, exercise, anytime anywhere, a pair of shoes
3. after, hurry, every day, three times a week, sports
4. library, going swimming, How often, Once a week, feel down, Not really, together
5. hate, boring, history homework, best, good at math, You are right

UNIT 3
She is tall and thin.

Getting Ready   p. 21

1.

Body 몸	Hair 머리	Age 나이
tall	long	in his early forties
athletic	dark	in her teens
thin	curly	young
heavy	bald	middle-aged
slim	blond	
	straight	

2. 1. b   2. c   3. e   4. a   5. d

1. 다음 단어들이 묘사하는 것은 무엇인가? 맞는 제목 아래에 단어들을 적으시오.

긴	10대의	짙은 색의
곱슬거리는	키가 큰	운동을 잘하는
여윈	젊은	몸무게가 많이 나가는
대머리의	금발의	직모의
날씬한	중년의	40대 초반의

2. 질문을 답과 연결시키시오.

1. 그는 키가 크니?   b. 응, 키가 커.
2. 그는 키가 얼마나 크니?   c. 그는 6피트야.
3. 그녀는 어떻게 생겼니?   e. 그녀는 진한 갈색 머리야.
4. 그는 턱수염을 길렀니?   a. 아니, 그렇지 않아.
5. 그녀는 안경을 끼고 있니?   d. 아니, 그렇지 않아.

Listening Task   p. 22~23

Listening 1	1. Hair, Age	2. Hair	3. Body	
	4. Hair	5. Age		
Listen Again	A	1. a	2. c	3. a	4. c
	B	5. a		
Listening 2	1. b	2. a	3. b	4.a
Listen Again	A	1. a	2. b	3. c	
	B	4. a		

Listening 1   p. 22

아래의 묘사는 무엇에 관한 것인가? 알맞은 곳에 표시하시오.

1. He is in his twenties, I mean, early twenties. Yes, he is pretty young. But he looks older,

because he is kind of bald.

2. It is long, straight and black. It is really beautiful and shiny. You've got to see her.

3. Yes, he is tall and big too. He is a heavy man. He looks like a football player. But he never plays football. He has very fair skin.

4. It is light-colored, kind of blond. It is curly and very short. It is kind of cute. She never keeps it long.

5. Is he young? No. He looks young. But he is middle-aged. He is in his late fifties. He is a grandfather. But he doesn't look old. He always exercises to keep fit.

해석

1. 그는 20대, 다시 말해 20대 초반이다. 그렇다, 그는 매우 젊다. 그러나 그는 머리가 좀 벗겨진 편이기 때문에 늙어 보인다.

2. 길고, 곧으며, 검정색이다. 윤기가 흐르고 정말 아름답다. 당신은 그녀를 만나봐야 한다.

3. 그렇다, 그는 키가 크고 덩치도 크다. 우람한 사람이다. 그는 미식축구 선수 같다. 하지만 미식축구를 전혀 하지 않는다. 그는 살결이 아주 희다.

4. 밝은 색깔인데, 약간 금발이다. 곱슬곱슬하고 매우 짧다. 그녀는 약간 귀여운 편이다. 그녀는 절대 머리를 기르지 않는다.

5. 그는 젊은가? 아니, 젊어 보인다. 그러나 그는 중년이다. 그는 50대 후반이다. 할아버지이다. 그러나 그렇게 늙어 보이지 않는다. 그는 건강을 유지하기 위해 항상 운동을 한다.

Listen Again
p. 22

A. 다시 듣고 맞는 것을 고르시오.

1★a. 그는 나이보다 늙어 보인다.　　b. 그는 30대이다.
   c. 그는 매우 친절하다.

2. a. 그녀는 갈색 머리이다.
   b. 그녀의 머리칼은 짧고 곱슬곱슬하다.
  ★c. 그녀는 머리칼에서 윤기가 난다.

3★a. 그는 키가 크고 우람하다.
   b. 그는 미식축구 선수이다.
   c. 그는 피부 색이 검다.

4. a. 그녀는 머리 색이 진하다.
   b. 그녀는 가끔씩 머리를 기른다.
  ★c. 그녀의 머리칼은 곱슬곱슬하다.

B. 다시 듣고 가장 적절하게 요약한 것을 고르시오.

5. a. ★　그는 중년의 남자이지만 젊어 보인다.
   b. □　그는 할아버지이며 아주 늙어 보인다.

Listening 2
p. 23

그들은 누구에 대해 이야기하고 있는가? 듣고 그림에 표시하시오.

스크립트

1.
Jeff　You know Kimberly Clark, don't you?
Chris　Maybe I just don't remember. What does she look like?
Jeff　She is a little plump and has a lot of freckles.
Chris　I know who you mean. The cute little girl from Texas, right?
Jeff　_____You got it._____

2.
W　I want a young man with a big build—tall, big and heavy.
M　An athletic man. I see. And when you say he is young, how young do you mean?
W　In his early twenties.
M　I see. Does he have to be good-looking?
W　_____No, he doesn't._____

3.
W　Oh, my son has been missing all day. I can't find him anywhere.
M　What does he look like?
W　He is six years old, with short curly brown hair. He is not very tall and not very big for his age, just medium-height and medium-build.
M　What is he wearing?
W　_____He's wearing a blue shirt._____

4.
Man I　Look at that girl. Isn't she cute?
Man II　You mean the one with big brown eyes and long straight black hair?
Man I　No, not that one. The one in the white dress next to her.
Man II　Well, I don't know. She looks too thin to me.
Man I　_____No. She's just slim._____

해석

1. Jeff　너 Kimberly Clark 알지?
   Chris　기억 안 나는데. 어떻게 생겼니?
   Jeff　약간 포동포동하고 주근깨가 많아.
   Chris　누구를 말하는지 알겠어. 텍사스에서 온 귀엽고 작은 여자애 말이지, 맞지?
   Jeff　_____맞아._____

2. W 나는 체격이 큰 즉, 키가 크고, 우람하고 덩치 좋은 젊은 남자를 원해요.

   M 운동 잘하게 생긴 남자요. 알았어요. 그리고 젊다고 한 것은 얼마나 젊다는 말이죠?

   W 20대 초반이요.

   M 알겠어요. 잘생겨야 하나요?

   W _____ 아니, 그럴 필요 없어요.

3. W 오, 우리 아들이 하루 종일 안 보여요. 어디에도 찾을 수가 없어요.

   M 어떻게 생겼나요?

   W 짧고 꼬불꼬불한 갈색 머리에, 6살이에요. 나이에 비해 키도 몸집도 크지 않고, 보통 키에 보통 체격이에요.

   M 무엇을 입고 있나요?

   W _____ 파란 셔츠를 입고 있어요.

4. Man I 저 여자애 좀 봐. 귀엽지 않니?

   Man II 큰 갈색 눈에 곧고 긴 검정 머리를 가진 애를 말하는 거야?

   Man I 아니, 걔 말고. 그 애 옆에 하얀 드레스를 입은 애야.

   Man II 음, 모르겠어. 내가 보기엔 너무 말랐어.

   Man I _____ 아냐. 그냥 날씬한 거야.

Listen Again   p. 23

A. 다시 듣고 알맞은 답을 고르시오.

1. Jeff가 할 말로 알맞은 것은?

   ★a. 맞아.   b. 괜찮아.   c. 그녀는 몰라.

2. 남자가 할 말로 알맞은 것은?

   a. 아니, 그건 사실이 아니에요.

   ★b. 아니, 그럴 필요 없어요.

   c. 아니에요.

3. 여자가 할 말로 알맞은 것은?

   a. 아니, 그렇지 않아요.   b. 그 애는 몰라요.

   ★c. 파란 셔츠를 입고 있어요.

B. 다시 듣고 가장 어울리는 응답을 고르시오.

4. a. ★ 아냐. 그냥 날씬한 거야.

   b. ☐ 그래.

   c. ☐ 아냐. 귀여워.

스크립트

```
a. No. She's just slim.
b. I do.
c. No. She's just cute.
```

Review   p. 24

1. What, heavy, heavy, tall
2. cute, blond, blue, years
3. brown, wear, one
4. old, early, fifty, gray, bald
5. tall, feet, teens, young, pretty

✻ 듣고 빈칸을 채우시오.

해석

1. W 네 남동생은 어떻게 생겼니? 너처럼 덩치가 크니?

   M 아니, 그는 덩치가 크지 않아. 그는 말랐고, 키가 크고 잘생겼어.

2. 내 여동생은 매우 귀여워. 그 애는 금발 머리에 크고 파란 눈을 가지고 있어. 그 애는 다음달에 세 살이 될 거야.

3. M 이 분이 너희 어머니셔?

   W 아니야, 우리 이모야. 우리 엄마는 짧은 갈색 머리이시고, 안경을 끼지 않으셨어.

   M 긴 갈색 코트를 입고 계신 분이 네 엄마니?

   W 맞아.

4. Smith 씨는 그렇게 늙지 않았는데 많은 사람들이 늙었다고 생각한다. 그는 사십 대 초반 밖에 안 됐지만, 사람들은 50세를 넘었을 거라고 생각한다. 그는 머리가 회색이고, 약간 대머리이다. 그래서 그렇게 생각하는 모양이다.

5. W Sharapova는 굉장해! 경기하는 것 좀 봐.

   M 키가 아주 크네. 6피트는 넘을 것 같아.

   W 응. 그녀는 10대이고 세계 챔피언이야.

   M 그렇게 어려?

   W 응. 그리고 정말 예뻐, 그렇지 않니?

On Your Own   p. 25

LISTEN & WRITE

들리는 질문을 써 보세요.

스크립트

```
How tall are you?
How old are you?
Do you look younger or older than you really are?
Do you have long hair?
Do you wear glasses?
```

해석

당신은 키가 몇입니까?

당신의 나이는 어떻게 됩니까?

당신은 실제 나이보다 나이 들어 보입니까, 젊어 보입니까?

당신은 머리가 깁니까?

당신은 안경을 낍니까?

PRONUNCIATION

/ r / **vs** / I /

☞ 듣고 따라해 보시오.

올바른, 읽다, 잘못된, 비율,

바위, 광선, 기름에 튀기다, 정확한

☞ 듣고 따라해 보시오.

빛, 이끌다, 긴, 늦은,

잠그다, 놓다, 날다, 모으다

☞ 잘 들어보고 차이점을 발견해 보시오.

올바른 / 빛, 읽다 / 이끌다, 잘못된 / 긴,

비율 / 늦은, 바위 / 잠그다, 광선 / 놓다,

기름에 튀기다 / 날다, 정확한 / 모으다

듣고 들리는 단어를 체크하시오.

스크립트 light, read, long, late, rock, ray, fly,
correct

올바른	☐	빛	★
읽다	★	이끌다	☐
잘못된	☐	긴	★
비율	☐	늦은	★
바위	★	잠그다	☐
광선	★	놓다	☐
기름에 튀기다	☐	날다	★
정확한	★	모으다	☐

Practice Test   p. 26~27

1. 1) c   2) b   2. 1) c   2) d   3. 1) b
4. 1) b   2) b   5. 1) b

✻ 듣고 알맞은 답을 고르시오.

1. 8살인 남자 아이가 한 여자 아이에 대해서 이야기하고 있다.

스크립트

I like Jenny. She is very pretty. Her big blue eyes are like an ocean. Her long blond hair moves like grass in the wind. Her skin is fair and silky. She smiles like an angel. She has some freckles on her face and I love them, too. I always look at her but she never looks at me.

해석
나는 Jenny를 좋아해요. 그녀는 매우 예뻐요. 그녀의 큰 파란 눈은 바다 같아요. 그녀의 긴 금발 머리는 바람 속의 잔디같이 움직여요. 그녀의 피부는 희고 부드러워요. 그녀는 천사같이 미소 지어요. 그녀의 얼굴에는 약간의 주근깨가 있는데 나는 그것들도 좋아요. 나는 항상 그녀를 보지만, 그녀는 절대 나를 보지 않아요.

1) 여자 아이에 대해 언급되지 않은 것은?
   a. 머리   b. 피부   ★c. 키   d. 눈

2) 여자 아이에 대해 일치하는 것은?
   a. 머리칼이 검정색이다.   ★b. 주근깨가 있다.
   c. 눈동자가 갈색이다.   d. 피부 색이 검다.

2. 한 어머니가 실종된 자기 아들에 대해 경찰관에게 이야기하고 있다.

스크립트

W Excuse me, officer. Please find my son. He's been missing all day.

M Calm down and tell me. What does he look like?

W He's tall for his age.

M How old is he?

W Nine.

M What about his hair?

W He has short curly black hair.

M Anything else? Is he wearing glasses or something?

W Not glasses, but he's wearing a red T-shirt and white shorts.

해석

W 실례합니다, 경찰관 아저씨. 제 아들 좀 찾아 주세요. 하루 종일 안 보여요.

M 진정하시고 제게 말씀을 해 주세요. 애가 어떻게 생겼죠?

W 나이에 비해 키가 커요.

M 몇 살인데요?

W 아홉 살이요.

M 머리 모양은 어때요?

W 짧고 곱슬거리는 검은 머리요.

M 다른 건요? 안경을 꼈다거나 뭘 입고 있나요?

W 안경은 안 꼈는데, 빨간 티셔츠에 하얀 반바지를 입었어요.

1) 남자 아이는 _____.
   a. 키가 작다.   b. 말랐다.   ★c. 아홉 살이다.   d. 집에 있다.

2) 다음 중 소년에 대한 내용과 일치하지 않는 것은?
   a. 검은 머리이다.   b. 키가 크다.
   c. 빨간 티셔츠를 입고 있다.   ★d. 안경을 끼고 있다.

3. 한 여자가 그녀의 친구에 대해 이야기하고 있다.

스크립트

My friend Jane is in her late thirties, not very tall, not very short. She's a little plump, but not heavy. She has gray eyes and short brown hair. She likes casual wear so maybe she will be wearing jeans and a shirt.

해석

내 친구 Jane은 30대 후반에, 키는 크지도 않고, 작지도 않아요. 약간 통통하긴 하지만, 큰 몸집은 아니에요. 회색 눈에 짧은 갈색 머리예요. 캐주얼한 옷을 좋아해서, 아마도 청바지에 셔츠를 입고 있을 거예요.

4. 한 남자가 해변 휴양지에서 아내를 찾고 있다.

스크립트

> M Can you help me find my wife? I really need to find her right away.
> W Sure. What does she look like?
> M Well, she's kind of tall, and she's thin.
> W Do you remember what kind of clothes she is wearing?
> M She is wearing a skirt and a red one piece swimsuit.
> W I think I saw her at the swimming pool.

해석

M 제 아내를 찾는 것을 도와주시겠습니까? 지금 당장 그녀를 찾아야 합니다.
W 물론이죠. 부인께서는 어떻게 생기셨습니까?
M 음, 키가 크고 마른 편입니다.
W 부인께서 어떤 옷을 입으셨는지 기억나십니까?
M 치마와 붉은색 원피스 수영복을 입고 있었습니다.
W 수영장에서 부인을 본 것 같습니다.

1) 남자는 그의 아내가 _____고 말한다.

    a. 키가 작다   ★b. 키가 크다
    c. 뚱뚱하다   d. 늙었다

2) 남자가 다음에 할 행동은 무엇일까?

    a. 저녁 식사를 한다.
    ★b. 수영장에 간다.
    c. 집으로 간다.
    d. 음료수를 마신다.

5. Sarah와 Mike는 함께 Mike의 앨범을 보고 있다.

스크립트

> Sarah Who's this cute fat baby?
> Mike Doesn't he look like me?
> Sarah Not at all! Who's this little, thin girl wearing big glasses?
> Mike She was my next door neighbor when I was young. We used to play all the time.
> Sarah I see. What about this tall, handsome man? Is he your dad?
> Mike No, my grandpa in his twenties.
> Susan Really? He looks like a movie star.

해석

Sarah 이 통통하고 귀여운 아기는 누구니?
Mike 나처럼 안 생겼어?
Sarah 전혀! 이 안경을 낀 작고 마른 소녀는 누구니?
Mike 나 어렸을 때 우리 옆집에 살던 애. 우리는 항상 함께 놀았었지.
Sarah 그렇구나. 이 키 크고 잘생긴 남자는? 너희 아버지시니?
Mike 아니, 우리 할아버지 20대일 때.
Susan 정말? 영화배우 같아.

1) 대화 내용과 일치하지 <u>않는</u> 것은?

    a. Mike는 아기였을 때 귀엽고 통통했다.
    ★b. Mike의 할아버지는 영화배우다.
    c. Mike의 할아버지는 젊었을 때 미남이셨다.
    d. Mike는 어렸을 때 옆집 아이와 놀곤 했다.

Dictation   p. 28

1. pretty, big blue eyes, blond, fair, silky, freckles
2. been missing, look like, tall, his age, hair, curly black, glasses, wearing
3. in her late thirties, short, plump, heavy, gray, jeans
4. right away, tall, thin, what kind of clothes, skirt
5. fat, thin, big glasses, used to, handsome, in his twenties, looks like

UNIT 4
What time do you get up?

Getting Ready
p. 29

1. 1. 6   2. 6 : 30   3. 7, 8   4. 8:20
   5. 9, 6   6. 7   7. 9
2. 1. f   2. e   3. d   4. a   5. c   6. b

1. 그림은 John의 전형적인 하루이다. 빈칸에 시간을 적으시오.

   1. John은 ___6___ 시에 일어난다.
   2. 그는 _6시 30분_ 에 커피를 마신다.
   3. 그는 ___7___ 시부터 ___8___ 시까지 운동을 한다.
   4. 그는 _8시 20분_ 에 출근한다.
   5. 그는 ___9___ 시부터 ___6___ 시까지 일한다.
   6. 그는 ___7___ 시에 집에 온다.
   7. 그는 ___9___ 시에 잠자리에 든다.

2. 질문을 답과 연결시키시오.

   1. 몇 시에 일어나니?   f. 7시 30분이요.
   2. 방과 후에 무엇을 하니?   e. 야구를 해요.
   3. 어떻게 학교에 가니?   d. 자전거 타고요.
   4. 수업이 몇 교시나 있니?   a. 여섯 개요.
   5. 숙제가 많니?   c. 아니요, 그렇지 않아요.
   6. 아침에 누가 깨워주니?   b. 엄마가 깨워줘요.

Listening Task
p. 30~31

Listening 1	1. 7:30	2. 8:10
	3. 8:30, 12:00	
	4. 3:30, 6:00, 10:30	
Listen Again A	1. b 2. a 3. c	
B	4. b	
Listening 2	1. b 2. a 3. a 4. a	
Listen Again A	1. b 2. c 3. b	
B	4. a	

Listening 1
p. 30

Jeff는 그의 하루 일과에 대해 이야기하고 있다. 듣고, 시간을 적으시오.

월요일 일정

1. ___7:30___ 기상
2. ___8:10___ 스쿨버스 타기
3. ___8:30___ 수업 시작
   ___12:00___ 점심 먹기
4. ___3:30___ 학교에서 집으로 오기
   ___6:00___ 시까지 자유시간
   ___10:30___ 취침

스크립트

1. I get up at 7:30 on weekdays, but not on weekends. I sleep until 10 on Saturdays and Sundays. I don't set my alarm clock on weekends. I love spending the morning hours in my warm bed.

2. I always take a long shower right after I get up. It wakes me up. If I don't shower, I can't really wake up. I can't eat breakfast and I am still sleepy at school. I take the school bus to school at 8:10 a.m.

3. School starts at 8:30. I have three classes in the morning. Each class is sixty minutes long. Lunch time is at 12:00. My friends and I usually play basketball after lunch. At 12:40 the bell rings and our lunchtime is over. We go back to our classes.

4. I come home from school at 3:30. My mom gives me a snack then. I have free time for fun and exercise until 6 o'clock. After dinner I do my homework and some reading. I go to bed at 10:30.

해석

1. 나는 평일에는 7시 30분에 일어난다. 그러나 주말에는 그렇지 않다. 나는 토요일과 일요일에는 10시까지 잠을 잔다. 주말에는 자명종 시계를 맞춰 놓지 않는다. 나는 따뜻한 침대에서 아침 시간을 보내는 것을 좋아한다.

2. 나는 항상 일어난 후에 바로 긴 샤워를 한다. 이것은 내 잠을 깨워준다. 만약 샤워를 하지 않는다면, 나는 잠에서 제대로 깨지 못한다. 나는 아침을 먹지 못하고 학교에서도 여전히 졸리다. 나는 오전 8시 10분에 스쿨버스를 타고 학교에 간다.

3. 수업은 8시 30분에 시작한다. 아침에는 3개의 수업이 있다. 각각의 수업은 60분이다. 점심시간은 12시이다. 내 친구들과 나는 보통 점심을 먹은 뒤 농구를 한다. 12시 40분에 벨이 울리고 점심시간이 끝난다. 우리는 교실로 돌아간다.

4. 나는 3시 30분에 학교에서 집으로 온다. 그때 엄마는 나에게 간식을 주신다. 6시까지 놀이와 운동을 위한 자유 시간을 갖는다. 저녁 식사 후 나는 숙제를 하고 책을 읽는다. 10시 30분에 잠을 잔다.

Listen Again

p. 30

A. 다시 듣고 알맞은 답을 고르시오.

1. 그는 아침에 어떻게 일어나는가?
   a. 그의 엄마가 깨운다.   ★b. 자명종 시계가 깨운다.
   c. 혼자서 일어난다.

2. 무엇을 먼저 하는가?
   ★a. 샤워   b. 아침 식사   c. 신문 읽기

3. 점심시간이 끝나고 바로 무엇을 하는가?
   a. 야구   b. 수업   ★c. 농구

B. 다시 듣고 가장 적절하게 요약한 것을 고르시오.

4. a. □ 그는 3시 30분에 집에 돌아와서 6시에 잠을 잔다.
   b. ★ 그는 3시 30분에 집에 돌아와서 6시까지 자유 시간을 가진다.

Listening 2

p. 31

사람들이 자신의 의사와 이야기하고 있다. 무엇이 문제인가?

1. a. 그는 7시 30분에 일어난다.
   ★b. 그는 아침에 커피를 마신다.

2. ★a. 그녀는 일을 너무 많이 한다.
   b. 그녀는 전화를 너무 많이 한다.

3. ★a. 그녀는 전혀 놀지 않는다.
   b. 그녀는 잠을 너무 많이 잔다.

4. ★a. 그녀는 너무 늦게 일어난다.
   b. 그녀는 그녀의 엄마를 좋아하지 않는다.

스크립트

1.

Doctor So what time do you get up in the morning?
Man Around 6:30.
Doctor What is the first thing you do in the morning?
Man I drink a cup of coffee and read the newspaper.
Doctor That's the problem. Your stomach doesn't agree with coffee in the morning.

2.

Doctor How long are you at work?
Woman From 9:00 a.m. till 5:00 p.m. But I work overtime pretty often.
Doctor What time do you come home when you work overtime?
Woman About 11:30.
Doctor You need some rest. Your body calls for that.

3.

Doctor What is your day like, Mrs. White?
Mrs. White It's like most mothers'. I clean, cook, wash and do other small things around the house.
Doctor Do you have any fun?
Mrs. White Well, I don't know.
Doctor Have some fun. Go outside and get some fresh air.

4.

Doctor You look sleepy. What time do you go to bed?
Pat One or two in the morning. But please don't tell my mom.
Doctor What do you do until then?
Pat I play computer games. Once I start, I can't stop.

해석

1. Doctor 아침에 몇 시에 일어납니까?
   Man 대략 6시 30분에요.
   Doctor 아침에 당신이 처음으로 하는 일은 무엇입니까?
   Man 나는 커피 한 잔을 마시고 신문을 읽어요.
   Doctor 그게 문제예요. 당신의 위는 아침 커피에 탈이 나는 겁니다.

2. Doctor 얼마 동안 근무를 하나요?
   Woman 오전 9시부터 오후 5시까지요. 그러나 저는 초과 근무를 꽤 자주 해요.
   Doctor 초과 근무를 할 때는 몇 시에 집에 오나요?
   Woman 11시 30분쯤에요.
   Doctor 당신은 휴식이 필요해요. 당신의 몸이 그것을 필요로 해요.

3. Doctor 하루 일과가 어떤가요, White 부인?
   Mrs. White 여느 엄마들과 같아요. 청소하고, 요리하고, 설거지하고, 그리고 집안의 다른 작은 일들을 하죠.
   Doctor 재미있는 일은 하시는 게 있나요?
   Mrs. White 글쎄요, 잘 모르겠어요.
   Doctor 좀 즐기세요. 밖으로 나가서 상쾌한 공기를 마셔요.

4. Doctor 졸려 보이네요. 몇 시에 잠을 자나요?
   Pat 새벽 1시나 2시요. 엄마에게는 말하지 마세요.
   Doctor 그때까지 무엇을 하나요?
   Pat 컴퓨터 게임을 해요. 일단 시작하면 멈출 수가 없어요.

Listen Again

p. 31

A. 다시 듣고 알맞은 답을 고르시오.

1. 그는 _____ 에 일어난다.
   a. 6시   ★b. 6시 30분   c. 7시 30분

2. 그녀는 _____ 에 매일의 업무를 시작한다.

    a. 8시   b. 8시 30분   ★c. 9시

3. 그녀는 보통 _____ .

    a. 즐기며 지낸다

  ★b. 대부분의 엄마들이 하는 일을 한다

    c. 외출한다

B. 다시 듣고 맞는 문장을 고르시오.

4. a. ★ 여자 아이는 컴퓨터 게임을 너무 좋아해서 잠자리에 늦게 든다.

    b. ☐ 여자 아이는 수면 장애가 있기 때문에 새벽 1시나 2시에 잠자리에 든다.

스크립트

  a. The girl goes to bed too late because she likes to play computer games.

  b. The girl goes to bed at one or two in the morning because she has a sleeping problem.

Review   p. 32

1. get up, 7, do, take
2. classes, homework, take, help, 6:30
3. How long, 9, 4, go to bed, 10 p.m.
4. starts, hours, during, day, 9
5. walks, afternoon, come, 30, 4:30

※ 듣고 빈칸을 채우시오.

해석

1. W 아침에 몇 시에 일어나니?

  M 7시에 일어나요.

  W 그러고 나서 무엇을 하니?

  M 보통 샤워를 해요.

2. 엄마, 나 피곤해요. 나는 하루에 수업이 5개 있어요. 방과 후에는 숙제를 해요. 고양이 Lucy를 돌봐요. 그리고 가끔은 엄마를 도와 집안일을 해요. 지금이 유일한 내 자유 시간이에요. 6시 30분까지는 저를 쉬게 해 주세요.

3. M 얼마 동안 근무하나요?

  W 오전 9시부터 오후 4시까지요.

  M 언제 잠자리에 드나요?

  W 저녁 10시에요.

4. 우리 언니는 부지런하다. 그녀는 5시에 하루를 시작한다. 하루에 5시간을 자고 낮 시간 동안 많은 일을 한다. 그녀는 밤 9시쯤에 집에 돌아온다.

5. W Amy 어디 있어?

  M 나갔어. 오후에 우리 집 개 Max를 산책시켜.

  W 언제 돌아와?

  M 30분 후에. 4시 30분에 피아노 레슨이 있어.

On Your Own   p. 33

LISTEN & WRITE

들리는 질문을 써 보세요.

스크립트

What time do you get up?
What time do you go to school?
How do you go to school?
How long are you in school?
What time do you come home?
What do you do after school?

해석

아침에 몇 시에 일어납니까?

몇 시에 학교에 갑니까?

학교에 어떻게 갑니까?

학교에 얼마나 오랫동안 있습니까?

몇 시에 집에 옵니까?

방과 후에 무엇을 합니까?

PRONUNCIATION

/ s / vs / z /

☞ 듣고 따라해 보시오.

  노래하다, 한 모금, 도장, 곧, 보내다, Sue

☞ 듣고 따라해 보시오.

  쌩쌩 소리 내다, 지퍼로 잠그다, 열성, 확대(축소)시키다, 참선, 동물원

☞ 잘 들어보고 차이점을 발견해 보시오.

  노래하다 / 쌩쌩 소리 내다, 한 모금 / 지퍼로 잠그다

  도장 / 열성, 곧 / 확대(축소)시키다

  보내다 / 참선, Sue / 동물원

듣고 들리는 단어를 체크하시오.

스크립트 zing, sip, seal, zoom, zen, Sue

노래하다 ☐	쌩쌩 소리 내다 ★
한 모금 ★	지퍼로 잠그다 ☐
도장 ★	열성 ☐
곧 ☐	확대(축소)시키다 ★
보내다 ☐	참선 ★
Sue ★	동물원 ☐

※ 듣고 알맞은 답을 고르시오.

1. 기자가 대형 레스토랑 체인점의 CEO인 Coleman 씨와 인터뷰를 하고 있다.

스크립트

M1　How do you start your day?
M2　I have a cup of coffee.
M1　And then what do you do?
M2　I take a shower and read the newspaper.
M1　You do a lot of things in the morning. What time do you get up?
M2　Around 12:30.
M1　You mean in the morning?
M2　No, in the afternoon. I come home from work after midnight. I go to bed at 2:00 in the morning.

해석

M1　하루를 어떻게 시작하나요?
M2　커피 한 잔을 마셔요.
M1　그러고 나서 무엇을 하나요?
M2　샤워를 하고 신문을 읽어요.
M1　아침에 많은 일을 하시는군요. 몇 시에 일어나나요?
M2　12시 30분쯤에요.
M1　새벽 말인가요?
M2　아니요, 오후에요. 저는 자정이 지나야 직장에서 집에 와요. 저는 새벽 2시에 잠을 자요.

1) Coleman 씨에 대해 일치하는 것은?
　　a. 그는 매우 일찍 일어난다.
　　b. 그는 운동으로 걷기를 한다.
　★c. 그는 자정 이후에 잠을 잔다.
　　d. 그는 정오 이전에 하루를 시작한다.

2) 그는 하루 중 몇 시에 첫 번째 커피를 마실까?
　　a. 오전 7시 30분　　b. 오전 2시
　　c. 오전 1시　　★d. 오후 1시

2. 이것은 Bill의 직업에 관한 것이다.

스크립트

Bill is in a hurry all the time. When there are big and small things happening around town, he is there. There are good and bad events all the time. They happen every day and night. Sometimes he goes to bed at 1:00 a.m., and sometimes at 2:00 p.m. In between he writes reports and shows up on TV.

해석

Bill은 항상 바쁘다. 동네 주변에 크고 작은 사고가 있을 때면, 그는 거기에 있다. 좋고 나쁜 사건은 항상 있다. 사건은 매일 밤 낮으로 일어난다. 가끔 그는 새벽 1시에 잠을 자고, 가끔은 오후 2시에 잔다. 기사를 쓰는 중간 중간에는 TV에 나온다.

1) 그의 직업은 무엇일까?
　　a. 의사　　★b. 기자
　　c. 비행기 조종사　　d. 경찰

2) Bill의 하루에 대해 일치하는 것은?
　　a. 항상 같은 시간에 침대에 든다.
　　b. 낮 시간에는 항상 일을 한다.
　★c. 가끔 TV에 나온다.
　　d. 밤에만 아주 바쁘다.

3. Pat는 Jeff의 일정을 묻고 있다.

스크립트

Pat　Hi, Jeff! I need to see you today. Are you busy schedule this afternoon?
Jeff　I have a piano lesson at 4:30. That's it.
Pat　When does it end?
Jeff　At 5:30. It takes just one hour.
Pat　Can I drop by your house at 6 then?
Jeff　Sure. Bye. Hey, Pat! Bring the board game with you.

해석

Pat　안녕, Jeff! 오늘 나 너 좀 만나야 하는데. 오늘 오후에 바쁜 일 있어?
Jeff　4시 30분에 피아노 레슨이 있어. 그게 다야.
Pat　언제 끝나?
Jeff　5시 30분. 1시간 밖에 안 해.
Pat　그러면 6시에 너희 집에 들러도 되겠어?
Jeff　물론이지. 잘 가. 야, Pat! 보드게임 가져와.

1) 이들은 몇 시에 만날 것인가?

    a. 오후 4시 30분

    b. 오후 5시 30분

    ★c. 오후 6시

    d. 오후 6시 30분

2) 다음 중 일치하는 것은?

    a. Jeff는 오늘 할 일이 많다.

    b. 피아노 레슨은 30분 동안 한다.

    ★c. Jeff는 피아노 레슨이 끝난 다음 Pat을 만날 것이다.

    d. 이들은 아마도 컴퓨터 게임을 할 것이다.

4. Sophie는 오후에 잠에서 깨어난다.

스크립트

Ah~ that was a good sleep. Oh my goodness, It's 2 p.m.? What am I going to do? I missed all the final exams! I was supposed to wake up at 5:30, revise math, science and English for two hours, eat my breakfast, and leave home at 8 o'clock. I don't believe this! Sophie, you stupid! Wait, what day is it today? Ah~ it's summer vacation. That schedule was for yesterday. Phew!

해석

아~ 달콤한 잠이었어. 오 이런, 낮 2시야? 어떻게 하지? 기말 시험을 모두 놓쳤어! 5시 반에 일어나서 2시간 동안 수학, 과학 그리고 영어를 다시 보고, 아침을 먹고, 8시에는 집을 나서려고 했는데. 믿을 수가 없네! Sophie, 얼간이! 기다려 봐, 오늘이 무슨 요일이지? 아~ 여름 방학이구나. 그 계획은 어제 것이었어. 휴우!

1) Sophie에게 무슨 일이 일어났는가?

    a. 늦게 일어나서 모든 기말 시험을 놓치는 꿈을 꾸었다.

    b. 늦게 일어난 후 시험을 놓친 것을 깨달았다.

    ★c. 오후에 일어나서 모든 기말 시험을 놓쳤다고 생각했다.

    d. 이번 학기를 망쳐서 화가 났다.

2) Sophie는 몇 시에 수학, 과학, 그리고 영어를 다시 보는 것을 끝낼 계획이었는가?

    a. 5시 30분   b. 7시   ★c. 7시 30분   d. 8시

5. Sarah와 Sophie는 전화로 통화하고 있다.

스크립트

Sophie Hi, is Sarah there?

Sarah Hi, Sophie! It's me.

Sophie About shopping tomorrow—what time is good for you?

Sarah I'm free in the afternoon.

Sophie Well, I have to pick my little brother up at 3:30 and then take him to his football club at 5:30. Six o'clock is too late, isn't it?

Sarah Yeah, I think so. Shall we make it noon?

Sophie Good. See you then.

해석

Sophie 여보세요, Sarah 있어요?

Sarah 안녕, Sophie! 나야.

Sophie 내일 쇼핑 말인데. 몇 시가 좋아?

Sarah 난 오후에 한가해.

Sophie 음, 내가 3시 반에 남동생을 데리고 와서 5시 반에 걔를 축구 클럽에 데려다줘야 한다는 것을 깜빡했어. 6시는 너무 늦지?

Sarah 응, 그런 것 같아. 12시에 갈 수 있을까?

Sophie 물론. 그때 보자.

1) Sophie와 Sarah는 내일 어디에 갈 것인가?

    a. 학교   b. 축구 클럽   ★c. 쇼핑몰   d. 집

2) Sophie와 Sarah는 내일 몇 시에 쇼핑을 갈 것인가?

    a. 3시 30분   ★b. 12시   c. 5시 30분   d. 7시

Dictation   p. 36

1. start, And then, take a shower, get up, Around, midnight

2. in a hurry, happening, events, goes to bed, between, shows up

3. Are you busy, piano lesson, end, takes, at 6, Bring

4. 2 p.m., missed, supposed to, breakfast, what day is it today, schedule

5. Shopping, good for you, I'm free, too late, noon, See you

UNIT 5
What's the weather like?

Getting Ready   p. 37

1.

dry	sunny	windy	snowy
70°F (22°C)	95°F (36°C)	32°F (0°C)	20°F (-7°C)
April	August	October	January

2. 1. d   2. a   3. b   4. c   5. e   6. f

1. 달의 이름, 온도, 그리고 날씨의 단어를 그림 밑에 적으시오.

건조한	맑은	바람 부는	눈 내리는
95°F(36℃)	32°F(0℃)	70°F(22℃)	20°F(-7℃)
1월	4월	8월	10월

*F: 화씨, C: 섭씨

2. 질문을 답과 연결시키시오.

1. 도쿄의 날씨는 어떤가요?   d. 도쿄는 몹시 추워요.
2. 온도는 어때요?   a. 섭씨 35도예요.
3. 아직 비가 오나요?   b. 아니요, 오지 않아요.
4. 겨울에 눈이 많이 오나요?   c. 네, 그래요.
5. 서울의 날씨는 어떤가요?   e. 좋고 따뜻해요.
6. 번개와 천둥이 치나요?   f. 네, 그래요.

Listening Task   p. 38~39

Listening 1	3, 4, 2, 1			
Listen Again	A	1. b	2. b	3. c
	B	4. a		
Listening 2	1. a	2. c	3. a	4. b
Listen Again	A	1. a	2. c	3. b
	B	4. a		

Listening I   p. 38

날씨에 대해 듣고 그림에 번호를 붙이시오.

스크립트

1.
M   How about a picnic this afternoon?
W   It's too hot and humid to go out. It's nice and cool inside with air-conditioning. What's the temperature outside?
M   It's over 33 degrees.

2.
W   Hello?
M   Hello, Auntie, what's the weather like there in London?
W   It's warm but very foggy.
M   It's always foggy there. How warm is it?
W   It's about 23 degrees.

3.
W   Amy is in Washington D.C. for a field trip. How is the weather there?
M   The weatherman says it's stormy and freezing.
W   I'm worried. She doesn't have a warm sweater. What's the temperature?
M   They say today's low is minus 5 degrees and the high is 2.

4.
W   Look at the clouds. They're getting dark.
M   Yeah, it's going to rain. It's getting chilly.
W   We get a lot of rain this time of year, don't we?
M   I know. This year it's a lot colder. The temperature is as low as 3 degrees Celsius.

해석
1. M 오늘 오후에 소풍 갈래?
   W 밖에 나가기엔 너무 덥고, 습도가 높아. 에어컨이 있어서 실내는 시원한데. 바깥 온도는 얼마나 되니?
   M 33도 이상이야.

2. W 여보세요?
   M 안녕하세요, 이모. 런던의 날씨는 어때요?
   W 따뜻한데 안개가 많이 짙구나.
   M 거긴 항상 안개가 끼네요. 얼마나 따뜻한데요?
   W 약 23도야.

3. W Amy가 현장 학습으로 워싱턴에 있어. 거기 날씨는 어때?
   M 기상 캐스터가 폭풍이 치고 몹시 춥다고 했어요.
   W 걱정된다. 걔는 따뜻한 스웨터도 없는데. 온도는 어떠니?
   M 오늘 최저 온도는 영하 5도, 최고 온도는 2도라고 했어요.

4. W 구름을 봐. 어두워지고 있어.
   M 응, 비가 올 거야. 으스스해지고 있어.
   W 이번 해에는 비가 더 많이 내려, 그렇지 않니?
   M 맞아. 올해가 훨씬 더 추워. 온도가 섭씨 3도 밖에 안 돼.

Listen Again   p. 38

A. 다시 듣고 틀린 것을 고르시오.

1. a. 밖은 습기가 많다.   ★b. 밖은 시원하다.
   c. 에어컨을 틀어놓고 있다.

2. a. 런던은 보통 안개가 낀다.
　★b. 런던은 춥다.
　c. 남자는 그의 이모와 전화하고 있다.

3. a. Amy는 집을 떠나 있다.
　b. Amy는 추운 날씨에 대해 준비가 되어 있지 않다.
　★c. 워싱턴 D.C.에는 눈이 많이 내리고 있다.

B. 다시 듣고 가장 적절하게 요약한 것을 고르시오.

4. a. ★ 날이 쌀쌀해지고 비가 올 것이다. 다른 해보다 춥다.
　b. □ 날은 점점 어두워지고 비가 올 것이다. 예년처럼 춥다.

Listening 2　　　　　　　　　　p. 39

일기 예보를 듣고 알맞은 답을 고르시오.

1. 오늘 날씨는 어떤가?
　★a. 맑다.　　　　b. 춥다.　　　　c. 바람이 분다.

2. 오늘 날씨는 어떤가?
　a. 폭풍이 분다.　　b. 눈이 온다.　　★c. 아주 춥다.

3. 오늘 날씨는 어떤가?
　★a. 안개가 매우 짙다.　b. 아주 덥다.　　c. 습도가 매우 높다.

4. 오늘 날씨는 어떤가?
　a. 맑지만 춥다.
　★b. 덥고 비가 온다.
　c. 흐리고 바람이 분다.

스크립트

1.
Good morning. This is the weather report for Tuesday, October 2. It is nice and sunny around the country. The temperature this morning is 18 degrees Celsius. It's perfect weather for a picnic. This nice weather will continue until the weekend. Enjoy your fine autumn day.

2.
Good afternoon. This is today's weather for Friday, December 20. It is partly cloudy and windy nationwide. It's freezing. The temperature is well below zero. There is no snow but it will get even colder tomorrow.

3.
Good morning. This is the weather for today, Thursday, May 3. It's very foggy. Be careful while you're driving. It's warm and the temperature is at 18 degrees Celsius. There is good news though—the sun will be shining tomorrow.

4.
Good afternoon. This is the Channel 4 weather report for Monday, July 27. We are having the worst weather of the season. There is heavy rain and thunderstorms. The temperature is at a high of 37 degrees Celsius. This hot stormy weather will continue for a couple of more days.

해석

1. 안녕하세요. 10월 2일 화요일 일기 예보입니다. 전국적으로 맑습니다. 오늘 아침 온도는 섭씨 18도입니다. 소풍 가기에 완벽한 날씨입니다. 이 멋진 날씨는 주말까지 계속될 것입니다. 멋진 가을날을 즐기세요.

2. 안녕하세요. 12월 20일 금요일, 오늘의 날씨입니다. 부분적으로 구름이 끼고, 전국적으로 바람이 붑니다. 몹시 춥습니다. 온도는 영하로 많이 내려갑니다. 눈은 내리지 않지만, 내일은 더 추워질 것입니다.

3. 안녕하세요. 5월 3일 목요일, 오늘의 날씨입니다. 안개가 매우 짙습니다. 운전하는 동안 조심하십시오. 따뜻하고 온도는 섭씨 18도입니다. 하지만 좋은 소식이 있습니다. 내일은 화창할 것입니다.

4. 안녕하세요. 7월 27일 월요일, 채널 4 일기 예보입니다. 이번 계절 중 가장 최악의 날씨입니다. 강한 비와 뇌우가 있습니다. 온도는 섭씨 37도로 높습니다. 이런 덥고 폭풍우 치는 날씨는 앞으로 이삼 일 정도 계속되겠습니다.

Listen Again　　　　　　　　　　p. 39

A. 다시 듣고 알맞은 답을 고르시오.

1. 내일 날씨는 ＿＿＿＿＿ 것이다.
　★a. 오늘과 같을　　b. 더 좋아질　　c. 더 나빠질

2. 내일 날씨는 ＿＿＿＿＿ 것이다.
　a. 더 좋아질　　b. 화창하고 햇볕이 잘 들　★c. 더욱 추울

3. 내일 날씨는 ＿＿＿＿＿ 것이다.
　a. 여전히 안개가 짙을　　★b. 화창할　　c. 비가 올

B. 다시 듣고 맞는 문장을 고르시오.

4. a. ★ 오늘 날씨는 매우 더우며 많은 비와 뇌우를 동반할 것이다.
　b. □ 오늘 날씨는 날씨가 정말 안 좋지만 기온이 그리 높지는 않을 것이다.

스크립트

　a. Today's weather is really hot with heavy rain and thunderstorms.
　b. Today's weather is really bad but the temperature is not too high.

21

Review   p. 40

1. weather, humid, temperature, degrees
2. cloudy, highs, low, lows, high, forties, warmer
3. How, rainy, Is it, cold
4. week, forecast, stormy, Monday, Thursday, weather
5. freezing, snowing, wind

✻ 듣고 빈칸을 채우시오.

해석
1. M 오늘 날씨 어때?
   W 덥고 습도가 높아.
   M 온도가 어떻게 돼?
   W 화씨 96도야.

2. 전국적으로 따뜻하고 부분적으로 흐립니다. 최고 온도는 70도 초반이고, 최저 온도는 50도 후반입니다. 밤으로 가면서 온도는 40도 후반까지 떨어질 것이고, 내일은 더 따뜻해질 것입니다.

3. M 거기 런던의 날씨는 어때?
   W 기상 캐스터가 비가 온다고 했어.
   M 거기 따뜻하니?
   W 아니, 꽤 추워.

4. 일기에게,
   아마 우리 다음 주 여행은 취소해야 할 것 같아. 기상 캐스터가 폭풍이 칠 거라고 했어. 월요일에서 목요일까지 계속될 거라고 해. 정말 가고 싶어서 날씨가 좋아지기를 정말로 바라.

5. M 부들부들… 정말 춥다.
   W 여전히 눈이 오니?
   M 아니야. 하지만 바람이 점점 강해지고 있어.
   W 창문이 다 닫혔는지 확인해야겠다.

On Your Own   p. 41

LISTEN & WRITE

들리는 질문을 써 보세요.

스크립트

What is the weather like today?
What is the temperature today?
Do you like rain?
What is your favorite season?
Why?

해석
오늘 날씨가 어떻습니까?
오늘 기온은 어떻습니까?

PRONUNCIATION

/ v / vs / b /

☞ 듣고 따라해 보시오.
소형 트럭, 아주, 투표하다, (소, 코끼리 등이) 새끼를 낳다, 비둘기, 자이브(스윙 춤)

☞ 듣고 따라해 보시오.
금지, 베리, 배, 택시, 새로 녹음하다, 일치하다

☞ 잘 들어보고 차이점을 발견해 보시오.
소형 트럭 / 금지, 아주 / 베리,
투표하다 / 배, (소, 코끼리 등이) 새끼를 낳다 / 택시
비둘기 / 새로 녹음하다, 자이브(스윙 춤) / 일치하다

듣고 들리는 단어를 체크 하시오.

스크립트   ban, very, vote, calve , dub, jibe

소형 트럭	☐	금지	★
아주	★	베리	☐
투표하다	★	보트	☐
새끼를 낳다	★	택시	☐
비둘기	☐	새로 녹음하다	★
자이브	☐	일치하다	★

Practice Test   p. 42~43

1. 1) a   2) d   2. 1) c   2) c   3. 1) c   2) d
4. 1) c   2) b   5. 1) a   2) c

✻ 듣고 알맞은 답을 고르시오.

1. 주간 일기 예보이다.

스크립트

The weather will be very changeable this week. On Monday it will be warm and cloudy. Tuesday through Thursday it will be rainy and very windy. There will even be thunderstorms and lightning. The stormy weather will clear up from Thursday evening, and on Friday morning we'll see clear blue skies all over the nation. The weekend will be sunny and clear.

해석
이번 주 날씨는 매우 변덕스럽겠습니다. 월요일은 따뜻하고 구름이 많습니다. 화요일부터 목요일까지는 비가 오고 바람이 매우

강할 것입니다. 뇌우와 번개도 있을 것입니다. 폭풍우 치는 날씨는 목요일 저녁부터 갤 것이고, 금요일 아침에는 전국에 걸쳐 맑은 파란 하늘을 볼 것입니다. 주말은 화창하고 맑겠습니다.

1) 날씨가 어떻게 변화하겠는가? [두 번 들으시오.]

★a. 흐리다 → 폭풍우 친다 → 맑다

b. 흐리다 → 맑다 → 폭풍우 친다

c. 맑다 → 흐리다 → 비 온다

d. 비 온다 → 폭풍우 친다 → 맑다

2) 파란 하늘은 언제 볼 수 있는가?

a. 월요일에   b. 화요일에   c. 목요일에   ★d. 금요일에

2. 두 사람이 계절에 대해 이야기하고 있다.

스크립트

M Look at the color of the trees. I like this season. It's cool and dry. It's comfortable.

W Same here. The summer was too hot and humid. I could hardly breathe in the summer.

M That's true. But this season is too short. The leaves are already starting to fall. I don't like cold weather either.

해석

M 나무의 색을 봐. 난 이 계절이 좋아. 시원하고 건조해. 쾌적해.

W 나도 마찬가지야. 여름은 너무 덥고 습도가 높았어. 난 여름에는 거의 숨을 쉴 수가 없었어.

M 맞아. 그런데 이 계절은 너무 짧아. 나뭇잎들이 이미 떨어지기 시작했어. 나는 추운 날씨도 싫어.

1) 지금은 무슨 계절인가?

a. 봄   b. 여름   ★c. 가을   d. 겨울

2) 여름에는 날씨가 어땠는가?

a. 덥고 건조했다.   b. 따뜻하고 습도가 높았다.

★c. 덥고 습도가 높았다.   d. 춥고 건조했다.

3. 두 사람이 날씨에 대해 이야기하고 있다.

스크립트

W I am all wet. I am really tired of this rain.

M Me, too. There is too much rain this summer.

W The weather is crazy this year. It was very cold in the spring.

M Yes, it even snowed.

W How about tomorrow? Did you hear the weather forecast for tomorrow?

M Yes. It will be worse tomorrow. There will be thunderstorms.

해석

W 나 다 젖었어. 비가 정말 지겨워.

M 나도 그래. 이번 여름에는 비가 너무 많이 와.

W 올해는 날씨가 이상해. 봄에는 아주 추웠잖아.

M 어, 눈까지 왔지.

W 내일은 어떨까? 내일 일기 예보 들었어?

M 응. 내일은 더 안 좋을 거래. 폭풍우가 친대.

1) 오늘 날씨가 어떤가?

a. 눈이 온다.   b. 폭풍우가 친다.

★c. 비가 온다.   d. 춥다.

2) 다음 중 대화 내용과 일치하지 않는 것은?

a. 내일은 날씨가 더 나빠질 것이다.

b. 내일은 비가 올 것이다.

c. 올해 날씨는 여느 때와 다르다.

★d. 봄에는 날씨가 따뜻했다.

4. 다음 글은 이메일 메시지이다.

스크립트

Hi, Regina!
I'm now in the Vatican City in Rome. It's a beautiful city but I'm not happy. Can you guess why? It's not snowing! The weather forecast said it won't snow all December. People here tell me that it's the rainy season. It's raining every day.
I will write again soon.
Say hello to Sarah for me!

Love,
Jane

해석

안녕, Regina!
나는 지금 로마의 바티칸시티에 있어. 여긴 아름다운 도시지만 난 즐겁지가 않아. 왜 그런지 알아? 눈이 오지 않는다는 거야! 일기 예보에서 12월에는 한 번도 눈이 오지 않는대. 여기 사람들은 12월이 장마철이라고 말해. 매일 비가 와.
곧 다시 메일 쓸게.
Sarah에게 안부 전해 줘!
사랑하는 Jane으로부터.

1) 이 메일은 누가 누구에게 썼는가?

a. Regina가 Jane에게 썼다.

b. Jane이 Sarah에게 썼다.

★c. Jane이 Regina에게 썼다.

d. Regina가 Sarah에게 썼다.

2) 12월에 로마의 날씨는 어떠한가?

a. 눈이 많이 온다.

★b. 보통 비가 온다.

c. 춥다.

d. 흐리다.

5. Tom은 엄마와 이야기하고 있다.

스크립트

Tom	Mom, I feel hot. Can you get me a glass of water?
Mom	What's the weather like outside?
Tom	It's really hot. It's 33 degrees today. Didn't you listen to the weather forecast?
Mom	No. Do you know what the weather will be like this weekend? I'm going on a picnic.
Tom	On Saturday, it'll be sunny and about 22 degrees.
Mom	That's a great news.

해석

Tom 엄마, 더워요. 물 한 컵만 갖다 주실래요?

Mom 바깥 날씨가 어떠니?

Tom 정말 더워요. 오늘 33도에요. 일기 예보 못 들으셨어요?

Mom 아니. 이번 주말 날씨가 어떤지 아니? 야유회를 갈 계획인데.

Tom 토요일엔 맑고 22도 정도가 될 거예요.

Mom 좋은 소식이구나.

1) 이어질 대답으로 가장 적절한 것은?
★a. 좋은 소식이구나.   b. 더운 날씨가 싫어.
 c. 비 오는 날이 좋아.   d. 오늘 날씨는 참 좋구나.

2) 대화는 무엇에 관한 것인가?
 a. 오늘의 기온   b. 토요일의 기온
★c. 오늘과 토요일의 날씨   d. 토요일의 야유회

Dictation   p. 44

1. changeable, warm, cloudy, rainy, windy, stormy, clear
2. season, comfortable, hot, humid, cold weather
3. wet, rain, cold, snowed, weather forecast, thunderstorms
4. beautiful, snowing, rainy season, Say hello
5. outside, really hot, degrees, weekend, picnic, sunny

UNIT 6
Where is my shirt?

Getting Ready   p. 45

1. 4, 5, 1, 2, 3
2. 1. e   2. a   3. b   4. c   5. d

1. 그림에서 물건을 찾고, 빈칸에 번호를 적으시오.

탁자 위에 있습니다.	4
문 옆에 있습니다.	5
소파 뒤에 있습니다.	1
방 한가운데 있습니다.	2
소파 옆에 있습니다.	3

2. 질문을 답과 연결시키시오.

1. 책꽂이는 어디에 있나요?   e. 소파 옆에 있어요.
2. 방에 탁자가 있나요?   a. 네, 있어요.
3. 몇 개의 찬장이 있나요?   b. 3개 있어요.
4. 어디에서 식물을 볼 수 있나요?   c. 모퉁이에서 볼 수 있어요.
5. 창문 맞은편에 난로가 있나요?   d. 네, 있어요.

Listening Task   p. 46~47

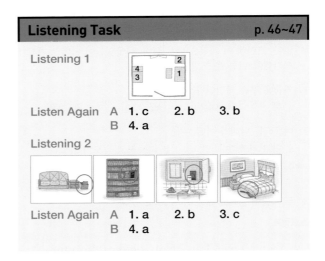

Listening 1

Listen Again A 1. c   2. b   3. b
              B 4. a

Listening 2

Listen Again A 1. a   2. b   3. c
              B 4. a

Listening 1   p. 46

Sue가 이사를 하고 있다. 그녀는 어디에 물건을 두어야 할지를 도우미에게 말하고 있다. 번호를 넣으시오.

스크립트

1. I want the sofa on the right side of the room. I can have fresh air beside me that way. Yes, thank you.

2. And please put the nightstand in the far right corner, near the sofa.

3. Next, the bookshelf... Where do you think would be good? Okay, I'll put it on the left side of the room, opposite the sofa. Is that okay? Fine.

4. What next? The TV. Okay, we have to see TV on the sofa, so I'll put it by the window next to the bookshelf.

해석

1. 나는 소파를 방 오른쪽에 두고 싶어요. 옆에서 상쾌한 공기를 마실 수 있잖아요. 네, 고마워요.

2. 그리고 협탁은 소파 옆 맨 오른쪽 구석으로 놔 주세요.

3. 다음에는, 책장이지... 어디가 좋을까요? 좋아요, 방 왼쪽에 놓아야겠어요. 소파 건너편에요. 괜찮아요? 좋아요.

4. 다음에는 뭐죠? TV에요. 우리가 대부분 TV를 소파에서 보니까 책장 옆에 놓아야겠어요.

Listen Again
p. 46

A. 다시 듣고 맞는 것을 고르시오.

1. a. 소파는 창문 앞에 있다.
   b. 소파는 창문 옆에 있다.
   ★c. 소파는 방의 오른쪽에 있다.

2. a. 협탁은 소파 가까이에 있지 않다.
   ★b. 협탁은 오른쪽 구석에 있다.
   c. 소파는 왼쪽 구석에 있다.

3. a. 책장은 소파 옆에 있다.
   ★b. 책장과 소파는 서로 마주보고 있다.
   c. 책장은 방의 오른쪽에 있다.

B. 다시 듣고 가장 적절하게 요약한 것을 고르시오.

4. a. ★ TV는 소파를 마주보게 놓일 것이다.
   b. □ TV와 소파는 방의 같은 쪽에 놓일 것이다.

Listening 2
p. 47

Jeff와 Brown 부인은 무언가를 찾고 있다. 각 그림에서 그 물건에 동그라미 치시오.

스크립트

1.
M Where is it?
W It's on the floor in front of the sofa.
M I can't find it.
W Oh, I forgot. It's in the box next to the nightstand. I put it in there.
M In the box next to the nightstand... Yes, here it is.

2.
M Oh, I can't find it anywhere.
W It's on the bookshelf by the window.
M Where on the bookshelf?
W On the third shelf from the top. See? Next to the thick green book.
M Third from the top? I got it.

3.
M Oh, I need it, and it's nowhere.
W It's in the kitchen cabinet above the sink.
M Where?
W See? Behind the sugar bowl.
M Behind the sugar bowl? Yeah, I found it.

4.
M Where is it?
W Are you still looking? I'm sure it's in your room.
M No, Mom. I have already looked through it.
W Try again. It must be somewhere under the bed.
M Under the bed... Yes. You're right, Mom. Thanks.

해석

1. M 그거 어디에 있어요?
   W 소파 앞 바닥에 있어.
   M 못 찾겠어요.
   W 아, 깜박했다. 협탁 옆 상자에 있어. 내가 그 안에 넣어 두었어.
   M 협탁 옆 상자 안이라... 네, 여기 있네요.

2. M 오, 어디에서도 못 찾겠어요.
   W 그거 창문 옆 책장에 있어.
   M 책장 어디에요?
   W 꼭대기에서 세 번째 선반에 있어. 보이니? 두꺼운 초록색 책 옆에.
   M 꼭대기에서 세 번째요? 여기 찾았어요.

3. M 오, 난 그게 필요한데, 아무데도 없어요.
   W 그건 싱크대 위 부엌 찬장 안에 있단다.
   M 어디에요?
   W 보이니? 설탕 통 뒤에.
   M 설탕 통 뒤요? 네, 찾았어요.

4. M 그거 어디에 있어요?
   W 아직도 찾고 있니? 확실히 네 방 안에 있어.
   M 아니에요, 엄마. 이미 다 찾아봤어요.
   W 다시 찾아 봐. 분명히 침대 밑 어디엔가 있을 거야.
   M 침대 밑이라... 네. 엄마 말이 맞아요. 고마워요.

Listen Again

p. 47

A. 다시 듣고 알맞은 답을 고르시오.

1. Jeff 는 _____ 물건을 찾았다.
   ★a. 상자 안에서
   b. 상자 뒤에서
   c. 상자 옆에서

2. 물건은 위에서 _____ 선반 위에 있었다.
   a. 두 번째   ★b. 세 번째   c. 네 번째

3. Jeff는 물건을 설탕 통 _____ 찾았다.
   a. 앞에서   b. 안에서   ★c. 뒤에서

B. 다시 듣고 맞는 문장을 고르시오.

4. a. ★ Jeff는 무언가를 찾고 있었는데 침대 밑에서 찾았다.
   b. ☐ Jeff는 무언가를 찾고 있었는데 엄마가 찾아 주셨다.

스크립트

> a. Jeff was looking for something and found it under the bed.
> b. Jeff was looking for something and his mom found it for him.

Review

p. 48

1. Where, on, in, under
2. what, left, right, by, on, in front of
3. anywhere, among, next to
4. keys, in, on
5. next to, behind, found

※ 듣고 빈칸을 채우시오.

해석

1. W 내 안경 어디에 있니?
   M 거실 탁자 위에서 봤어요.
   W 아니야, 거기에는 없어. 아, 여기 있구나. 탁자 아래에 있어.

2. 내 방이 어떻게 생겼는지 말해 줄게. 문은 왼편에, 창문은 오른편에 있어. 문 옆에 작은 탁자가 있고, 탁자 위에는 전화기가 있어. 창문 앞에 소파가 있어.

3. W 내 MP3 플레이어 봤니?
   M 네 책상 위에 있는 책들 사이에 있었어.
   W 그래, 여기 사전 옆에 있구나.

4. 나는 아침에 출근할 때 자동차 열쇠를 자주 잊어버린다. 방 어딘가에 놔두고 오는데, 보통은 책상 위에 놓고 온다. 내 아내 Karen은 항상 열쇠를 찾아다 준다.

5. M 벽 옆 바로 여기에 놔둔 것 같은데. 아무 데도 없어.
   W 소파 뒤는 봤어?
   M 아니. 응, 여기 있다. 고마워.

On Your Own

p. 49

LISTEN & WRITE

들리는 질문을 써 보세요.

스크립트

> Where is your bag?
> Where are your books?
> How many chairs are there in your classroom?
> Is there a painting on the wall?

해석
당신의 가방은 어디에 있습니까?
당신의 책은 어디에 있습니까?
당신의 교실엔 얼마나 많은 의자가 있습니까?
벽에는 그림이 있습니까?

PRONUNCIATION

> ### / f / vs / p /
>
> ☞ 듣고 따라해 보시오.
>   요금, 멋진, 느끼다, 빠른, 뚱뚱한, 아내
>
> ☞ 듣고 따라해 보시오.
>   콩, 소나무, 껍질을 벗기다, 과거, 가볍게 치다, 닦아내다
>
> ☞ 잘 들어보고 차이점을 발견해 보시오.
>   요금 / 콩, 멋진 / 소나무, 느끼다 / 껍질을 벗기다,
>   빠른 / 과거, 뚱뚱한 / 가볍게 치다, 아내 / 닦아내다

듣고 들리는 단어를 체크 하시오

스크립트 pea, fine, feel, past, fat, wipe

요금	☐	콩	★
멋진	★	소나무	☐
느끼다	★	껍질을 벗기다	☐
빠른	☐	과거	★
뚱뚱한	★	가볍게 치다	☐
아내	☐	닦아내다	★

Practice Test

p. 50~51

1. 1) b	2. 1) a	3. 1) b 2) a
4. 1) a	5. 1) a 2) c	

※ 듣고 알맞은 답을 고르시오.

1. Jenny는 그녀의 부엌을 묘사하고 있다.

스크립트

This is my kitchen. In my kitchen there is a round table in the middle. There are three chairs around it. On one of the chairs, my cat Lucy is sleeping. On another chair is my apron. Under the table is a wastepaper basket. There is some wastepaper on the floor around it. Behind the wastepaper basket are my old slippers. My kitchen is really messy.

해석

이건 내 부엌이야. 내 부엌에는 중앙에 원형 식탁이 있어. 의자 세 개가 식탁 둘레에 있고. 한 개의 의자 위에는 나의 고양이 Lucy 가 자고 있어. 또 다른 의자 위에는 내 앞치마가 있어. 식탁 아래 에는 휴지통이 있어. 휴지통 주변 바닥에 휴지 몇 장이 있어. 휴지 통 뒤에는 내 낡은 슬리퍼가 있어. 내 부엌은 정말 지저분해.

1) 맞는 그림을 고르시오.

2. 사람들이 그들의 고양이를 찾고 있다.

스크립트

M Where is Lucy? I haven't seen her all day.
W I saw her sleeping in the living room, behind the sofa this morning.
M She is not there.
W She was on the mat by the front door.
M When was that?
W Just a while ago.
M No, she's gone.
W Check under the basement stairs. She likes dark places.

해석

M Lucy는 어디 있니? 하루 종일 못 봤어.
W 오늘 아침에 거실 소파 뒤에서 자고 있는 것을 봤어.
M 거기 없어.
W 현관문 옆, 매트 위에 있었어.
M 그게 언제였는데?
W 바로 잠시 전에.
M 아니야, 없어.
W 지하실 계단 아래를 확인해 봐. Lucy는 어두운 곳을 좋아해.

1) 가장 적절하게 요약한 것을 고르시오.
   a. ★ 고양이는 거실에 있었고 그 다음에는 현관에 있었으며 이제는 지하실 계단 아래에 있을지도 모른다.
   b. ☐ 고양이가 실종됐다. 고양이는 항상 지하실 계단 아래에 서 자는데 어두운 곳을 좋아하기 때문이다.

3. Jeff는 무언가를 찾고 있다.

스크립트

Jeff Mom, can you help me find my library card?
Mom Oh, you lost it again. It must be in the top drawer of your desk.
Jeff It's not there.
Mom Then it may be somewhere around the bookshelf.
Jeff I got it, Mom. It is under a book on the bookshelf.

해석

Jeff 엄마, 제 도서관 카드 찾는 것 좀 도와주실래요?
Mom 아, 너 또 잃어버렸구나. 분명히 네 책상 맨 위 서랍에 있을 거야.
Jeff 거기 없어요.
Mom 그러면 책꽂이 주변 어딘가에 있겠지.
Jeff 찾았어요, 엄마. 책꽂이에 있는 책 밑에 있어요.

1) 물건은 어디에 있는가? 맞는 그림을 고르시오.

2) 대화가 끝난 후 그는 어디로 갈까?
   ★a. 도서관   b. 식당
    c. 체육관   d. 상점

4. Sophie는 그녀의 침실을 묘사하고 있다.

스크립트

In my bedroom, there is a bed against the left side wall. The fan is beside the bed. My desk is next to the window on the right side of the room. On the right side of the desk, there is a bookcase. Oh, I forgot to tell you about my best friend—my computer! It's on the desk.

해석

내 침실에는, 왼쪽 벽에 기대어 침대가 있어요. 침대 옆에는 선풍 기가 있고요. 책상은 방 오른쪽 창문가에 있어요. 책상 오른쪽에 는 큰 책장이 있어요. 아, 내 제일 친한 친구인 컴퓨터를 말하는 것을 잊었네요! 그건 책상 위에 있어요.

1) 맞는 그림을 고르시오.

5. 남편과 부인이 아침에 이야기를 하고 있다.

Alex	Honey, have you seen my keys?
Emma	You lost them again? I think I saw them in the living room.
Alex	I already looked there, but I couldn't find them.
Emma	Aren't they on the sofa?
Alex	No.
Emma	Check if they are beside the phone. You picked up the phone when you came back home last night, didn't you?
Alex	Ah, here they are!

해석

Alex	여보, 내 열쇠 본 적 있어요?
Emma	또 잃어버렸나요? 거실 어딘가에서 봤는데.
Alex	거긴 이미 찾아봤는데, 찾질 못했어요.
Emma	소파 위에 없던가요?
Alex	없어요.
Emma	전화기 옆에 있는지 보세요. 어젯밤에 집에 왔을 때 전화기를 썼어요, 안 그래요?
Alex	아하, 여기 있군!

1) 대화 내용에 대해 일치하지 않는 것은 무엇인가?
★a. 부인은 열쇠를 찾고 있는 중이다.
  b. 남편은 어디에 열쇠를 두었는지 기억하지 못한다.
  c. 부인은 남편에게 어디를 확인해야 할지 말하고 있다.
  d. 남편은 열쇠를 자주 잃어버린다.

2) 열쇠는 어디에 있었는가?
  a. 커피테이블 밑
  b. 소파 위
★c. 전화기 옆
  d. 남편의 주머니 속

Dictation   p. 52

1. in the middle, On, Under, around, Behind, messy
2. Where is, in the living room, behind, by the front door, while ago, under
3. lost, in the top drawer, somewhere, bookshelf, I got it
4. against, beside the bed, right side, It's on
5. lost, living room, on the sofa, beside, here they are

UNIT 7
How much is it?

Getting Ready   p. 53

1. 1. price tag   2. used   3. household
   4. new arrival   5. out of season   6. tax
2. 1. e   2. f   3. a   4. d   5. b   6. c

1. 빠진 단어를 네모 안에서 찾아 빈칸에 써 넣으시오.

세금 가격표 가정용의 제철이 아닌 중고의 신제품

1. 얼마에요? ___가격표___ 가 없네요.
2. 이건 새 것이 아니에요. 이건 ___중고___ 예요.
3. 샴푸, 칫솔, 수건은 모두 ___가정용___ 이에요.
4. 이건 세일이 아니에요. 왜냐하면 ___신제품___ 이거든요.
5. 봄이에요. 크리스마스 품목은 ___철이 아니에요___.
6. ___세금___ 포함해서 총액은 57달러 80센트입니다.

2. 질문을 답과 연결시키시오.

1. 도와드릴까요?   e. 네, 저는 모자를 찾고 있어요.
2. 얼마에요?   f. 35달러 90센트입니다.
3. 어떻게 그렇게 싼가요?   a. 세일 중이에요.
4. 더 싼 것이 있나요?   d. 물론 있지요.
5. 조금만 깎아줄 수 있나요?   b. 죄송하지만, 그럴 수 없어요.
6. 계산해 드릴까요?   c. 네, 그래 주세요.

Listening Task   p. 54~55

Listening 1	1. c	2. a	3. b	4. d
Listen Again A	1. b	2. b	3. a	
B	4. a			
Listening 2	1. Yes	2. No	3. Yes	4. Yes
Listen Again A	1. b	2. b	3. c	
B	4. b			

Listening I   p. 54

듣고 물건과 가격표를 연결시키시오.

1.
M Can I help you?
W I'm looking for something special for my daughter. She's graduating from high school next week.
M How about this beautiful ring?

w How much is it?

m It's $1,056.

w Oh, I don't like the design. It's not quite right for a young girl.

2.

m How do you like these earrings?

w How much are they?

m They're $890.

w Oh, they are too big.

3.

m How about this necklace then? It is 18 karat gold.

w What's the price?

m It is only $425. It's the same design as the one Julia Roberts wore...

w It looks cheap.

4.

w How about this pin? It's silver, isn't it?

m No, it's not. It's stainless steel.

w How much is it?

m It's $6.89.

w I think that is perfect for my daughter. It's small and beautiful. She is a shy girl. She'll love it!

해석

1. M 도와드릴까요?

W 내 딸을 위한 특별한 것을 찾고 있어요. 걔는 다음 주에 고등학교를 졸업하거든요.

M 이 예쁜 반지는 어떤가요?

W 얼마에요?

M 1,056달러에요.

W 오, 디자인이 마음에 들지 않아요. 어린 여자아이에게는 알맞지 않네요.

2. M 이 귀걸이는 어떠세요?

W 얼만데요?

M 890달러에요.

W 오, 너무 커요.

3. M 그러면 이 목걸이는 어때요? 18캐럿의 금이에요.

W 얼마에요?

M 겨우 425달러에요. Julia Roberts가 한 목걸이와 같은 디자인인데……

W 싸구려로 보이네요.

4. W 이 핀은 어떤가요? 이거 은이죠?

M 아니에요. 스테인리스에요.

W 얼마인가요?

M 6달러 89센트에요.

w 그게 내 딸에게 딱일 것 같아요. 작고 아름다워요. 그녀는 수줍음이 많은 아이에요. 좋아할 거예요!

Listen Again   p. 54

A. 다시 듣고 알맞은 답을 고르시오.

1. White 부인은 왜 이 물건이 마음에 들지 않는다고 하는가?

   a. 가격이 마음에 들지 않아서

★b. 디자인이 마음에 들지 않아서

   c. 색깔이 마음에 들지 않아서

2. White 부인은 왜 이 물건이 마음에 들지 않는다고 하는가?

   a. 너무 작아서

★b. 너무 커서

   c. 너무 비싸서

3. White 부인은 왜 이 물건이 마음에 들지 않는다고 하는가?

★a. 싸구려처럼 보여서

   b. 무거워서

   c. 금을 좋아하지 않아서

B. 다시 듣고 가장 적절하게 요약한 것을 고르시오.

4. a. ★ 여자는 가격과 사이즈가 마음에 들어서 핀을 살 것이다.

   b. ☐ 그녀의 딸은 수줍음이 많아서 여자가 핀을 사고 있다.

Listening 2   p. 55

사람들이 각각 물건을 살까, 사지 않을까? 표시하시오.

1. 살 것이다 ___★___   사지 않을 것이다 _____
2. 살 것이다 _____   사지 않을 것이다 ___★___
3. 살 것이다 ___★___   사지 않을 것이다 _____
4. 살 것이다 ___★___   사지 않을 것이다 _____

스크립트

1.

Clerk   Good afternoon. You've got some shampoo, a towel, and three toothbrushes. It's $19.89 plus tax. That's $20.38 in total.

Mrs. Brown   Is there tax for household goods in this state?

Clerk   Yes, ma'am.

Mrs. Brown   Oh, I see. Here you are.

2.

Susie   I'll take this jacket.

Clerk   That's $170.98.

Susie   Isn't it $80.99? I thought it was on sale.

Clerk   No, sorry. It's not on sale. It is a new arrival.

Susie   Then maybe I'll come back later.

3.

Clerk How may I help you?

Jeff How much is the shirt, please?

Clerk It's $5.99.

Jeff It was $20 or something. How come it is so cheap?

Clerk It's on sale. It's out of season.

Jeff That's good.

4.

Clerk Can I ring them up for you?

Mr. Brown Yes.

Clerk Let's see... One blouse, one dress, and two belts... That comes to $320.68.

Mrs. Brown Do you take Master Card?

Clerk Sure.

해석

1. Clerk 안녕하세요. 샴푸, 수건, 칫솔 3개를 사셨군요. 19달러 89센트에 세금이 붙습니다. 총 20달러 38센트입니다.

　 Mrs.Brown 이 주(州)에서는 가정용품에 세금이 붙나요?

　 Clerk 네, 부인.

　 Mrs.Brown 오, 그렇군요. 여기 있어요.

2. Susie 이 재킷을 사겠어요.

　 Clerk 170달러 98센트입니다.

　 Susie 80달러 99센트 아닌가요? 세일 중이라고 생각했는데.

　 Clerk 아니에요. 죄송합니다. 그건 세일이 아니에요. 신상품이거든요.

　 Susie 그러면 나중에 다시 올게요.

3. Clerk 어떻게 도와드릴까요?

　 Jeff 이 셔츠는 얼마인가요?

　 Clerk 5달러 99센트에요.

　 Jeff 20달러나 그 정도였는데. 어떻게 이렇게 싼가요?

　 Clerk 세일 중이에요. 철이 지났으니까요.

　 Jeff 잘됐네요.

4. Clerk 계산해 드릴까요?

　 Mr.Brown 네.

　 Clerk 한 번 봅시다... 블라우스 한 벌, 드레스 한 벌, 그리고 벨트 두 개... 320달러 68센트에요.

　 Mrs.Brown 마스터 카드 받나요?

　 Clerk 물론이죠.

Listen Again   p. 55

A. 다시 듣고 틀린 것을 고르시오.

1. a. 그녀는 세금을 냈다.

　★b. 그녀는 비누를 샀다.

　 c. 그녀는 가정용품에 세금이 붙는 줄 몰랐다.

2. a. 그 재킷은 신상품이다.

　★b. 이 상점은 세일을 하고 있지 않다.

　 c. 오래된 품목만 세일한다.

3. a. 이 셔츠는 지난 시즌 상품이다.

　 b. 그는 전에 이 상점에 와 본 적이 있다.

　★c. 셔츠에 문제가 있어서 싼 것이다.

B. 다시 듣고 맞는 문장을 고르시오.

4. a. □ 그녀는 블라우스 한 벌, 드레스 한 벌, 벨트 두 개와 마스터 카드를 사고 싶어한다.

　 b. ★ 그녀는 네 가지 물건을 사고 있으며, 카드 결제를 하고 싶어한다.

스크립트

　 a. She wants to buy one blouse, one dress, two belts and a master card.

　 b. She is buying four items and she wants to pay by credit card.

Review   p. 56

1. much, 55, expensive, season, one
2. warm, expensive, on sale, new arrival
3. price, 100, 80, 12, price tag
4. ring, comes, tax, credit cards

❋ 듣고 빈칸을 채우시오.

해석

1. W 이 모자 얼마예요?

　 M 55달러입니다.

　 W 믿을 수 없어요. 너무 비싸네요.

　 M 이번 계절에 가장 잘 인기 있는 물건이에요. 모두들 하나씩 쓰고 있잖아요.

2. 가장 내 마음에 드는 옷은 이 스웨터이다. 그것은 100% 양모다. 가볍고, 따뜻하고, 예쁘다. 그것은 140달러 60센트였다. 비싼데 신상품이라서 세일을 하지 않기 때문이다. 하지만 그만한 가치가 있다고 생각한다. 정말 마음에 든다!

3. M 봐! 나 신제품 선글라스를 샀어. 얼마인지 맞춰 봐.

　 W 100달러.

　 M 더 싸.

　 W 그럼 80달러.

　 M 더 싸. 겨우 12달러에 샀어.

　 W 믿을 수 없어!

　 M 나도 믿을 수 없어. 중고품을 판매하는 온라인 경매에서 이걸 샀어. 하지만 이건 새거야. 가격표까지 붙어 있다니까. 운이 좋았어!

4. W 네, 계산해 드릴게요. 세금 포함해서 296달러 65센트네요.

　 M 신용 카드도 받나요?

　 W 네, 비자, 아메리칸 익스프레스, 마스터 카드를 받아요.

　 M 여기 있어요.

LISTEN & WRITE

들리는 질문을 써 보세요.

스크립트

Did you buy anything this week?
How much was it?
Do you like to buy something on sale or a new arrival?
Where is your favorite shopping place?

해석

이번 주에 물건을 샀습니까?
그것은 얼마였습니까?
세일 중인 것과 신제품 중 어느 것을 사는 걸 좋아합니까?
당신이 가장 좋아하는 쇼핑 장소는 어디입니까?

PRONUNCIATION

/ ai /
☞ 듣고 따라해 보시오.
나는, 얼음, 죽다, 나의, 싸우다, 좋아하다,
타이, 마음, 서명하다, 안녕, 사다, ~에 의해

아래 문장을 읽고 'ai' 소리가 있는 단어에 동그라미 치시오.

1. 나는 내 타이를 좋아한다.
2. 나는 내 생각을 좋아했던 그 남자를 찾고 있다.

이제 듣고 답을 확인하시오.

1. I like my tie.
2. I am finding the guy who liked my idea.

Practice Test   p. 58~59

1. 1) b 2) a   2. 1) a   3. 1) b 2) c
4. 1) d 2) c   5. 1) c 2) c

✻ 듣고 알맞은 답을 고르시오.

1. 한 남자가 상점에 있다.

스크립트

W How may I help you, sir?
M I'm looking for a briefcase.
W Here we have a large collection of them.
M Hmm... How much is this one?
W It's $89.90.
M I want something a little cheaper. Can you come down a little?

W No, sir. It's already on sale.
M All right. I'll take it.
W So, your final total is $93.80.
M Wasn't it eighty something?
W There is tax, sir.
M Oh, I see.

해석

W 어떻게 도와드릴까요?
M 서류 가방을 찾고 있어요.
W 우리는 다양한 종류의 서류 가방이 있어요.
M 흠... 이건 얼마인가요?
W 89달러 90센트에요.
M 조금 더 싼 걸 원해요. 깎아 주실 수 있어요?
W 안 됩니다, 손님. 이미 세일 중이거든요.
M 좋아요. 사겠어요.
W 그러면, 손님의 최종 가격은 93달러 80센트입니다.
M 80 몇 달러 아닌가요?
W 세금이 있습니다, 손님.
M 아, 알겠어요.

1) 남자는 _____ 을(를) 사고 있다.
  a. 신발   ★b. 서류 가방   c. 여행 가방

2) 대화 내용과 일치하는 것은?
  ★a. 남자는 세금을 지불해야 한다.
    b. 남자는 가방이 싸다고 생각한다.
    c. 남자는 이 물건을 사지 않을 것이다.
    d. 남자는 90달러보다 적게 지불할 것이다.

2. 손님이 점원의 말을 잘 못 듣는다.

스크립트

W What can I do for you?
M I really like this pair of pants. What's the price? There's no price tag.
W $580.89
M $158.89?
W No, $580.89

해석

W 무엇을 도와드릴까요?
M 이 바지가 정말 마음에 들어요. 얼마에요? 가격표가 없네요.
W 580달러 89센트입니다.
M 158달러 89센트요?
W 아니요, 580달러 89센트요.

1) 맞는 가격을 고르시오
★a. 580달러 89센트
  b. 518달러 89센트
  c. 158달러 89센트

3. Jeff가 상점에 있다.

Clerk	What can I do for you?
Jeff	I'm looking for a present for my mom.
Clerk	How much can you spend?
Jeff	Around $20.
Clerk	How about some accessories, like belts or hats?
Jeff	Show me some belts, please.
Clerk	Here you are. This one is $18.90 and it's very pretty.

해석

Clerk 무엇을 도와드릴까요?

Jeff 엄마께 드릴 선물을 찾고 있어요.

Clerk 얼마 정도를 쓰실 수 있나요?

Jeff 20달러쯤이요.

Clerk 벨트나 모자 같은 액세서리는 어떠세요?

Jeff 벨트 좀 보여 주세요.

Clerk 여기 있습니다. 이건 18달러 90센트이고 아주 예뻐요.

1) Jeff는 무엇을 사고 있는가?
   a. 여자 친구에게 줄 선물　★b.엄마께 드릴 선물
   c. 선생님께 드릴 선물　　　d. 스스로에게 줄 선물

2) Jeff가 할 말로 적당하지 않은 것은?
   a. 좀 깎아 주실 수 있나요?　b. 그걸로 살게요.
   ★c. 제가 계산해 드릴게요.　d. 엄마가 좋아하실 거예요.

4. Sarah는 가게 주인과 이야기를 하고 있다.

Shopkeeper	May I help you?
Sarah	Well, I'm looking for a present for my mom.
Shopkeeper	How about this bag? It is hand-made, but not that expensive.
Sarah	How much is it?
Shopkeeper	$40. Isn't it cheap?
Sarah	Yeah, but I can't afford it.
Shopkeeper	I'll give you a discount. How about $30?
Sarah	It's very kind of you, but I've got only $25 now.
Shopkeeper	Deal.
Sarah	Thank you so much.

해석

Shopkeeper 무엇을 도와드릴까요?

Sarah 음, 엄마를 위한 선물을 찾고 있어요.

Shopkeeper 이 가방은 어때요? 수제품이지만, 그다지 비싸지 않아요.

Sarah 얼만데요?

Shopkeeper 40달러요. 싸지 않나요?

Sarah 네, 하지만 전 그걸 살 여유가 없네요.

Shopkeeper 제가 깎아 드릴게요. 30달러는 어때요?

Sarah 정말 친절하시네요. 하지만 전 25달러 밖에 없어요.

Shopkeeper 그 가격에 해 드리죠.

Sarah 정말 감사합니다.

1) 가방의 원래 가격은 얼마인가?
   a. 20달러　　b. 25달러　　c. 30달러　　★d. 40달러

2) 가게 주인은 Sarah에게 왜 할인을 해 주었는가?
   a. Sarah가 학생이라서.
   b. Sarah가 좋은 손님이라서.
   ★c. Sarah가 가방을 살 만한 충분한 돈이 없어서.
   d. Sarah가 엄마에게 선물을 사 드리기를 원해서.

5. Patrick은 그가 오늘 무엇을 샀는지 여동생에게 말하고 있다.

Sophie, guess what I bought for you today. You'll like it. On my way home, I saw an old lady selling summer hats. The hats were hand-made. I asked how much they were, and the old lady said, "$15 each." I had $50 in my pocket, so I picked two, the green one and the red one. Look, aren't they beautiful?

해석

Sophie, 오늘 너에게 주려고 뭘 샀는지 맞춰 봐. 아마 마음에 들 거야. 집에 오는 길에, 나이 든 부인이 여름 모자를 팔고 있는 걸 봤어. 수제품이야. 모자가 얼마인지 물었더니, 그 부인이 "하나에 15달러입니다."라고 했어. 주머니에 50달러가 있어서, 초록색 하나와 빨간색 하나, 그렇게 두 개를 샀어. 봐, 멋지지 않아?

1) Patrick이 구입한 물건은 무엇인가?

2) Patrick은 모자에 얼마를 지불했는가?
   a. 15달러　　b. 20달러　　★c. 30달러　　d. 50달러

Dictation　　　　　　　　　　　　　　p. 60

1. I'm looking for, large collection, cheaper, come down, eighty
2. price, price tag, $580.89, $580.89
3. present, spend, 20, belts, 18.90
4. looking, bag, hand-made, cheap, I can't afford it, discount
5. bought, selling, 15, 50, picked

UNIT 8
Don't cross the road!

Getting Ready
p. 61

1. 1. school zone 2. handicapped
   3. ticket 4. fasten
   5. driver's license 6. crosswalk
   7. Jaywalking
2. 1. d 2. e 3. a 4. c 5. b 6. f

1. 빠진 표현을 네모 안에서 찾아 빈칸에 써 넣으시오.

| 운전면허증 | 장애인의 | 딱지 | 스쿨존(어린이 보호 구역) |
| 횡단보도 | 무단 횡단 | 매다 | |

1. 속도를 줄이세요! ___스쿨존___ 입니다. 주변에 어린이들이 많아요.
2. 나는 ___장애인___ 주차 구역에 주차했다.
3. 나는 속도위반 ___딱지___ 를 떼었다.
4. 당신은 항상 안전벨트를 ___매야___ 한다.
5. 운전할 때는 ___운전면허증___ 을 가지고 다녀야 한다.
6. 항상 ___횡단보도___ 에서 길을 건너라.
7. ___무단 횡단___ 은 위험하다.

2. 같은 의미를 지닌 표현을 연결하시오.

1. 우회전하시오. d. 여기서 우회전할 수 있습니다.
2. 멈추시오. e. 여기서 완전히 멈춰야 합니다.
3. 안전벨트를 매시오. a. 안전벨트를 매야 합니다.
4. 여기서 길을 건너지 마시오. c. 여기서 길을 건너면 안 됩니다.
5. 주차 금지! b. 여기에 주차하면 안 됩니다.
6. 진입 금지. f. 여기로 들어가면 안 됩니다.

Listening Task
p. 62~63

Listening 1		1. T	2. F	3. T	4. F
Listen Again	A	1. b	2. a	3. c	
	B	4. a			
Listening 2		4, 3, 1, 2			
Listen Again	A	1. c	2. b	3. c	
	B	4. b			

Listening 1
p. 62

듣고 True(참)이나 False(거짓)에 표시하시오.

1. 그들은 길을 건너고 있다. (T)
2. 여자는 운전 중이다. (F)
3. 여자와 경찰관 사이의 대화이다. (T)
4. 지하철 안에서 이야기하고 있다. (F)

스크립트

1.
W You can't jaywalk here. There's a crosswalk right over there.
M It's too far.
W But it's a busy street. Jaywalking is dangerous.
M Yeah, but the road is not busy right now.
W ___You still shouldn't jaywalk.___

2.
W Stop! What are you doing?
M Why? Don't shout!
W You ran a red light!
M Uh uh... A police car is coming.
W ___Oh, no!___

3.
M Excuse me. You were speeding.
W I'm sorry. I didn't see the sign. I'm new here.
M Anyway I have to give you a ticket. Can I see your driver's license please?
W ___Oh, please, officer.___

4.
W Buckle up, kids.
M I don't want to.
W You have to fasten your seat belt on the highway.
M Then I can't move.
W ___But you have to.___

해석

1. W 여기서 무단 횡단하면 안 돼. 바로 저기에 횡단보도가 있어.
   M 너무 멀어요.
   W 그러나 이곳은 붐비는 거리야. 무단 횡단은 위험해.
   M 알아요, 그러나 지금 당장은 붐비지 않잖아요.
   W ___그래도 무단 횡단은 안 돼.___

2. W 멈춰! 너 뭐 하는 거야?
   M 왜? 소리 지르지 마!
   W 너 빨간 불에서 안 멈췄잖아!
   M 어, 경찰차가 온다.
   W ___오, 안 돼!___

3. M 실례합니다. 속도를 위반하셨습니다.
   W 죄송합니다. 신호를 보지 못했어요. 여기 처음 왔거든요.
   M 어쨌든 위반 딱지를 떼야겠습니다. 운전면허증 좀 볼 수 있을까요?
   W ___제발요, 경관님.___

4. W 애들아, 안전벨트 매렴.
   M 싫어요.

W 고속 도로에서는 안전벨트를 매야만 해.
M 그러면 움직일 수가 없잖아요.
W _____ 그래도 해야 돼.

Listen Again

p. 62

A. 다시 듣고 알맞은 답을 고르시오.

1. 이어질 말로 가장 어울리는 것은?
   a. 넌 괜찮아.   ★b. 그래도 무단 횡단은 안 돼.
   c. 여기서 길을 건너도 돼.

2. 이어질 말로 가장 어울리는 것은?
   ★a. 오, 안 돼!   b. 알았어.   c. 만세!

3. 이어질 말로 가장 어울리는 것은?
   a. 당연히 안 됩니다.   b. 절대 안 돼요.   ★c. 제발요, 경관님.

B. 다시 듣고 가장 어울리는 응답을 고르시오.

4. a. ★ 그래도 해야 돼.   b. ☐ 물론이지.   c. ☐ 확실해요.

스크립트

a. But you have to.   b. Certainly.   c. I am sure.

Listening 2

p. 63

듣고 표지판의 번호를 쓰시오.

스크립트

1. My family was on the way home from shopping yesterday. Suddenly we heard a siren. My dad stopped the car. A police officer came up and gave my dad a ticket. It was a school zone and he was driving over 20 mph. You must not drive over 20 mph in the school zone.

2. Last week my mom paid a 100-dollar fine. She parked in a handicapped parking area. She was in a hurry and didn't see the sign. You can't park in the handicapped parking area. The fine is very heavy.

3. My brother had a car accident the other day. He entered a road and bumped into a car face to face. It was a one-way road. There was a 'Do Not Enter' sign. You really have to be careful not to miss the sign.

4. My mom and I dropped by the public library last Friday. When we got out of the library, our car was gone. It was towed away. How come? It was parked on the street. Don't ever park your car on the street.

해석

1. 우리 가족은 어제 쇼핑을 하고 집으로 돌아오는 길이었어. 갑자기 사이렌 소리가 들렸어. 우리 아빠가 차를 멈췄어. 경찰관이 와서 아빠에게 딱지를 뗐어. 스쿨존이었는데 시속 20마일보다 빠르게 운전하고 있었던 거야. 스쿨존에서는 시속 20마일보다 빠르게 운전하면 안 돼.

2. 지난주에 우리 엄마는 벌금을 100달러 물었어. 장애인 주차 구역에 주차를 한 거야. 너무 바빠서 표지판을 못 보셨나봐. 장애인 주차 구역에 주차하면 안 돼. 벌금이 아주 비싸거든.

3. 우리 형이 얼마 전에 자동차 사고를 냈어. 길로 들어가다가 정면으로 어떤 차를 받은 거야. 거긴 일방통행로였어. '진입 금지' 표지판이 있었어. 표지판을 놓치지 않도록 정말 조심해야 돼.

4. 우리 엄마와 나는 지난 금요일에 공공도서관에 들렀어. 도서관을 나왔는데, 우리 차가 없어졌어. 견인이 된 거야. 왜냐고? 길에다 주차를 했거든. 절대로 길에다 주차하지 마.

Listen Again

p. 63

A. 다시 듣고 알맞은 답을 고르시오.

1. 스쿨존의 제한 속도는 얼마인가?
   a. 시속 40마일   b. 시속 30마일   ★c. 시속 20마일

2. 그녀는 _____ 벌금을 냈는데, _____ 주차 구역에 주차했기 때문이다.
   a. 큰, 무료   ★b. 많은, 장애인의   c. 큰, 특별한

3. 그는 _____ 도로에 진입했다가 사고를 냈다.
   a. 작은   b. 혼잡한   ★c. 일방통행

B. 다시 듣고 맞는 문장을 고르시오.

4. a. ☐ 자동차가 견인됐는데 공원에 있었기 때문이다.
   b. ★ 길에 주차했기 때문에 그들의 차가 견인됐다.

스크립트

a. Their car was towed away because it was in a park.
b. Their car was towed away because it was parked on the street.

Review

p. 64

1. speed limit, 60, fasten
2. accident, entered, bumped, miss
3. speeding, sign, zone
4. parked, gone, towed, street
5. cross, busy, jaywalk, crosswalk

✽ 듣고 빈칸을 채우시오.

해석

1. W 고속 도로에서 제한 속도는 얼마인가요?
   M 시속 60마일이에요.
   W 빠르군요. 안전벨트를 꼭 매세요.

34

2. 며칠 전에 우리 아빠는 자동차 사고를 당하셨다. 아빠가 퇴근해서 집으로 돌아오시던 길이었다. 아빠는 작은 길에 들어섰고 트럭과 부딪쳤다. 다행스럽게도 아빠는 다치지 않았지만 정말 위험했다. 표지판을 놓치지 마세요.

3. M 속도 위반입니다.
   W 아니에요.
   M 저기 있는 표지판 안 보이세요? 여긴 스쿨존입니다.
   W 오, 몰랐어요.

4. 어젯밤, 나는 잠깐 뭘 좀 사려고 길에 차를 주차했습니다. 돌아왔을 때, 차가 없더라고요. 사람들이 견인됐다고 하더군요. 절대로 길에다 주차하지 마세요.

5. M 너는 여기서 길을 건너면 안 돼.
   W 지금 별로 혼잡하지도 않잖아요.
   M 그래도 무단 횡단은 안 돼. 봐! 저기 횡단보도가 있어.

On Your Own   p. 65

LISTEN & WRITE

들리는 질문을 써 보세요.

스크립트

Have you ever jaywalked?
Do you usually fasten your seat belt?
What is the speed limit for your school area?

해석
무단 횡단을 해 본 적이 있습니까?
평상시에 안전벨트를 맵니까?
당신의 학교 주변의 제한 속도는 몇입니까?

PRONUNCIATION

/ au /

☞ 듣고 따라해 보시오.

밖에, 암소, 어떻게, 지금, ~에 대하여, 갈색,
구름, ~ 아래에, 집, 입, 소리, 마을

아래 문장을 읽고 'au' 소리가 있는 단어에 동그라미 치시오.

1. 시내에 있는 그 갈색 집 어때요?
2. 밖에 얼마나 많은 소가 있습니까?

이제 듣고 답을 확인하시오.

1. How about the brown house in downtown?
2. How many cows can you count outside?

Practice Test   p. 66~67

1. 1) b 2) b   2. 1) b 2) a   3. 1) a 2) c
4. 1) c 2) a   5. 1) b 2) c

❋ 듣고 알맞은 답을 고르시오.

1. Brian은 경찰관과 이야기하고 있다.

스크립트

Police Officer	You ran a red light.
Brian	I didn't, sir.
Police Officer	Yes, you did. I was watching you. I need to see your license, please.
Brian	Maybe I was nervous driving. This is actually my first time driving.
Police Officer	I am sorry, but I have to give you a ticket.
Brian	I don't have a license. This is my father's car.
Police Officer	I have to take you to the police station then.

해석

Police Officer	빨간 불에서 달리셨습니다.
Brian	안 그랬어요.
Police Officer	그러셨습니다. 제가 당신을 보고 있었어요. 당신의 면허증을 봐야겠습니다.
Brian	아마 제가 운전하느라 긴장했나봐요. 사실 제 첫 번째 운전이거든요.
Police Officer	죄송하지만, 딱지를 끊어야겠습니다.
Brian	전 운전면허증이 없어요. 이건 아빠 차예요.
Police Officer	그렇다면 당신을 경찰서로 데려가야겠군요.

1) 대화 내용과 일치하지 않는 것은?
   a. Brian은 빨간 불을 지나쳤다.
   ★b. Brian은 속도를 위반했다.
   c. Brian은 자기 아버지 차를 운전하고 있었다.
   d. 경찰관은 Brian을 경찰서로 데려갈 것이다.

2) Brian은 _____ 때문에 경찰서에 가야 한다.
   a. 아버지 차로 운전했기   ★b. 운전면허증이 없기
   c. 음주 운전을 했기   d. 빨간불에서 지나쳤기 때문에

2. 다음은 길에 관한 것이다.

스크립트

It is a busy street. It's dangerous. There are many cars. There are many people passing by. There is an overpass over there. There is a crosswalk over here.
So _____ don't jaywalk here _____.

해석
분주한 거리이다. 위험하다. 차들이 많다. 많은 사람들이 지나간다. 저기에 육교가 있다. 이쪽에 횡단보도가 있다.
그러니까 _____ 여기서 무단 횡단을 하지 마세요 _____.

1) 이어질 표현으로 가장 어울리는 것은?

    a. 속도를 줄이세요.   ★b. 여기서 무단 횡단을 하지 마세요.

    c. 달리지 마세요.   d. 서두르세요.

2) ＿＿＿＿＿＿ 가 있어서 길이 위험하다.

    ★a. 많은 자동차   b. 많은 육교

    c. 많은 횡단보도   d. 많은 나무

3. 다음은 Brown 부인과 Jeff의 대화이다.

스크립트

Mom	What is this? It's a 50 dollar-fine from the police station.
Jeff	I am sorry, Mom. I drove your car and got a ticket.
Mom	What did you do?
Jeff	I was speeding.
Mom	How fast were you driving?
Jeff	It was just 40 mph, but it was a school zone.
Mom	You won't get any allowance next month.
Jeff	Sure.

해석

Mom 이게 뭐야? 경찰서에서 온 50달러 벌금 고지서네.

Jeff 죄송해요, 엄마. 엄마 차로 운전하다가 딱지를 떼었어요.

Mom 뭘 했는데?

Jeff 속도위반이요.

Mom 얼마나 빨리 달렸는데?

Jeff 시속 40마일밖에 안 됐는데, 스쿨존이었어요.

Mom 다음 달은 용돈 없다.

Jeff 네.

1) 대화 내용과 일치하는 것은?

    ★a. Jeff는 엄마 차로 운전했다.

    b. Jeff는 고속도로에서 속도를 위반했다.

    c. Jeff가 벌금을 낼 것이다.

    d. Jeff는 다음 달에 용돈을 받을 것이다.

2) Jeff는 시속 ＿＿＿＿＿＿마일로 달렸고 벌금은 ＿＿＿＿＿＿ 달러이다.

    a. 50, 40   b. 40, 40   ★c. 40, 50   d. 50, 50

4. 세 사람이 이야기하고 있다.

스크립트

Mom	Peter, don't play near the street. Okay?
Peter	Okay, okay. Don't worry, Mom. I won't.
Man	Is this your son?
Mom	Yes, he is. What's the matter?
Man	I nearly ran over your son. He was playing on the street with other kids.
Mom	I'm so sorry. I told him not to play near

the street. Thank you for telling me what happened.

Man (to Peter) Listen, young man, it's very dangerous to play near the street, okay?

해석

Mom Peter, 도로변에서 놀지 말거라, 알았지?

Peter 네, 네. 걱정 마세요, 엄마. 안 그럴게요.

Man 이 아이가 부인 아들인가요?

Mom 네, 그런데요. 무슨 일인가요?

Man 제가 당신 아들을 거의 칠 뻔했네요. 얘가 도로에서 다른 아이들과 놀고 있었거든요.

Mom 정말 죄송합니다. 도로변에서 놀지 말라고 일렀는데. 무슨 일이 일어났는지 말씀해 주셔서 감사합니다.

Man (Peter에게) 들어라, 애야, 도로 변에서 노는 것은 아주 위험한단다, 알겠지?

1) 대화는 어디에서 이루어지고 있는가?

    a. 도로에서   b. 차에서

    ★c. Peter의 집에서   d. 남자의 집에서

2) 대화의 올바른 요약을 고르시오.

    a. ★ Peter는 도로에서 놀고 있었고 한 운전자가 그를 거의 칠 뻔했다. 그래서 그 운전자는 Peter와 그의 엄마에게 주의를 주기 위해 집으로 왔다.

    b. ☐ 한 운전자가 Peter가 도로에서 놀고 있었는지 물어보기 위해 Peter의 집으로 왔다.

5. 다음은 경찰관과 한 여성의 대화이다.

스크립트

M	Excuse me, lady, this space is for the handicapped.
W	Well, it's my husband's car, and he is handicapped.
M	But I can't find any sticker for the handicapped on your car.
W	Oh, maybe he forgot to put it on.
M	You better tell me the truth.
W	All right, I'm sorry. I couldn't find a space anywhere, so I came here. I promise I won't do this again.
M	I understand, but you have to pay the fine of $100.
W	$100!

해석

M 실례합니다, 부인, 이 공간은 장애인 전용입니다.

W 음, 제 남편의 차인데요, 남편은 장애인이에요.

M 하지만 부인 차에는 장애인을 표시하는 어떤 스티커도 보이지 않는데요.

W 아, 아마 남편이 그걸 붙이는 걸 깜빡했을 거예요.

M 사실대로 이야기하시는 게 좋으실 텐데요.

W 알았어요, 죄송합니다. 주차할 공간을 어디에서도 찾을 수가 없어서 여기로 왔어요. 다시는 이런 짓을 하지 않겠습니다.

M 이해합니다만, 벌금 100달러를 내셔야 합니다.

W 100달러요!

1) 대화는 어디서 이루어지고 있는가?
    a. 도로에서   ★b. 주차장에서
    c. 경찰서에서   d. 운전면허 시험장에서

2) 왜 경찰관이 그녀에게 벌금을 물렸는가?
    a. 그녀가 경찰에게 거짓말을 해서
    b. 그녀가 스티커에 대한 돈을 지불하지 않아서
    ★c. 그녀가 장애인 전용 주차 공간에 주차를 해서
    d. 그녀가 장애인 남편을 기다리고 있어서

Dictation   p. 68

1. ran, license, first time, ticket, my father's car, police station
2. busy, dangerous, passing, crosswalk
3. fine, drove, speeding, fast, 40
4. near the street, matter, ran over, happened, dangerous
5. handicapped, sticker, put it on, space, fine

UNIT 9
What do you do?

Getting Ready   p. 69

1. 1. c   2. d   3. a   4. f   5. e   6. b   7. g
2. 1. a   2. e   3. c   4. b   5. d

1. 아래 네모 안에 있는 단어들의 기호를 빈칸에 쓰시오.

| a. 치과 의사 | b. 간호사 | c. 승무원 | d. 주방장 |
| e. 미용사 | f. 관광안내원 | g. 사서 | |

1. 이 사람은 비행 중에 승객을 돌본다.   c
2. 이 사람은 레스토랑에서 음식을 만든다.   d
3. 이 사람은 당신의 이를 돌본다.   a
4. 이 사람은 관광객을 안내한다.   f
5. 이 사람은 당신의 머리를 자른다.   e
6. 이 사람은 의사를 돕는다.   b
7. 이 사람은 책을 찾는 것을 도와준다.   g

2. 질문을 답과 연결시키시오.

1. 직업이 무엇인가요?   a. 레스토랑을 운영해요.
2. 당신의 직업은 어떤가요?   e. 지루해요.
3. 당신은 당신의 직업을 얼마나 좋아하나요?
    c. 별로 좋아하지 않아요.
4. 근무 시간이 어떻게 되세요? b. 오전 9시부터 오후 1시까지요.
5. 일은 어떻게 되어 가나요? d. 아주 잘 돼요.

Listening Task   p. 70~71

Listening 1	1. b	2. c	3. b	4. a
Listen Again A	1. c	2. c	3. c	
B	4. a			
Listening 2	1. c	2. c	3. a	4. b
Listen Again A	1. b	2. c	3. a	
B	4. a			

Listening 1   p. 70

사람들이 그들의 직업에 대해서 이야기하고 있다. 어떤 직업에 대해 이야기하고 있는가?

1. a. 비행사   ★b. 승무원   c. 여행사 직원
2. a. 의사   b. 농부   ★c. 간호사
3. a. 식당 종업원   ★b. 주방장   c. 가게 종업원
4. ★a. 경찰관   b. 운동선수   c. 의사

1.

My job? It's wonderful. I can travel a lot. I can meet many different people. I learn a lot from them. I enjoy serving them. The problem is I can't sleep during the flight.

2.

What do I do? I work in the hospital. I look after sick people. I do help doctors. Now I'm tired of my job. I have to work at night from time to time and I hate it.

3.

What's my job? I like cooking, and that's my job. It doesn't make me much money but I am happy when people enjoy my food. Someday I'll have my own restaurant. The only problem is I am getting fat.

4.

What is my husband's job like? It's a tough job, but I am proud of him. He keeps people safe. One thing I don't like about his job is it's dangerous.

해석

1. 내 직업? 굉장해. 나는 여행을 많이 갈 수 있어. 많은 다양한 사람들을 만날 수 있어. 그 사람들에게서 많은 걸 배우지. 그 사람들 접대하는 것도 재미있고, 문제는 내가 비행 중에는 잘 수가 없다는 거야.

2. 내 직업이 뭐냐고? 나는 병원에서 일해. 나는 아픈 사람들을 돌봐. 나는 의사들을 도와주지. 이제 내 직업에 싫증이 나. 가끔 밤에 일해야 하는데 난 그게 싫어.

3. 내 직업이 뭐냐고? 나는 요리하는 것을 좋아하고, 그게 내 직업이야. 돈을 많이 벌지는 않지만 사람들이 내 음식을 즐길 때 나는 행복해. 언젠가 나는 내 식당을 차릴 거야. 유일한 문제는 내가 뚱뚱해지고 있다는 거지.

4. 내 남편 직업이 뭐냐고? 그건 매우 거친 직업이지만, 나는 그가 자랑스러워. 그는 사람들을 안전하게 보호해. 그의 직업에 대해 한 가지 내가 싫어하는 점은 위험하다는 거야.

Listen Again
p. 70

A. 다시 듣고 알맞은 답을 고르시오.

1. 그녀가 자신의 직업을 좋아하는 이유가 <u>아닌</u> 것은?
   a. 다양한 사람들을 만난다.
   b. 여행을 많이 할 수 있다.
   ★c. 돈을 많이 벌 수 있다.

2. 그가 하는 일이 <u>아닌</u> 것은?
   a. 아픈 사람들을 돌본다.
   b. 의사를 돕는다.
   ★c. 밤에만 일한다.

3. 문제는 _____ 이다.
   a. 그가 돈을 많이 못 번다는 것
   b. 그가 자신의 식당을 가지고 있지 않다는 것
   ★c. 그가 뚱뚱해지고 있다는 것

B. 다시 듣고 가장 적절하게 요약한 것을 고르시오.

4. a. ☒ 그녀의 남편은 거친 직업을 가지고 있고 그녀는 그가 자랑스럽지만 그의 직업은 위험하다.
   b. ☐ 그녀의 남편은 거칠다. 그녀는 그의 직업이 위험하기 때문에 그를 자랑스러워한다.

Listening 2
p. 71

※ 듣고 빈칸에 알맞은 말을 고르시오.

1. Peterson 씨는 _____ 이다.
   a. 우체부   b. 공장 근로자   ★c. 버스 기사

2. 소녀는 _____ 일을 하고 싶어 한다.
   a. 간호사   b. 유치원 교사   ★c. 베이비시터

3. Pat은 _____ 일하고 있다.
   ★a. 식당에서   b. 정규직으로   c. 매니저로

4. Cindy는 _____ 이다.
   a. 식당 종업원   ★b. 미용사   c. 승무원

스크립트

1.

Jeff	Good afternoon, Mr. Peterson!
Mr. Peterson	Good afternoon, Jeff! Put 50 cents in the box.
Jeff	I have to get off at the post office.
Mr. Peterson	I'll let you know when.
Jeff	Thanks. How are you doing?
Mr. Peterson	Fine. It's nice to see my good neighbors while working.
Jeff	How many hours a day do you work?
Mr. Peterson	Nine hours.

2.

W	Hello, are you still looking for a babysitter?
M	Yes.
W	What are the working hours?
M	From 9 a.m. to 5 p.m., Monday through Friday. It's a full-time job.
W	Can I ask how much is the pay?
M	$300 a week.

3.

W How's your part-time job going, Pat?

M Terrible.

W Why is that?

M The restaurant has a new manager and she is so mean. She shouts at waiters all the time. I think I'm going to quit.

W _____ Sorry to hear that.

4.

Man Thanks for the wonderful job, Cindy. I like my new hair.

Cindy Thanks. I'm glad you like it.

Man How many customers do you have a day?

Cindy About 30.

Man That's a lot. How long have you been working here?

Cindy _____ For three years.

해석

1. Jeff 안녕하세요, Peterson 씨!

   Mr. Peterson 안녕, Jeff! 통에 50센트를 넣어.

   Jeff 전 우체국에서 내려야 돼요.

   Mr. Peterson 내릴 때가 되면 가르쳐 줄게.

   Jeff 고맙습니다. 어떻게 지내세요?

   Mr. Peterson 좋아. 근무 중에 좋은 이웃을 만나니 반갑구나.

   Jeff 하루에 몇 시간 일하세요?

   Mr. Peterson _____ 9시간.

2. W 안녕하세요, 아직도 베이비시터를 찾고 계신가요?

   M 네.

   W 근무 시간은 어떻게 되나요?

   M 월요일부터 금요일까지, 오전 9시부터 오후 5시까지요. 정규직이에요.

   W 급여가 얼마인지 여쭤어 봐도 될까요?

   M _____ 주당 300달러요.

3. W 아르바이트는 어때, Pat?

   M 끔찍해.

   W 왜 그러는데?

   M 식당에 새 지배인이 왔는데 너무 못됐어. 종업원들에게 항상 소리를 질러. 그만 둘까 해.

   W _____ 안됐네.

4. Man 정말 잘 해줘서 고마워요, Cindy. 새로운 머리가 마음에 들어요.

   Cindy 고마워요. 마음에 드신다니 기쁘네요.

   Man 하루에 손님이 몇 명이나 되세요?

   Cindy 30명쯤이요.

   Man 많네요. 여기서 일한 지 얼마나 되셨어요?

   Cindy _____ 3년간 했어요.

Listen Again

p. 71

A. 다시 듣고 알맞은 답을 고르시오.

1. 이어질 응답으로 가장 어울리는 것은?

   a. 하루에 세 번.

   ★b. 9시간.

   c. 오래 전이야.

2. 이어질 응답으로 가장 어울리는 것은?

   a. 일주일에 한 번이요.

   b. 하루에 7시간이요.

   ★c. 주당 300달러요.

3. 이어질 응답으로 가장 어울리는 것은?

   ★a. 안됐네.

   b. 괜찮아.

   c. 문제 없어.

B. 다시 듣고 가장 어울리는 응답을 고르시오.

4. a. ★ 3년간 했어요.

   b. ☐ 2004년에요.

   c. ☐ 아뇨, 별로 안 됐어요.

스크립트

a. For three years.

b. In 2004.

c. No, it's not very long.

Review
p. 72

1. do, dentist, job, indoors
2. for, store, hours, hour
3. work, How long, 5 hours
4. work, boss, co-workers, 2800, new job
5. like, 3, hour, late

✱ 듣고 빈칸을 채우시오.

해석

1. W 직업이 뭐니?

   M 나는 치과 의사야.

   W 네 직업은 어때?

   M 음, 괜찮아. 실내에서 일하는 것은 싫어하지만, 적어도 나는 사람들을 도울 수 있어.

2. 신발 가게 점원을 찾습니다. 근무 시간은 오전 11시부터 오후 8시입니다. 초봉은 시급 7달러입니다. 스페인 어를 좀 할 수 있는 사람을 원합니다.

3. W 어디에서 일하니?

   M 주유소에서 일해.

   W 얼마나 일하니?

   M 하루에 다섯 시간.

4. 오늘 직장 첫날이었어요. 잘 해낸 것 같아요. 상사도 좋고, 직장 동료들도 마음에 들어요. 그리고 월급이 2800달러니까 급여도 좋고요. 이 새 직장을 얻다니 전 운이 좋았던 것 같아요.

5. M 나 새 아르바이트 구했어, Susan.
   W 어때?
   M 하루 3시간 일하고, 시급 7달러야.
   W 나쁘진 않네.
   M 응. 문제는 근무 시간이야. 밤 늦게 일해야 돼.

On Your Own   p. 73

LISTEN & WRITE

듣고 질문을 써 보세요.

스크립트

> Do you have a part-time job?
> What is your job like?
> What do you want to do in the future?
> Why?

해석
아르바이트를 하고 있습니까?
그 일은 어떻습니까?
미래에 어떤 일을 하고 싶습니까?
그 이유는 무엇입니까?

PRONUNCIATION

> **/ ei /**
>
> ☞ 듣고 따라해 보시오.
>   하나의, 낮, Jay, 놓다
>   아마 ~일 것이다, 말하다, 케이크, 주었다
>   주요한, 고통, 그들, 기다리다

아래 문장을 읽고 'ei' 소리가 있는 단어에 동그라미 하시오.
1. Jay는 언젠가는 케이크를 구울지도 모른다.
2. 기다려 봐. 그들이 우리에게 고통을 줬다고 말하지 마.
3. May는 David의 생일을 위해 케이크를 만들었다.

이제 듣고 답을 확인하시오.
1. Jay may bake a cake one day.
2. Wait. Don't say they gave us pain.
3. May made a cake for David's birthday.

Practice Test   p. 74~75

1. 1) b   2) a   2. 1) b   2) d   3. 1) b   2) c
4. 1) c   5. 1) d

※ 듣고 알맞은 답을 고르시오.

1. 한 남자가 자신의 직업에 대해서 말하고 있다.

스크립트

> W How are you doing?
> M Pretty busy. The roads are very slippery these days. And there are many car accidents.
> W How many cars do you fix a day?
> M I work on about ten cars a day.
> W Wow, that's a lot.

해석
W 잘 지내니?
M 꽤 바빠. 요즘은 길이 아주 미끄러워. 그래서 교통사고가 많아.
W 하루에 몇 대의 차를 수리하니?
M 하루에 10대 정도를 수리해.
W 와, 많구나.

1) 남자의 직업은 무엇인가?
   a. 수도 배관공   ★b. 자동차 정비사
   c. 택시 운전사   d. 치과 의사

2) 대화 내용과 일치하지 않는 것은?
   ★a. 지금은 날씨가 춥다.
   b. 그는 일하느라 바쁘다.
   c. 그는 하루에 열 대의 차를 수리한다.
   d. 요즘 교통사고가 많이 난다.

2. 한 남자가 자신의 직업에 대해 이야기하고 있다.

스크립트

> People come to me when they have problems with their teeth. These days there are more children coming to my office. They eat too many sweets, don't they? Anyway I like my job because I can help other people. The problem is that I work indoors. I can't get fresh air very much. That's the hardest part of my job.

해석
사람들은 치아에 문제가 있을 때 저에게 옵니다. 요즘에는 더 많은 어린이들이 진료실에 옵니다. 그들은 사탕을 너무 많이 먹어요, 그렇지 않나요? 어쨌든 저는 다른 사람들을 도울 수 있어서 제 직업을 좋아합니다. 문제는 실내에서 일한다는 거지요. 신선한 공기를 많이 마실 수가 없어요. 그게 제 직업의 가장 힘든 점이죠.

1) 남자의 직업은 무엇인가?

    a. 간호사   ★b. 치과 의사   c. 교사   d. 엔지니어

2) 남자에 대한 설명으로 옳은 것은?

    a. 사탕을 좋아한다.

    b. 실내에서 일하는 것을 좋아한다.

    c. 아이들을 좋아하지 않는다.

   ★d. 사람들을 돕는 것을 즐긴다.

3. 한 여자가 자신의 직업에 대해 이야기하고 있다.

스크립트

M What do you do for a living?
W I work as a cashier at a supermarket.
M How many hours do you work a day?
W Five hours.
M So you are a part-time worker.
W Yes, I go to school in the evening. I am studying to be a teacher.

해석

M 무슨 일을 하세요?
W 슈퍼마켓에서 계산원으로 일해요.
M 하루에 몇 시간 일하세요?
W 5시간이요.
M 그러니까 아르바이트를 하시는군요.
W 네. 저녁에는 학교에 가요. 교사가 되려고 공부하고 있어요.

1) 여자는 _____(으)로 일한다.

    a. 식당 종업원 ★b. 계산원   c. 교사   d. 지배인

2) 여자에 대한 설명으로 옳지 <u>않은</u> 것은?

    a. 아르바이트를 한다.

    b. 저녁에는 학교에 간다.

   ★c. 식당에서 일한다.

    d. 교사가 되고 싶어한다.

4. Emily와 아빠가 이야기를 하고 있다.

스크립트

Emily Dad, what do you do every day?
Dad I work from 9 to 5.
Emily What is your job?
Dad Well, I work with books around.
Emily Really?
Dad Yes. I help other people to find the books they want to read.

해석

Emily 아빠, 아빠는 매일 무엇을 하나요?
Dad 9시부터 5시까지 일을 하지.
Emily 무슨 일이요?

Dad 음, 책과 관련된 일을 하지.
Emily 정말요?
Dad 응. 사람들이 읽고 싶어 하는 책을 찾는 것을 도와준단다.

1) Emily의 아빠는 무슨 일을 한다고 생각하는가?

    a. 의사   b. 치과 의사 ★c. 사서   d. 사업가

5. 두 소년이 이야기하고 있다.

스크립트

Philip Peter, what do you want to be?
Peter Well, I'm interested in biology, so maybe I'll be a biology teacher. What about you, Philip?
Philip I don't know. But I'm good at English, particularly writing.
Peter That's true. Hey, you can be a writer!
Philip Sounds good but my father wants me to be a doctor.
Peter A doctor?

해석

Philip Peter, 넌 무엇이 되고 싶어?
Peter 음, 난 생물학에 관심이 있어서 생물 교사가 될지도 모르겠어. 넌 어때, Philip?
Philip 모르겠어. 하지만 나는 영어, 특히 작문을 잘해.
Peter 맞아. 그래, 넌 작가가 될 수 있을 거야!
Philip 좋은 생각이지만 우리 아빠는 내가 의사가 되길 원하셔.
Peter 의사?

1) Philip에 관해 사실인 것은?

    a. 그는 작가가 되고 싶어하지 않는다.

    b. 그는 아마 생물 교사가 될 것이다.

    c. 그는 의사가 되기를 원한다.

   ★d. 그의 아버지는 그가 의사가 되기를 원하신다.

Dictation   p. 76

1. How are you doing, busy, a day, work on, that's a lot

2. come to me, problems, my office, my job, hardest, my job

3. What do you do, cashier, How many hours, part-time worker, to be a teacher

4. I work from 9 to 5, I work with books around, I help

5. what, want to be, teacher, I don't know, good at, writer, to be a doctor

UNIT 10
How can I get there?

p. 77

Getting Ready

1.
1. post office 2. drugstore
3. parking lot 4. City Hall
5. drugstore 6. cinema
7. police station

1. 지도를 보고 네모 안에 있는 단어로 빈칸을 채우시오.

주차장	우체국	시청	약국	영화관	경찰서

1. _____우체국_____ 은 레스토랑 건너에 있다.
2. _____약국_____ 은 신호등을 지나서 있다.
3. _____주차장_____ 은 공원 뒤에 있다.
4. _____시청_____ 은 경찰서 맞은편에 있다.
5. _____약국_____ 은 병원 옆에 있다.
6. _____영화관_____ 은 Third 가와 Elm 가 코너에 있다.
7. _____경찰서_____ 는 버스 정류장 근처, Lincoln 가에 있다.

Listening Task

p. 78~79

Listening 1

Listen Again 1. two 2. right
3. past 4. right, second

Listening 2 1. b 2. a 3. b 4. a

Listen Again 1. two, right, third, right
2. down, past, left
3. High, facing, Pine
4. two, right, not far

Listening 1

p. 78

사람들이 방향을 알려주고 있다. 듣고 지도 위에 숫자를 쓰시오.

스크립트

1.
Go straight two more blocks.
It is around the corner on your right.

2.
Go one more block and turn right.
It is across from the bank.

3.
Go down the street and take the second left.
It is past the cinema on your left. It's easy to find.

4.
Go straight and turn right at the second traffic light. It is at the end of the street on your left.
You can't miss it.

해석
1. 두 블록 더 직진하세요.
당신의 오른쪽 코너 주변에 있어요.

2. 한 블록 더 가서 오른쪽으로 도세요.
은행 건너편에 있어요.

3. 길을 따라 내려가서 두 번째 왼쪽 길로 가세요.
영화관을 지나서 왼쪽에 있어요. 찾기 쉬워요.

4. 직진하다가 두 번째 신호등에서 오른쪽으로 도세요.
왼쪽 길 끝에 있어요. 꼭 찾으실 거예요.

Listen Again

p. 78

다시 듣고 맞는 말에 동그라미 치시오. (위의 지도는 보지 마시오.)
1. 그녀는 (한 / 두) 블록을 똑바로 가야 한다.

2. 그녀는 (오른쪽 / 왼쪽)으로 돌아가야 한다.

3. 극장 (지나서 / 옆에) 있다.

4. 그녀는 (첫 번째 / 두 번째) 신호등에서 (오른쪽 / 왼쪽)으로 돌아가야 한다.

Listening 2

p. 79

사람들이 방향을 묻고 알려 주고 있다. 듣고 알맞은 지도를 고르시오.
스크립트

1.
w Excuse me, sir. Where is City Hall?
m Go down two more blocks and turn right. It's the third building on your right.
w Two more blocks and right. Third on the right. Thanks.

2.
m How can I get to the movie theater?
w It is two blocks down this road. It is past the restaurant on your left. You can't miss it.
m Two blocks down, past the restaurant. Thanks a lot.

42

3.

W Can I help you? You seem lost.

M Yes, I am. Where can I buy some medicine?

W So you're looking for a drugstore. It's on High Street, between Maple and Pine. It's across from the hotel.

M On High, between Maple and Pine. Thank you very much.

4.

M Is there a toy store around here?

W Yes, it's on Willow Street.

M Where is Willow Street?

W Uh... Go up two more blocks, and you're on Willow. You just turn right and you will see it.

M Thanks.

해석

1. W 실례합니다. 시청은 어디에 있나요?

   M 두 블록 더 내려가서서 오른쪽으로 도세요. 오른쪽에 있는 세 번째 빌딩이에요.

   W 두 블록 더, 그리고 오른쪽. 오른쪽에서 세 번째. 감사합니다.

2. M 영화관에 어떻게 가나요?

   W 이 길에서 두 블록 아래에 있어요. 당신의 왼쪽에 있는 레스토랑을 지나서 있어요. 금방 찾을 수 있을 거예요.

   M 두 블록 아래, 레스토랑 지나서. 고마워요.

3. W 도와드릴까요? 길을 잃으신 것 같네요.

   M 네, 그래요. 어디에서 약을 살 수 있죠?

   W 그렇다면 당신은 약국을 찾고 있군요. Maple과 Pine 사이 High 가에 있어요. 호텔 건너편에 있어요.

   M Maple과 Pine 사이에 있는 High 가요. 정말 감사합니다.

4. M 이 근처에 장난감 가게가 있나요?

   W 네, Willow 가에 에 있어요.

   M Willow 가가 어디인가요?

   W 어... 두 블록 더 올라가면, Willow 가가 나와요. 오른쪽으로 돌기만 하면 돼요. 바로 보일 거예요.

   M 고마워요.

Listen Again

p. 79

다시 듣고 맞는 말에 동그라미 치시오. (위의 지도는 보지 마시오.)

1. 시청은 (두 / 세) 블록 떨어져 있다. (오른쪽 / 왼쪽)으로 돌아야 한다. 당신의 (오른쪽 / 왼쪽)에 있는 (네 번째 / 세 번째) 건물이다.

2. 영화관은 이 길 (위 / 아래)로 세 블록 가야 한다. 당신의 (오른쪽 / 왼쪽)에 있는 식당 (옆에 / 지나서) 있다.

3. 약국은 (Hill / High) 가에 있다. 호텔 (맞은편에 / 뒤에) 있다. Maple 가와 (Spruce / Pine) 가 사이에 있다.

4. 장난감 가게는 (한 / 두) 블록 더 올라가야 한다. Willow 가에서는 (오른쪽 / 왼쪽)으로 돌아야 한다. 모퉁이에서 (멀다 / 멀지 않다).

1. Excuse, get, blocks, corner
2. down, right, traffic, more, between
3. buy, on, on, past, can't miss
4. side, left, take, third
5. next to, past, across, behind, wrong

✻ 듣고 빈칸을 채우시오.

해석

1. W 실례합니다. 가장 가까운 지하철역에 어떻게 가나요?

   M 두 블록 더 내려가서서 오른쪽으로 도세요. 코너 근처에 있어요.

   W 고마워요.

2. 먼저, 이 길을 따라 걸어 내려가세요.
   세 번째 신호등에서 오른쪽으로 도세요.
   그리고 한 블록 더 가면 High 가예요.
   그곳은 극장과 약국 사이에 있어요.

3. M 어디에서 전구를 살 수 있나요?

   W Maple 가에 철물점이 있어요.

   M Maple 가 어디인가요?

   W 소방서 바로 지나서 오른쪽에 있어요. 금방 찾을 수 있을 거예요.

4. 저희가 이사를 했습니다. 저희의 새 주소는 Spruce 가 256번지입니다. 강 건너편에 있습니다. 다리 끝에서 왼쪽으로 돌아 두 번째 오른쪽 길로 들어오십시오. 오른쪽 세 번째 건물입니다. 거기서 뵙게 되길 바랍니다.

5. M 엄마, 못 찾겠어요. 서점 옆에 있어요, 아니면 약국 지나서 있어요?

   W 둘 다 아니야. 호텔 건너편, 주차장 뒤편에 있어.

   M 아, 길을 잘못 들었어요. 호텔은 Maple 가에 있죠?

   W 그래.

LISTEN & WRITE

듣고 질문을 써 보세요.

스크립트

Where is your school?
How far is your school from your house?
Is there a hospital near your school?

해석
당신의 학교는 어디입니까?

당신의 학교는 집에서 얼마나 멉니까?

당신의 학교 근처에는 병원이 있습니까?

PRONUNCIATION

> **/ ou /**
>
> ☞ 듣고 따라해 보시오.
>
> 가다, Joe, 낮은, 알다, 아니오, 바느질하다
> 뼈, 황금, 오로지, 전화기, ~위쪽에

아래 문장을 읽고 'ou' 소리가 있는 단어에 동그라미 하시오.

1. 아니요, 오로지 Joe만이 어디에 두 개의 황금 전화기가 있는지 압니다.
2. Tony와 Moe는 우리 집 옆에 있는 떡갈나무를 소유하고 있지 않다.

이제 듣고 답을 확인하시오.

1. No, only Joe knows where both of the gold phones are.
2. Tony and Moe don't own the oak tree by my home.

Practice Test				p. 82~83
1. 1) c	2. 1) b	3. 1) b	4. 1) d	5. 1) c

※ 듣고 알맞은 답을 고르시오.

1. 두 사람이 방향을 묻고 알려주고 있다.

스크립트

> M How can I get there?
> W Walk up High Street and take the second left. It's the third building on your left.
> M Second left on High. Third on the right.
> W No, not on the right, on the left.
> M Oh, thanks.
> W No problem.

해석

M 거기에 어떻게 갈 수 있죠?

W High 가에서 걸어 올라가서 두 번째 길에서 왼쪽으로 도세요. 당신 왼쪽에 있는 세 번째 빌딩이에요.

M High 가에서 두 번째 길에서 좌회전. 오른쪽의 세 번째 빌딩이요.

W 아니요, 오른쪽이 아니고 왼쪽이요.

M 아, 고마워요.

W 천만에요.

1) 남자가 찾고 있는 장소는 어디인가? 지도에서 찾으시오.
   a. 은행   b. 슈퍼마켓   ★c. 호텔   d. 식당

2. 다음은 위치에 관한 내용이다.

스크립트

> First, get out of the hotel. Turn right and walk until you see the church. There's a bridge. Cross the bridge and go down for a few minutes. You'll see a tall building at the intersection. It is the small building next to it.

해석

우선, 호텔에서 나오세요. 오른쪽으로 돌아 교회가 보일 때까지 걸으세요. 다리가 있어요. 다리를 건너서 몇 분 동안 걸어 내려가세요. 교차로에서 높은 빌딩을 볼 수 있을 거예요. 그 빌딩 옆에 있는 작은 건물이에요.

1) 어떤 지도가 알맞게 표시되어 있는가?

3. 다음은 위치에 관한 내용이다.

스크립트

> M Where is the restaurant?
> W Do you know where City Hall is?
> M Yes, it's on North Street.
> W Let's start from City Hall. Go up the street three more blocks.
> M Yes, three blocks from City Hall.
> W It is High Street. Turn left on High and go two more blocks.
> M Yes.
> W This time turn right. It's just around the corner, next to the shoe store.

해석

M 식당이 어디 있습니까?

W 시청이 어디 있는지 아세요?

M 네, North 가에 있어요.

W 시청에서부터 시작하죠. 세 블록 더 위로 올라가세요.

M 네, 시청에서부터 세 블록.

W 거기가 High 가예요. High 가에서 왼쪽으로 돈 다음 두 블록 더 가세요.

M 네.

W 이번엔 오른쪽으로 돌아서요. 바로 그 모퉁이 근처에 신발가게 옆이에요.

1) 맞는 지도를 찾으시오.

4. Maria가 한 신사에게 뭔가를 묻고 있다.

스크립트

Maria	Excuse me, could you tell me how to get to the nearest subway station?
Gentleman	Sure. Go straight two blocks.

Maria	Yes.
Gentleman	On the corner, there is a big post office. There, turn left.
Maria	Post office, left.
Gentleman	Then walk a block and you'll see the subway station. You can't miss it.
Maria	Thank you.
Gentleman	You're welcome.

해석

Maria	실례합니다만, 여기서 가장 가까운 지하철역으로 가는 길을 알려 주시겠습니까?
Gentleman	물론이죠. 두 블록을 쭉 가세요.
Maria	네.
Gentleman	모퉁이에, 큰 우체국이 있어요. 거기서, 왼쪽으로 도세요.
Maria	우체국, 왼쪽.
Gentleman	그러고 나서 한 블록을 걸어가시면 지하철역이 보일 거예요. 곧 찾으실 거예요.
Maria	감사합니다.
Gentleman	천만에요.

1) 사실이 아닌 것은?

  a. 우체국은 지하철역에서 한 블록 떨어져 있다.

  b. 지하철역은 우체국에서 멀지 않다.

  c. 우체국은 그들이 있는 곳에서 두 블록 떨어져 있다.

  ★d. 우체국은 경찰서와 가깝다.

5. Sarah는 집에서 Jenny를 기다리고 있다.

스크립트

Jenny	Hi, Sarah. It's Jenny.
Sarah	Hi, where are you?
Jenny	I'm lost. I'm at Royal York and Kingsway. How do I get to your house from here?
Sarah	Okay. Do you see the Humber Plaza?
Jenny	Yeah, across the street.
Sarah	All right. Cross the street and get to the Humber Plaza. Walk east one block along Kingsway Road. My house is on the corner.
Jenny	Okay. I'll be there soon!

해석

Jenny	여보세요, Sarah. 나 Jenny야.
Sarah	응, 어디야?
Jenny	길을 잃었어. Royal Yock와 Kingsway 사이에 있어. 여기서 너희 집에 어떻게 가지?
Sarah	좋아. Humber 광장이 보여?

Jenny	응. 길 건너에.
Sarah	맞아. 길을 건너서 Humber 광장으로 가. Kingsway 거리를 따라서 동쪽으로 한 블록 가. 우리 집은 모퉁이에 있어.
Jenny	알았어. 곧 갈게!

1) Sarah의 집은 어느 것인가?

Dictation   p. 84

1. How can I get there, take, on your left, right, left, No problem
2. Turn right, Cross, go down, see, building, next to
3. it's on, Go up, three more blocks, This time turn left, around the corner
4. how to get, Go straight, On the corner, left, walk a block, Thank you
5. where are you, How do I get, from here, across the street, Walk east

UNIT 11
I'd like a steak.

Getting Ready
p. 85

1.

곡물	야채	고기와 생선	디저트	음료
rice	carrots	beef	cake	coffee
cereal	onions	chicken	cookie	milk
	peas	fish	ice cream	juice
			pie	tea

2. 1. d   2. a   3. b   4. c   5. e

1. 단어들을 알맞은 네모 안에 열거하시오.

쌀	쇠고기	케이크	닭고기	쿠키	커피
생선	우유	주스	아이스크림	파이	시리얼
당근	차	양파	완두콩		

2. 질문을 대답과 연결시키시오.

1. 뭐 좀 마실래?   d. 네, 오렌지 주스 주세요.
2. 무엇을 원하세요?   a. 스테이크 주세요.
3. 주문하시겠어요?   b. 네. 미트볼 스파게티 주세요.
4. 샌드위치 어때요?   c. 아니오. 그건 질렸어요.
5. 피자 어때?   e. 그거 좋겠다.

Listening Task
p. 86~87

Listening 1		1. b	2. c	3. b	4. c
Listen Again	A	1. a	2. a	3. c	
	B	4. a			
Listening 2		1. b	2. b	3. a	4. b
Listen Again	A	1. a	2. b	3. b	
	B	4. b			

Listening 1
p. 86

듣고 사람들이 이야기하는 식사를 고르시오.

1. a. 아침 식사   ★b. 점심 식사   c. 저녁 식사
2. a. 아침 식사   b. 점심 식사   ★c. 저녁 식사
3. a. 아침 식사   ★b. 점심 식사   c. 저녁 식사
4. a. 아침 식사   b. 점심 식사   ★c. 저녁 식사

스크립트

1.
M I'm hungry. I didn't have much for breakfast.
W Do you feel like a sandwich for lunch?
M No, I don't. I'm tired of sandwiches now.
W How about some Mexican food?
M That's a good idea.

2.
M Let's eat out this evening.
W I don't feel like going out today. I'm tired.
M Shall we order a pizza at home?
W Anything you say.

3.
M It's lunch break. I don't know where to go though.
W Did you try the new Chinese restaurant downtown?
M No. Is it good?
W Yes. I heard the food is wonderful and the service is good.

4.
M How about some fast food?
W No. I had a long week. I'd like something special for tonight.
M Then let's go to a seafood restaurant. You like lobster.
W Sounds great to me.

해석
1. M 나 배고파. 아침을 많이 못 먹었어.
   W 점심으로 샌드위치 어때?
   M 아니. 이제 샌드위치는 싫증나.
   W 멕시코 음식은 어때?
   M 좋은 생각이야.

2. M 오늘 저녁은 외식하자.
   W 오늘은 나가고 싶지 않아. 피곤해.
   M 집에서 피자 시켜 먹을까?
   W 그렇게 하자.

3. M 점심시간이야. 하지만 어디로 가야 할지 모르겠어.
   W 시내에 새로 생긴 중국 식당 가봤니?
   M 아니. 거기 좋아?
   W 응. 음식도 맛있고 서비스도 좋다고 들었어.

4. M 패스트푸드 먹는 거 어때?
   W 아니. 이번 주는 정말 힘들었어. 오늘 밤엔 특별한 것을 먹고 싶어.
   M 그러면 해산물 식당에 가자. 너 바닷가재 좋아하잖아.
   W 좋은 생각이야.

Listen Again

p. 86

A. 다시 듣고 알맞은 답을 고르시오.

1. 대화 내용과 일치하는 것은?
   ★a. 남자는 샌드위치를 많이 먹었다.
   b. 그는 아침 식사를 하지 않았다.
   c. 그들은 샌드위치를 먹을 것이다.

2. 그들은 무엇을 먹을 것인가?
   ★a. 피자
   b. 해산물
   c. 스테이크

3. 대화 내용과 일치하지 않는 것은?
   a. 중국 음식점은 새로 생긴 곳이다.
   b. 중국 음식점은 시내에 있다.
   ★c. 음식은 맛있지만 서비스는 좋지 않다.

B. 다시 듣고 가장 적절하게 요약한 것을 고르시오.

4. a. ★ 그녀는 힘든 한 주를 보냈고 좋은 음식을 먹고 싶기 때문에 그들은 해산물 음식을 먹을 것이다.
   b. □ 그녀가 가장 좋아하는 요리는 바닷가재이기 때문에 패스트푸드는 먹고 싶어 하지 않는다.

Listening 2

p. 87

듣고 그들이 먹을 음식을 선택하시오.

스크립트

1.
M Next in line, please. May I help you?
W Yes, I'd like a double cheese burger and a small French fries.
M Anything to drink?
W A small Coke, please.
M For here or to go?
W _____ To go. _____

2.
M May I take your order?
W Well, I'd like to have a steak.
M How would you like your steak, ma'am?
W Well-done, please.
M Which dressing would you like on your salad?
W _____ French dressing, please. _____

3.
W What would you like, sir?
M I'll have spaghetti with salad.
W Which salad would you like?
M Caesar.
W Anything to drink?
M _____ Coke, please. / Just water, please. _____

4.
M So are you ready to order?
W Not yet. We haven't decided on dessert.
M How about the chocolate fudge cake? It's everyone's favorite.
W Okay, then I'll have grilled ribs with garden salad. And for dessert a chocolate fudge cake.
M How about you, ma'am?
W2 _____ I'll have the same. _____

해석

1. M 다음 손님이요. 주문하시겠습니까?
   W 네, 더블치즈버거와 감자튀김 작은 걸로 주세요.
   M 마실 것은요?
   W 콜라 작은 걸로 주세요.
   M 여기서 드실 건가요, 가져가실 건가요?
   W _____ 가져갈 거예요. _____

2. M 주문하시겠습니까?
   W 음, 스테이크로 주세요.
   M 스테이크는 어떻게 해드릴까요?
   W 완전히 익혀 주세요.
   M 샐러드에 어떤 드레싱을 원하시나요?
   W _____ French Dressing으로 주세요. _____

3. W 뭘 드시겠습니까?
   M 샐러드를 곁들인 스파게티요.
   W 어떤 샐러드 드실래요?
   M 시저 샐러드로 주세요.
   W 마실 것은요?
   M _____ 콜라 주세요. / 그냥 물 주세요. _____

4. M 주문할 준비 되셨나요?
   W 아직 안 됐어요. 디저트를 아직 못 골랐어요.
   M 초콜릿 퍼지 케이크 어떠세요? 모든 사람들이 좋아하는 것이랍니다.
   W 좋아요, 그러면 가든 샐러드를 곁들인 구운 갈비로 하겠어요. 그리고 디저트는 초콜릿 퍼지 케이크를 주세요.
   M 부인은 어떠세요?
   W2 _____ 같은 걸로 주세요. _____

Listen Again

p. 87

A. 듣고 알맞은 답을 고르시오.

1. 이어질 말로 가장 어울리는 것은?
   ★a. 가져갈 거예요. b. 제 것이 아니에요. c. 저는 가기 싫어요.

2. 이어질 말로 가장 어울리는 것은?
   a. 사양할게요. ★b. French Dressing이요. c. 네, 주세요.

3. 이어질 말로 어울리지 않는 것은?
   a. 콜라 주세요. ★b. 아니에요. c. 그냥 물 주세요.

B. 다시 듣고 가장 어울리는 응답을 고르시오.

4. a. ☐ 아직 배가 고파요.　　　　b. ★ 같은 걸로 주세요.
   c. ☐ 감사합니다.

스크립트

> a. I'm still hungry. b. I'll have the same. c. Thank you.

Review　　　　　　　　　　　　　　p. 88

1. take, order, like, soup
2. food, service, desserts, try
3. dinner, Where, How about, tired, pizza
4. dessert, ice cream, the best thing
5. out, long, special, seafood

✳ 듣고 빈칸을 채우시오.

해석

1. W 주문하시겠습니까?
   M 스위트 케이준 쉬림프로 주세요.
   W 어떤 수프로 드릴까요?
   M 클램 차우더 수프로 주세요.

2. 이곳은 훌륭해. 음식은 맛있고, 서비스는 더 좋아. 나는 특히 디저트를 좋아해. 치즈 케이크는 정말 훌륭해. 꼭 먹어봐.

3. W 함께 저녁 먹자.
   M 좋아. 어디로 가고 싶니?
   W 스파게티 팰리스 어때?
   M 스파게티는 싫증났어. 변화를 줘서 피자 먹자.

4. 내가 제일 좋아하는 디저트는 아이스크림이야. 우리 엄마는 내가 아이스크림을 너무 많이 먹어서 걱정하셔. 하지만 어쩔 수 없어. 이 세상에 Toska Rabbins의 초콜릿 아이스크림보다 더 좋은 건 없는 걸.

5. W 오늘 저녁은 외식하자. 한 주 동안 힘들었으니까, 뭔가 특별한 것을 먹고 싶어.
   M 어디 가고 싶은데?
   W 해산물 요리 어때?
   M 좋아.

On Your Own　　　　　　　　　　　p. 89

LISTEN & WRITE

듣고 질문을 써 보세요.

스크립트

> What do you usually have for lunch?
> What would you like for today's dinner?
> How about some Chinese food?
> Where are you going to eat tonight?

해석
점심으로 보통 무엇을 먹습니까?
오늘 저녁은 무엇을 드시겠습니까?
중국 음식은 어떻습니까?
오늘 밤 식사는 어디에서 할 것입니까?

PRONUNCIATION

/ oi /
☞ 듣고 따라해 보시오. 　소년,　기쁨,　즐기다,　Roy,　장난감,　기름 　끓다,　코일,　동전,　잇다,　소음,　가리키다

아래 문장을 읽고 'oi' 소리가 있는 단어에 동그라미 하시오.

1. Roy는 저 시끄러운 장난감을 가지고 있는 소년이다.
2. 소년들은 코일과 기름을 사기 위해 동전 몇 개를 가지고 있다.

이제 듣고 답을 확인하시오.

1. Roy is the boy with that noisy toy.
2. The boys have a few coins to buy coils and oil.

Practice Test　　　　　　　　　　p. 90~91

1. M, M, W, W, M, W
2. 1) d　　2) a　　　　3. 1) c　　2) d
4. Mom - a glass of wine, seafood spaghetti, chocolate fudge cake

   Patrick - baked potato, water with ice, beef steak, chocolate fudge cake
5. 1) b　　2) d

✳ 듣고 알맞은 답을 고르시오.

1. 그들은 무엇을 주문하고 있는가? 메뉴의 M(남자)이나 W(여자)에 체크 ☑ 하시오.

스크립트

Waiter	Good evening! Are you ready to order?
Man	Yes, I'd like a T-bone steak.
Waiter	How would you like your steak, sir?
Man	Medium rare. And I'll have the salad with French dressing, please.
Waiter	And you, ma'am?
Woman	Roast beef and onion soup, please.
Waiter	Would you like anything to drink?
Man	Coffee, please.
Woman	I'll have orange juice.
Waiter	Okay. Your food will be ready in ten minutes.

해석
Waiter　안녕하세요! 주문할 준비 되셨나요?
Man　　네, 티본 스테이크 주세요.

48

Waiter	스테이크는 어떻게 해드릴까요?
Man	살짝 익혀 주세요. 그리고 프렌치 드레싱을 곁들인 샐러드를 주세요.
Waiter	부인은요?
Woman	구운 쇠고기와 양파 수프를 주세요.
Waiter	마실 것은요?
Man	커피 주세요.
Woman	저는 오렌지 주스 주세요.
Waiter	좋아요. 10분 안에 음식이 준비될 겁니다.

2. 사람들이 식당에서 음식을 주문하고 있다.

스크립트

Woman	What's on the menu?
Man	There's nothing special. What is the club sandwich?
Woman	Let me ask. Uh, excuse me. What's the club sandwich like?
Waiter	It is made with grilled beef and special sauce. It's great.
Woman	I'd like to try it. How about you?
Man	I'll have that too.

해석

Woman	메뉴에 뭐 있니?
Man	특별한 거 없어. 클럽 샌드위치는 뭐지?
Woman	물어 보자. 어, 실례합니다. 클럽 샌드위치가 뭐죠?
Waiter	구운 쇠고기와 특별한 소스로 만들어진 거예요. 맛있어요.
Woman	그걸로 먹어볼게요. 너는?
Man	나도 그거 먹어볼게.

1) 그들은 _____를 먹으려고 한다.
   a. 스테이크   b. 버거   c. 구운 쇠고기   ★d. 샌드위치

2) 대화 내용과 일치하는 것은?
   ★a. 그들은 같은 음식을 주문하고 있다.
   b. 그들은 거기에 여러 번 가본 적 있다.
   c. 그들은 중국 음식점에 있다.
   d. 그 샌드위치에는 닭고기가 들어 있다.

3. 엄마와 아들이 이야기하고 있다.

스크립트

Son	Mom, I'm hungry. What's for dinner?
Mom	Spaghetti. It's your favorite, isn't it?
Son	No, not any more. I'm tired of spaghetti. Let's eat out, please.
Mom	What do you want to eat?
Son	Pork rib barbecue at Bill's Barbecue.
Mom	Okay. But no more eating out this week.
Son	Hooray!

해석

Son	엄마, 배고파요. 저녁이 뭐예요?
Mom	스파게티야. 네가 제일 좋아하는 거지?
Son	이젠 아니에요. 스파게티는 질렸어요. 외식해요, 엄마.
Mom	뭘 먹고 싶니?
Son	Bill's Barbecue에서 파는 돼지갈비 바비큐요.
Mom	좋아. 하지만 이번 주에는 더 이상 외식은 없다.
Son	만세!

1) 그들은 무엇을 먹을 것인가?
   a. 스파게티
   b. 닭 바비큐
   ★c. 돼지갈비
   d. 구운 소고기

2) 대화 내용과 일치하는 것은?
   a. 소년은 스파게티를 좋아한 적이 없다.
   b. 그들은 점심 식사에 대해 이야기하고 있다.
   c. 그들은 아마도 이번 주 나중에 외식할 것이다.
   ★d. 그들은 오늘 저녁을 집에서 먹지 않을 것이다.

4. Patrick과 엄마가 식당에서 주문을 하고 있다.

스크립트

Waiter	Good evening, are you ready to order?
Mom	Yes, I would like the seafood spaghetti, please, with a glass of white wine.
Waiter	Yes, ma'am. And you, young man?
Patrick	I'll have the beef steak, cooked medium, with baked potatoes.
Waiter	And would you like anything to drink?
Patrick	Just water with ice, please.
Waiter	Anything for dessert?
Patrick & Mom	Chocolate fudge cake with fresh cream!

해석

Waiter	안녕하십니까, 주문할 준비가 되셨나요?
Mom	네, 전 해산물 스파게티로 할게요. 백포도주 한 잔도요.
Waiter	네, 부인. 그리고 젊은 신사 분은요?
Mom	전 중간으로 익힌 비프 스테이크와 구운 감자로 할게요.
Waiter	음료수는 무엇으로 하시겠습니까?
Mom	전 그냥 얼음물로 주세요.
Waiter	디저트는요?
Patrick & Mom	생크림을 곁들인 초콜릿 퍼지 케이크로 주세요!

1) 음식과 주문한 사람을 연결하시오.

	구운 감자
엄마	와인 한 잔
	초콜릿 퍼지 케이크
Patrick	얼음물
	해산물 스파게티
	비프 스테이크

5. Sarah와 Jim이 이야기를 하고 있다.

스크립트

Sarah	Have you ever tried Korean sushi, Jim?
Jim	What's that? Isn't sushi Japanese?
Sarah	Yeah, with raw fish. Korean sushi is different.
Jim	Oh!
Sarah	It's rice with ham, egg, cheese and lots of vegetables all rolled up in seaweed.
Jim	It sounds really healthy and yummy!
Sarah	It is. I love Korean sushi.
Jim	Well, why don't we have that for lunch? I'm getting hungry.
Sarah	Great!

해석

Sarah	Jim, 한국식 초밥 먹어 본 적 있어?
Jim	그게 뭐야? 초밥은 일본 거 아냐?
Sarah	응, 날생선으로 만들어. 한국식 초밥은 다르지.
Jim	아!
Sarah	햄, 달걀, 치즈, 그리고 갖가지 야채와 함께 밥을 김 속에 말아넣은 거야.
Jim	정말 영양가 있고 맛있을 것 같이 들리는데.
Sarah	정말 그래. 난 한국식 초밥이 좋아.
Jim	그럼, 점심에 그걸 먹는 게 어때? 배가 고파지려고 해.
Sarah	좋아!

1) 그들은 주로 무엇에 관해 이야기하고 있는가?
   a. 일본식 초밥
   ★b. 한국식 초밥
   c. 일본식 초밥과 한국식 초밥의 차이점
   d. 점심으로 먹을 것

2) 다음에 무슨 일이 벌어질 것인가?
   a. 그들은 일본 음식점으로 갈 것이다.
   b. 그들은 도서관에서 공부할 것이다.
   c. 그들은 수영하러 갈 것이다.
   ★d. 그들은 한국 음식점에서 식사를 할 것이다.

Dictation   p. 92

1. Are you ready to order, your steak, French dressing, anything to drink, I'll have, Your food
2. nothing special, sandwich, special, It's great
3. What's for dinner, I'm tired of, eat out, pork rib, eating out
4. would like, have, potatoes, drink, dessert, cream
5. tried, different, healthy, have that for lunch

UNIT 12
Can I speak to Amy, please?

Getting Ready   p. 93

1. | 1. b, l | 2. c, f | 3. j, m | 4. e, g |
   | 5. a, h | 6. d, k | 7. i, n | |

1. 각 상황에 따른 두 가지 표현을 고르시오.

   a. Nancy와 통화할 수 있을까요?
   b. 누구세요?
   c. 죄송하지만, 그는 다른 사람과 통화 중이에요.
   d. 전데요.
   e. 전화 잘못 거신 것 같은데요.
   f. 죄송하지만 그는 없습니다.
   g. 번호를 잘못 누르신 것 같아요.
   h. John 있나요?
   i. 잠깐만요. 그를 바꿔 드릴게요.
   j. 전하실 말씀 있으신가요?
   k. 전데요.
   l. 누구신가요?
   m. 메시지 남기실래요?
   n. 기다려 주세요.

   1. 전화 건 사람의 이름을 물을 때
   2. 그 사람이 전화를 받을 수 없다는 것을 말할 때
   3. 전화 건 사람이 무엇을 말하고 싶은지를 물을 때
   4. 전화를 잘못 걸었다고 말할 때
   5. 전화 건 사람이 누구랑 통화하고 싶은지 말할 때
   6. 전화 받은 사람이 전화 건 사람이 원하는 사람일 때
   7. 전화 건 사람에게 기다리라고 말할 때

Listening Task   p. 94~95

Listening 1		1. C	2. C	3. R	4. R
Listen Again	A	1. b	2. c	3. b	
	B	4. a			
Listening 2		1. Mr. Brown		2. Brian	
		3. Tim		4. Sarah	
Listen Again	A	1. c	2. c	3. a	
	B	4. b			

Listening 1   p. 94

어떤 것이 전화 건 사람의 메모이고, 어떤 것이 전화 받은 사람의 메모인가? C(전화 거는 사람)와 R(전화 받는 사람)을 쓰시오.

1. ___C___ 2. ___C___ 3. ___R___ 4. ___R___

스크립트

1.
Hi, Amy! This is Sue. I have something to ask you about our math homework. Please give me a call. I'll be home after 7 p.m. this evening.

2.
Hello, Ms. Grue. This is Mrs. White. I'm calling about my son, Fred. He's sick and may not be able to go to school tomorrow. Anyway, I'll try to call you again tomorrow morning. Bye!

3.
Hi! This is Jane and Tom's house. We're not home right now. Please leave your name and number. We'll get back to you as soon as we return. Bye! Have a nice day!

4.
Hello, you've reached Power Auto. Our business hours are from 9:00 a.m. to 8:00 p.m., Monday through Friday. We hope to have your call again. Thank you.

해석

1. 안녕, Amy! 나 Sue야. 수학 숙제에 관해서 물어볼 것이 있어. 나한테 전화해 줘. 난 오늘 저녁 7시 이후에 집에 있을 거야.

2. Grue 선생님, 안녕하세요. White 부인입니다. 제 아들 Fred 때문에 전화합니다. 그는 아파서 아마도 내일 학교에 가지 못할 것 같아요. 어쨌든 내일 아침에 다시 전화 드리겠습니다. 안녕히 계세요!

3. 안녕! Jane과 Tom의 집이에요. 우리는 지금 집에 없어요. 이름과 전화번호를 남겨 주세요. 우리가 돌아오는 대로 연락할게요. 안녕히 계세요. 좋은 하루 보내세요!

4. 안녕하세요, Power Auto입니다. 저희 영업 시간은 월요일부터 금요일, 오전 9시부터 오후 8시까지입니다. 다시 전화 주시기 바랍니다. 감사합니다.

Listen Again   p. 94

A. 다시 듣고 맞는 것을 고르시오.

1. a. Sue는 나중에 다시 전화할 것이다.
   ★b. Sue는 Amy가 연락해 주기를 바란다.
   c. Sue는 7시 이후에는 전화를 받을 수 없다.

2. a. 그녀는 Grue 선생님이 전화해 주기를 바란다.
   b. 그녀는 오늘 밤에 다시 전화할 것이다.
   ★c. 그녀의 아들이 아프다.

3. a. 전화 건 사람의 이름은 Jane이다.
   ★b. 전화 건 사람은 자신의 전화번호를 남길 것이다.
   c. 전화 건 사람은 나중에 다시 걸어야 한다.

B. 다시 듣고 가장 적절하게 요약한 것을 고르시오.

4. a. ★ Power Auto의 영업 시간은 월요일부터 금요일까지 9시에서 8시까지이다.
   b. ☐ Power Auto의 직원들은 월요일부터 토요일까지 일하며 손님들의 전화를 받는 것을 좋아한다.

Listening 2   p. 95

네 사람이 전화를 걸고 있다. 전화를 건 사람이 누구인지 표시하시오.

1. ___Mr. Brown___   2. ___Brian___
3. ___Tim___   4. ___Sarah___

스크립트

1.
M Hello? Can I speak to Mr. Smith, please?
W Who's calling, please?
M This is John Brown.
W Hold on a second. I'll get him for you.

2.
M Hello? Is Jane there?
W She's not in. Do you want to leave a message?
M Yes, thank you. This is Brian. Could you ask her to call me back?
W All right. I'll give her the message.

3.
M Hello? Is Jane in?
W Speaking. Who's this?
M Hi, Jane! This is Tim.
W Hi, Tim! What's up?
M There's no basketball game this afternoon. We'll meet tomorrow.
W I see. Thanks.

4.
W Hello? Can I talk to Amy, please? This is Sarah.
M There's no one here by that name. I think you've got the wrong number.
W Isn't this 405-2278?
M No. It's 405-2178.
W Oh, I'm sorry. I dialed the wrong number.

해석

1. M 안녕하세요? Smith 씨와 통화할 수 있을까요?
   W 누구세요?
   M John Brown입니다.
   W 잠시만 기다리세요. 바꿔 드릴게요.

2. M 안녕하세요? Jane 있나요?

   W 없어요. 메모 남기시겠어요?

   M 네, 고마워요. 전 Brian인데요. 그녀에게 전화해 달라고 전해 주시겠어요?

   W 좋아요. 그녀에게 전해 줄게요.

3. M 안녕하세요? Jane 있나요?

   W 전데요. 누구세요?

   M 안녕, Jane! Tim이야.

   W 안녕, Tim! 무슨 일이니?

   M 오늘 오후에는 농구 경기가 없어. 우린 내일 만날 거야.

   W 알겠어. 고마워.

4. W 안녕하세요? Amy와 통화할 수 있나요? 저는 Sarah인데요.

   M 여기 그 이름을 가진 사람은 없습니다. 전화를 잘못 거신 것 같습니다.

   W 405-2278 아닌가요?

   M 아니에요. 405-2178입니다.

   W 아, 죄송합니다. 제가 번호를 잘못 눌렀군요.

Listen Again   p. 95

A. 다시 듣고 맞는 것을 고르시오.

1. a. Smith 씨는 외출 중이다.
   b. Smith 씨는 전화를 받을 수가 없다.
   ★c. Smith 씨는 곧 전화를 받을 것이다.

2. a. Brian은 Jane과 통화를 했다.
   b. Brian은 전화를 다시 할 것이다.
   ★c. Brian은 Jane의 전화를 기다릴 것이다.

3★a. Tim은 Jane과 통화를 했다.   b. 그들은 오늘 만날 것이다.
   c. Tim이 메시지를 남겼다.

B. 다시 듣고 맞는 문장을 고르시오.

4. a. ☐ Sarah는 Amy에게 전화하고 싶지만 Amy가 이름을 바꿨다.
   b. ★ Sarah는 Amy에게 전화하고 싶지만 전화를 잘못 걸었다.

스크립트

> a. Sarah wants to call Amy but Amy changed her name.
> b. Sarah wants to call Amy but she dialed the wrong number.

Review   p. 96

1. speak, message, call
2. leave, possible
3. there, sorry, out, leave, tell
4. calling about, give me, call, 9
5. 2760, wrong, 314, 1766

※ 듣고 빈칸을 채우시오.

해석

1. W 안녕하세요, Brown 씨와 통화할 수 있나요?
   M 죄송합니다만, 그는 통화 중이에요. 메모 남기시겠어요?
   W 아니에요, 됐어요. 제가 나중에 다시 전화 걸게요.

2. 안녕하세요, 여기는 Jane의 집입니다. 저는 지금 집에 없어요. 메시지를 남겨 주시면 돌아오는 대로 연락 드리겠습니다. 고맙습니다.

3. W 안녕하세요, Mary 있나요?
   M 죄송합니다만 나갔는데요. 메모 남기시겠어요?
   W Jane이 전화했었다고만 말해 주세요.
   M 알겠어요, 그러겠습니다.

4. 안녕, Susan. 나 Joe야. 금요일 날 우리 데이트 때문에 전화했어. 내가 그날 밤 아마 늦게까지 일할지도 모르겠어. 나한테 전화 좀 해 줄래? 오늘 저녁 9시 이후에 아무 때나 우리 집으로 연락해 줘.

5. W 314-2760인가요?
   M 아니요, 전화 잘못 거셨어요. 314-1766이에요.
   W 아, 죄송합니다.
   M 괜찮아요.

On Your Own   p. 97

LISTEN & WRITE

듣고 질문을 써 보세요.

스크립트

> What is your phone number?
> Can I speak to your mother please?
> Who's calling?
> Leave a message for a friend.
> Will you be home by 8 o'clock?

해석

당신의 전화번호가 무엇입니까?
당신의 어머니와 통화할 수 있습니까?
누구세요?
친구에게 메시지를 남겨 놓으십시오.
8시까지 집에 올 것입니까?

PRONUNCIATION

단음절 단어

☞ 단음절 단어는 끊지 않고 발음해야 합니다.

☞ 듣고 따라해 보시오.

하나의, 그, 이다(단수 주어), 이다(복수 주어), 이다(I 주어), 당신, 먹다, 탔다, 보다, 다섯, Scott, 부유한, 검은, 기차, 밤, 장소, 실, 치다 아래 문장들은 단음절 단어들로만 되어 있습니다.
먼저 듣고 따라해 보세요.

1. Scott와 Rich는 5일 동안 밤낮으로 기차를 탔다.
2. 너와 네 검정색 자전거는 경기에서 잘 달릴 것이다.
3. 그는 거대한 스프링 밑에 깔렸지만, 지금은 괜찮다.

Practice Test   p. 98~99

1. 1) c   2. 1) d   2) c   3. 1) b   2) d
4. 1) c   2) c   5. 1) a

※ 듣고 알맞은 답을 고르시오.

1. 누군가 Wilson 씨에게 메시지를 남기고 있다. 알맞은 메모를
   고르시오.

   a. Tim Baker   최대한 빨리 전화 요망
      405-5356

   b. Wilson 씨가 전화하셨음   전화 요망
      405-0356

   ★c. Tim Baker   최대한 빨리 전화 요망
      405-0356

스크립트

M Hello, may I speak to Mr. Wilson, please?
W Sorry, but he's out to lunch right now. Can
   I take a message?
M Yes, please. This is Tim Baker from
   Boston. I'd like him to call me back as
   soon as he returns.
W Does he have your number?
M I think so, but just in case, it's 405-0356.
W 4-0-5-0-3-5-6. All right.
M Thank you.

해석

M 안녕하세요, Wilson 씨와 통화할 수 있나요?
W 죄송하지만, 그는 점심 먹으러 나갔어요. 메모 남기시겠어요?
M 네, 그럴게요. 보스턴의 Tim Baker입니다. 그가 돌아오는 대
   로 저에게 연락해 주었으면 합니다.
W 그가 당신의 번호를 가지고 있나요?
M 그렇게 생각하지만, 혹시 모르니까 405-0356이에요.
W 4-0-5-0-3-5-6. 알겠습니다.
M 고맙습니다.

2. 다음은 Debbie에게 남겨진 메시지이다.

스크립트

Hi, Debbie. This is Sue. How are you doing?
It's been years since I've talked to you. My
family is going to take a trip to Ohio next
week. My mom and dad are having a tennis
match there. I may be able to see you then. I'll
call you when I get to town. I miss you. Bye!

해석

안녕, Debbie. 나 Sue야. 잘 지내니? 오랜만이야. 우리 가족이 다
음주에 오하이오로 여행을 가. 우리 엄마, 아빠가 거기서 테니스
경기를 하셔. 그때 너를 볼 수 있을지도 몰라. 내가 도착하면 전
화를 할게. 보고 싶다. 안녕!

1) 메시지 내용과 일치하는 것은?
   a. Debbie와 Sue는 자매이다.
   b. Debbie와 Sue는 같은 마을에 살고 있다.
   c. Debbie는 Sue의 메시지를 듣고 그녀에게 연락을 할 것이다.
   ★d. Debbie는 Ohio에 산다.

2) 그들은 언제 만나게 될 것인가?
   a. 이번 주   b. 다음 달   ★c. 다음 주   d. 내일

3. 다음은 전화 통화이다.

스크립트

M   Hello? Can I speak to Susan, please?
W   May I ask who's calling?
M   This is Charles Hunt, Susan's classmate.
W   She's on another line. Would you hold or
    do you want to leave a message?
M   I'll hold.
W   Sure. Susan. There's a phone call for you.
W2 Hello?
M   It's me Charles, Susan.
W2 Oh, Charles! What's up?

해석

M   여보세요? Susan하고 통화할 수 있을까요?
W   누구신지요?
M   저는 Susan의 반 친구인 Charles Hunt입니다.
W   통화 중이에요. 기다리실래요, 아니면 메시지를 남기실래요?
M   기다릴게요.
W   그러세요. Susan. 너한테 전화 왔어.
W2 여보세요?
M   나야, Charles, Susan.
W2 아, Charles! 무슨 일이야?

1) 빈칸을 채울 알맞은 단어 묶음을 고르시오.

   _____는 _____에게 전화를 했으나 그녀는
   _____ 때문에 그는 _____.

   a. Susan - Charles - 바쁘기 - 기다린다
   ★b. Charles - Susan - 다른 전화를 하고 있기 - 기다린다
   c. Charles - Susan - 외출 중이기 - 메시지를 남긴다
   d. Charles - Susan - 바쁘기 - 메시지를 남긴다

2) Charles는 Susan의 _____ 이다.
   a. 남자 친구   b. 이웃   c. 사촌   ★d. 같은 반 친구

4. Tom은 Jenny에 전화를 하고 있다.

스크립트

M Hello! Is Jenny there?
W She's not here. Who's calling?
M It's Tom. I'm her classmate.
W Would you like to leave a message?
M Could you tell her to call me back?
W No problem. Does she know your phone number?
M I think so, but just in case, it's 237-1876.
W 237-1876. Okay, I'll make sure she gets it.
M Thanks. Bye!
W Bye!

해석

M 여보세요! Jenny 있나요?
W Jenny 여기 없는데. 누구니?
M Tom인데요. 반 친구예요.
W 메시지 남길래?
M 저에게 전화해 달라고 전해 주실래요?
W 그래. Jenny가 네 전화번호를 아니?
M 그럴 거라 생각하지만, 만약의 경우를 위해, 제 번호는 237-1876이에요.
W 237-1876. 알았다, Jenny에게 꼭 전할게.
M 감사합니다. 안녕히 계세요!
W 안녕!

1) 이 대화를 가장 잘 요약한 것은?
   a. Tom은 Jenny에게 전화를 했지만, 그녀는 집에 없다.
   b. Jenny가 집에 없어서, Tom은 그녀의 어머니에게 말하고 싶어한다.
   ★c. Jenny가 집에 없어서, Tom은 그녀가 그에게 전화해 주기를 바란다.
   d. Tom이 집에 없어서 Jenny는 자신의 전화번호를 남기고 있다.

2) Tom의 전화번호는 무엇인가?
   a. 237-8076   b. 273-8079
   ★c. 237-1876   d. 273-1870

5. 다음은 Lesley를 위한 메시지이다.

스크립트

Hi, Lesley. This is Mrs. Brown. My son James is in Grade 9 and he needs some help with writing essays. He wants to develop his writing skills. I wonder if you can give him writing lessons at my house once a week. If you could call me back when you get this, that'd be great. My phone number is 416-989-5668. Thank you. Bye!

해석

안녕하세요, Lesley 씨. Brown 부인입니다. 제 아들 James가 중학교 3학년인데, 글짓기를 하는 데 도움이 약간 필요합니다. 아들이 작문 실력을 늘리고 싶어 해요. Lesley 씨가 일주일에 한 번 저희 집에서 제 아들을 가르쳐 주실 수 있으신가 해서요. 이 메시지를 받고, 저에게 전화를 해 주시면 감사하겠습니다. 제 전화번호는 416-989-5668입니다. 감사합니다. 안녕히 계세요.

1) Brown 부인이 Lesley 씨에게 전화를 한 이유는?
   ★a. 그녀는 Lesley 씨가 James에게 글짓기 하는 것을 도와주기를 바란다.
   b. 그녀는 Lesley 씨를 만나서 무엇인가 의논하고 싶다.
   c. 그녀는 작문 실력을 향상시키는 법에 대한 정보를 원한다.
   d. 그녀는 Lesley 씨가 어디에서 James를 가르칠 수 있는지 알고 싶다.

Dictation   p. 100

1. speak to, Can I take a message?, number, 4-0-5-0-3-5-6
2. talked to you, mom, dad, able to see, I miss you
3. Can I speak to, who's calling, line, message, What's up
4. Is Jenny there, It's, phone number, 1876, Thanks
5. This is, writing skills, my house, call me back, 5668

UNIT 13
What do you do in your free time?

1. **Your own answers**
2. 1. e   2. f   3. a   4. c   5. b   6. d

1. 당신이 한 달에 한 번 이상 하는 활동들을 표시하시오.

영화 보러 가기 _____	외식하기 _____
콘서트 가기 _____	온라인 채팅 _____
쇼핑 가기 _____	자전거 타기 _____
낚시 가기 _____	컴퓨터 게임 하기 _____
공원 가기 _____	인터넷 서핑 _____

2. 질문을 답과 연결시키오.

1. 네가 제일 좋아하는 여가 활동이 뭐야?

    e. 컴퓨터 게임 하는 거야.

2. 이번 주말에 뭐 하니?   f. 나는 우리 숙모를 방문할 거야.

3. 이번 토요일에 바쁘니?   a. 아니, 그렇지는 않아. 왜?

4. 영화 보러 가고 싶니?   c. 응, 정말 가고 싶어.

5. 뭐 하고 싶니?   b. 테니스를 치고 싶어.

6. 우리 비디오 빌려서 보지 않을래?   d. 좋은 생각이야.

Listening 1	2, 3, 1, 4			
Listen Again	A	1. a	2. b	3. c
	B	4. a		
Listening 2	1. b	2. b	3. b	4. a
Listen Again	A	1. b	2. b	3. c
	B	4. a		

Listening 1   p. 102

사람들이 그들의 여가 활동에 대해 이야기하고 있다. 듣고 그림에 번호를 매기시오.

스크립트

1.

My favorite pastime is shopping. I go to the mall every weekend. There are things to see, things to eat, and things to buy. It's also fun to watch people. I like to be around people.

2.

What do I do on weekends? I go to the park with my family. After a long week, I need some quiet time. My children ride bikes and my wife and I read books on the grass. On a sunny Saturday, you will find me in the park.

3.

What do I do for fun? I just relax at home surfing the Internet. That's the best way to blow my stress away. I don't understand people going out for fun. It only makes them more tired.

4.

Mostly I have a good time with friends. We chat, dance or play games. Sometimes we go to the movies or concerts. I have no fun on weekdays, so I need some excitement on weekends.

해석

1. 내가 가장 좋아하는 여가 활동은 쇼핑이에요. 나는 주말마다 쇼핑몰에 가요. 그곳엔 볼거리가 있고, 먹을거리가 있고, 그리고 살 것들이 있어요. 또한 사람들을 구경하는 것도 재미있어요. 나는 사람들과 함께 있는 것이 좋아요.

2. 내가 주말에 뭘 하냐고요? 나는 가족들과 공원에 가요. 힘든 한 주를 보내고 나면, 나는 조용한 시간이 좀 필요하죠. 내 아이들은 자전거를 타고 내 아내와 나는 잔디 위에서 책을 읽어요. 맑은 토요일에는 공원에서 날 찾을 수 있을 거예요.

3. 내가 놀 때 무엇을 하냐고요? 나는 편안하게 집에서 인터넷 서핑을 해요. 그것이 내 스트레스를 날려버리는 최고의 방법이에요. 나는 사람들이 즐기기 위해 밖으로 나가는 것을 이해 못하겠어요. 그것은 날 더 피곤하게 만들 뿐이죠.

4. 대부분 나는 친구들과 함께 즐거운 시간을 가져요. 우리는 수다를 떨고, 춤을 추거나 게임을 해요. 때때로 우리는 영화나 콘서트를 보러 가요. 평일에는 재미있는 일이 없으니까, 주말에는 약간의 자극이 필요하죠.

Listen Again   p. 102

A. 다시 듣고 알맞은 답을 고르시오.

1. 다음 중 일치하지 않는 것은?

★a. 그녀는 사람들을 보는 것을 좋아하지 않는다.

   b. 그녀는 사야 할 것이 많기 때문에 쇼핑을 간다.

   c. 그녀는 때때로 그곳에 가서 먹는다.

2. 다음 중 일치하는 것은?

   a. 그는 그의 아이들과 함께 자전거를 탄다.

★b. 그는 그의 아내와 같은 여가 활동을 한다.

   c. 그는 공원에 사람이 많아서 간다.

3. 다음 중 일치하는 것은?

    a. 그는 스트레스를 전혀 받지 않는다.

    b. 그는 돈을 아끼기 위해 밖에 나가지 않는다.

  ★c. 그는 혼자 있는 것을 좋아한다.

B. 다시 듣고 가장 적절하게 요약한 것을 고르시오.

4. a. ★ 말하고 있는 사람은 주중에는 아무런 재미가 없기 때문에, 주말에 자신의 친구들과 밖에 나가는 것을 좋아한다.

    b. ☐ 말하고 있는 사람은 주중에 수다 떨기, 춤추기, 게임하기, 영화 보기를 좋아한다.

Listening 2   p. 103

두 번째로 말한 사람이 주말에 할 일은 무엇인가? 맞는 그림을 고르시오.

스크립트

1.

W Hey, Joe. There's a football match between the Giants and the Steelers next weekend.

M I know. I'm going to watch it on TV.

W On TV? You must be kidding. It's in our town. We've got to see it at the stadium.

M No, I'd enjoy it in my room. It's quieter and more relaxing.

2.

M What are you doing this weekend, Jan?

W Nothing special. I'll stay home and read some books.

M Why don't you play tennis with me?

W I'd love to. But I'm not sure if I could hit a single ball. I haven't played it for years.

M Don't worry. I am not very good either.

W Sorry but I'll stay home.

3.

M Angie, uh... Do you feel like going to a concert this Friday night?

W With you, Michael?

M Yes. I have tickets to a concert.

W Oh, I'd love to. But I have other plan that night. I'm going to the movies with my friends. I'm so sorry.

4.

W Hi, Jeff! Are you free this weekend?

M No, I have to help my mom clean up the house. Why?

W Tim and Jane are coming over to my house. I'd love you to join us.

M That would be fun, but I can't. I promised my mom. You guys have fun.

56

해석

1. W 이봐, Joe. 다음 주말에 자이언트와 스틸러스의 미식축구 경기가 있어.

  M 알아. 나는 TV로 보려고 해.

  W TV로? 농담하지 마. 우리 동네에서 한다고. 경기장에서 직접 봐야지.

  M 아니, 내 방에서 볼래. 더 조용하고 편하거든.

2. M Jan, 이번 주말에 뭐해?

  W 특별한 일은 없어. 집에 있으면서 책을 읽으려고 해.

  M 나랑 테니스 치지 않을래?

  W 나도 그러고 싶어. 하지만, 내가 공을 하나라도 칠 수 있을지 잘 모르겠어. 몇 년 동안 테니스를 치지 않았거든.

  M 걱정 마. 나도 그렇게 잘 치지 못해.

  W 미안해. 난 그냥 집에 있을래.

3. M Angie, 어... 이번 금요일 밤에 콘서트 가지 않을래?

  W 너랑, Michael?

  M 응. 콘서트 표가 있거든.

  W 오, 그러고 싶어. 그런데 그날 밤에 다른 계획이 있어. 내 친구와 영화를 보러 갈 거야. 정말 미안해.

4. W 안녕, Jeff! 이번 주말에 시간 있어?

  M 아니, 엄마 집 청소하시는 거 도와야 해. 왜?

  W Tim이랑 Jane이 우리 집에 올 거야. 너도 와.

  M 재밌겠다. 그런데 안 돼. 엄마에게 약속했거든. 너희들끼리 재밌게 놀아.

Listen Again   p. 103

A. 다시 듣고 알맞은 답을 고르시오.

1. Joe에 대한 설명으로 옳은 것은?

    a. 그는 운동을 좋아하지 않는다.

  ★b. 그는 시끄러운 관중과 함께 있고 싶지 않다.

    c. 그는 TV를 매우 좋아한다.

2. Jan에 대한 설명으로 옳은 것은?

    a. Jan은 테니스를 쳐 본 적이 없다.

  ★b. Jan은 이번 주말에 테니스를 치지 않을 것이다.

    c. Jan의 친구는 테니스를 굉장히 잘한다.

3. Angie에 대한 설명으로 옳은 것은?

    a. Angie는 콘서트보다 영화를 좋아한다.

    b. Angie는 콘서트를 싫어한다.

  ★c. Angie에게는 다른 계획이 있다.

B. 다시 듣고 맞는 문장을 고르시오.

4. a. ★ Jeff는 엄마가 집 청소하시는 걸 도와야 하기 때문에 친구네 집에 갈 수 없다.

    b. ☐ Jeff는 주말마다 엄마를 도와드리는 것을 좋아한다.

스크립트

a. Jeff cannot go to his friend's house because he has to help his mom clean up their house.

b. Jeff likes to help his mother on weekends.

Review   p. 104

1. pastime, play, skating
2. fun, relax, watch, Internet
3. are, doing, eat out, come over
4. pastime, movies, free, Friday, watching
5. feel like, fun, years, worry

※ 듣고 빈칸을 채우시오.

해석

1. W 네가 가장 좋아하는 여가 활동은 무엇이니?
   M 컴퓨터 게임을 하는 거야. 너는?
   W 나는 친구들과 스케이트를 타러 가. 동네에 새 아이스 링크가 생겼거든.

2. 나는 사람들이 즐기기 위해 밖에 나가는 걸 이해할 수 없어요. 난 주말에 쉬어야 해요. TV로 스포츠나 영화를 볼 수 있지요. 인터넷으로 물건을 살 수도 있어요.

3. M 너 이번 주말에 뭐하니?
   W 나는 가족들과 외식을 할 거야. 우리 엄마 생신이거든.
   M 나는 Tim이랑 보드게임을 할 거야. 그러니까 시간 있으면 놀러 와.

4. 내가 가장 좋아하는 여가 활동은 영화 감상이다. 오늘 새 DVD를 샀다. 오늘 나와 가장 친한 친구에게 금요일 저녁에 시간이 있냐고 물어볼 것이다. 그 애는 분명히 함께 DVD를 보는 걸 재미있어할 거라고 생각한다.

5. M 나랑 테니스 치지 않을래?
   W 재미있겠다. 그런데 난 잘 못 쳐. 몇 년 동안 안 쳤어.
   M 걱정 마. 나도 잘 못해.

On Your Own   p. 105

LISTEN & WRITE

듣고 질문을 써 보세요.

스크립트

What do you do for fun?
What are you going to do this weekend?
Do you like to play computer games?
Do you like to eat out?

해석
여가 활동으로 무엇을 합니까?
이번 주말에 무엇을 할 것입니까?
컴퓨터 게임 하는 것을 좋아합니까?
외식하는 것을 좋아합니까?

PRONUNCIATION

/ t / vs /d /

☞ 듣고 따라해 보시오.
꼬마, 10, 시간, 도시, 여행, 시도하다

☞ 듣고 따라해 보시오.
아빠, 동굴, 10센트 동전, 아래로, 똑똑 떨어지다, 건조한

☞ 잘 듣고 차이점을 발견해 보시오.
꼬마 / 아빠, 10 / 동굴, 시간 / 10센트 동전,
도시 / 아래로, 여행/똑똑 떨어지다, 시도하다 / 건조한

들리는 단어에 표시하시오.

스크립트 tad, den, dime, town, drip, try

꼬마	★	아빠	☐
10	☐	동굴	★
시간	☐	10센트 동전	★
도시	★	아래로	☐
여행	☐	똑똑 떨어지다	★
시도하다	★	건조한	☐

Practice Test   p. 106~107

1. 1) b   2) b   2. 1) c   2) d   3. 1) c   2) c
4. 1) a   5. 1) c   2) b

※ 듣고 알맞은 답을 고르시오.

1. 사람들이 주말 활동에 대해 이야기하고 있다.

스크립트

W What are you doing this weekend?
M I'm going to play computer games.
W Why don't you get out for some fresh air?
M Any good ideas?
W Sure. Let's go watch birds in the park.
M Watching birds? What a boring thing to do!
W It's better than playing computer games.
M I don't think so. Computer games are much more fun.

해석
W 이번 주말에 뭐해?
M 컴퓨터 게임 할 거야.
W 밖에 나가서 신선한 공기 좀 쐬지 그래?
M 무슨 좋은 생각이라도 있니?
W 물론. 공원으로 새 보러 가자.
M 새를 본다고? 너무 지루하잖아!
W 그게 컴퓨터 게임 하는 것보다 훨씬 나아.
M 나는 그렇게 생각하지 않아. 컴퓨터 게임이 훨씬 더 재밌어.

1) 남자는 여자의 제안을 _____.
   a. 받아들이고 있다   ★b. 거절하고 있다

2) 그들은 무슨 이야기를 하고 있는가? 다음 문장에서 빠진 말들을 찾으시오.

> 여자는 남자에게 _____에 가자고 제안하고 있지만, 남자는 집에서 _____싶어한다. 그는 여자의 생각이 _____고 생각한다.

   a. 공원 - 잠을 자고 - 재미있다
   ★b. 공원 - 컴퓨터를 하고 - 지루하다
   c. 산 - 컴퓨터를 하고 - 지루하다

2. 다음은 John에 대한 설명이다.

스크립트

> John is full of energy. He exercises to fight stress. But he is a little shy. He doesn't like people around when he exercises. He usually exercises alone.

해석

존은 활기가 넘친다. 그는 스트레스를 풀기 위해 운동을 한다. 그러나 그는 약간 수줍음을 탄다. 그는 운동할 때 주위에 사람이 있는 것을 좋아하지 않는다. 그는 보통 혼자 운동한다.

1) John이 가장 좋아하는 여가 활동은 _____이다.
   a. 축구하기   b. 독서
   ★c. 달리기   d. 컴퓨터 게임 하기

2) John에 대한 설명으로 사실이 아닌 것은?
   a. 약간 수줍음을 탄다.   b. 활기가 넘친다.
   c. 운동을 좋아한다.   ★d. 스트레스를 받지 않는다.

3. Amy가 주말 활동에 대해 친구와 이야기하고 있다.

스크립트

Amy	Are you free this Saturday?
Jenny	Yes. I have plenty of time.
Amy	Would you like to go shopping with me? There is a big sale for summer clothes in the mall.
Jenny	I'd love to. What time shall we meet?
Amy	How about 11 in the morning?
Jenny	Sounds great. I'll ask my mom to give us a ride.
Amy	Sounds good!

해석

Amy   이번 주 토요일에 시간 있어?
Jenny 응. 시간 많아.
Amy   나랑 쇼핑 갈래? 쇼핑몰에서 여름옷 세일 많이 하더라.

Jenny 좋아. 몇 시에 만날까?
Amy   오전 11시 어때?
Jenny 좋아. 우리 엄마에게 태워다 달라고 부탁할게.
Amy   그거 좋지!

1) 그들은 이번 토요일에 _____ 갈 것이다.
   a. 춤추러   b. 스케이트 타러
   ★c. 쇼핑하러   d. 외식하러

2) 대화 내용과 일치하지 않는 것은?
   a. 그들은 오전에 만날 것이다.
   b. 쇼핑몰에서 대대적인 세일을 한다.
   ★c. 그들은 아마 거기에 버스로 갈 것이다.
   d. 그들은 아마 옷을 좀 살 것이다.

4. 한 소년이 자신의 여가 시간에 대해 이야기하고 있다.

스크립트

> Believe or not, my favorite past time is volunteering to help disabled children. I eat, read and play together with them every Saturday. I enjoy spending time with them and I also learn a lot from them. Volunteering is the best way to spend some free time on weekends.

해석

믿거나 말거나, 내가 가장 좋아하는 여가 활동은 장애 아동들을 돕는 자원 봉사 활동이야. 난 매주 토요일 그들과 함께 먹고, 읽고, 그리고 놀기도 해. 난 그들과 함께 보내는 시간이 즐겁고 또 그들에게서 많은 것을 배워. 자원 봉사 활동은 주말이나 여름 방학에 남는 시간을 쓰는 최선의 방법이야.

1) 가장 적절하게 요약한 것을 고르시오.
   a. ★ 그가 가장 좋아하는 여가 활동은 장애 아동을 돕는 것이다.
   b. □ 그는 지루하기 때문에 장애 아동을 돕는 자원 봉사를 한다.

5. Sue는 파티를 열 계획이다.

스크립트

Sue	Hi, Monica! Are you free this Friday night?
Monica	I think so. Why?
Sue	I'm having a slumber party. Can you make it?
Monica	I'd love to. Who else is coming?
Sue	Andrea, Patricia, and Sarah. I'll borrow some DVDs.
Monica	Which ones?
Sue	Do you have any suggestions?

Monica	Not really. We can go together and I'll help you choose.
Sue	Wonderful. Let's meet after school on Friday.
Monica	Sure.

해석

Sue	안녕, Monica! 이번 주 금요일 밤에 시간 있어?
Monica	그런 것 같아. 왜?
Sue	파자마 파티를 할 거야. 올 수 있어?
Monica	좋아. 또 누가 와?
Sue	Andrea, Patricia, 그리고 Sarah. DVD도 몇 개 빌릴 거야.
Monica	어떤 DVD?
Sue	추천할 만한 게 있니?
Monica	아니. 같이 가서 네가 고르는 걸 도와줄게.
Sue	좋아. 금요일 방과 후에 만나자.
Monica	좋아.

1) Sue가 Monica에게 요구하고 있는 것은 무엇인가?
   a. 극장에 같이 가기
   b. DVD를 가지고 오기
   ★c. 다른 친구들과 그녀의 집에서 자기
   d. 볼만한 좋은 영화를 추천해 주기

2) Monica와 Sue는 언제 만날 것인가?
   a. 금요일 밤
   ★b. 금요일 오후
   c. 금요일 오전
   d. 오늘

Dictation   p. 108

1. doing, weekend, get out for, Let's go, boring, playing computer games, much more fun
2. exercises, doesn't like,
3. Are you free, plenty of time, go shopping, What time, in the morning, a ride
4. favorite, play together, spending time, the best way, free time
5. Are you free, I think so, Can you make it, Which ones, suggestions, I'll help you choose, after school

UNIT 14
Can you describe it?

Getting Ready   p. 109

1. 품목: sneakers, jacket, hat, wallet, sunglasses, backpack, suitcase, umbrella
   디자인/무늬: striped, checked, letters
   재료(소재): plastic, leather, wood
   색상: black, pink, tan

2. 1. f   2. a   3. g   4. c
   5. b   6. d   7. e

1. 단어들을 네 가지 분류로 그룹 짓고, 빈칸에 단어를 적으시오.

운동화	플라스틱	검정색의	줄무늬의	재킷
체크 무늬의	글자들	가죽	모자	나무
지갑	선글라스	배낭	여행 가방	우산
분홍색의	황갈색의			

2. 질문을 답과 연결시키시오.

1. 어떻게 생겼나요?   f. 그것은 크고 비싸 보여요.
2. 그것을 묘사할 수 있나요?   a. 네. 그것은 분홍색 모 스웨터에요.
3. 그것은 무슨 색깔인가요?   g. 검정과 하얀색이에요.
4. 그것은 무슨 모양인가요?   c. 사각형이에요.
5. 그것은 얼마나 무거운가요?   b. 그것은 약 2킬로그램이에요.
6. 그것은 얼마나 됐나요?   d. 그것은 3일 밖에 안 됐어요.
7. 무엇으로 만들어졌나요?   e. 플라스틱 소재에요.

Listening Task   p. 110~111

Listening 1		1, 3, 2, 4		
Listen Again	A	1. c	2. a	3. b
	B	4. b		
Listening 2		1. b	2. a	3. b	4. a
Listen Again	A	1. a	2. c	3. b
	B	4. b		

Listening 1   p. 110

사람들이 가방을 묘사하고 있다. 듣고 그림에 번호를 매기시오.

스크립트

1.
It's small and it's a leather bag.
There are some letters on the front.
I don't use it any more, as it's too old. I'm going to throw it away.

2.
It is a backpack with a checked design.
It looks like leather, but it is plastic.
It looks pretty but it is heavy. No one likes a heavy bag.

3.
It is a bag with a striped design.
It is light and strong.
I love it because I can always use it for short trips.

4.
It is a black suitcase.
It has wheels and a handle.
It can hold a lot, and it is not too big.
You can carry it onto an airplane.

해석
1. 이것은 작은 가죽 핸드백이에요.
   앞면에 몇 개의 글자가 있어요.
   너무 오래 되어서 나는 그 가방을 더 이상 사용하지 않아요.
   버릴 거예요.

2. 이것은 체크 무늬 디자인의 배낭이에요.
   가죽처럼 보이지만, 플라스틱 소재에요.
   예뻐 보이지만 무거워요. 무거운 가방을 좋아하는 사람은 없지요.

3. 줄무늬 디자인의 가방이에요.
   가볍고 튼튼해요.
   제가 아주 좋아하는데, 짧은 여행에서 항상 이용할 수 있기 때문이에요.

4. 검은색 여행 가방이에요.
   바퀴와 손잡이가 있어요.
   많이 담을 수 있고, 너무 크지도 않아요.
   당신은 비행기 탈 때 휴대할 수 있지요.

Listen Again
p. 110

A. 다시 듣고 알맞은 답을 고르시오.

1. 가방에 대한 설명으로 옳은 것은?
   a. 새것이다.   b. 너무 크다.   ★c. 가죽으로 만들어졌다.

2. 가방에 대한 설명으로 옳지 않은 것은?
   ★a. 가죽으로 만들어졌다.   b. 무겁다.   c. 예쁘다.

3. 가방에 대한 설명으로 옳은 것은?
   a. 무겁다.   ★b. 튼튼하다.   c.긴 여행에 적합하다.

B. 다시 듣고 가장 적절하게 요약한 것을 고르시오.

4. a. ☐ 검은색 바퀴와 손잡이가 달려 있다.
   b. ★ 물건이 많이 들어가는 검은색 여행 가방인데 별로 크지는 않다.

Listening 2
p. 111

그들은 무엇을 찾고 있는가? 알맞은 그림을 고르시오.

스크립트

1.
M I lost my umbrella. Has anyone turned in an umbrella?
W What does it look like?
M It is black and has a wooden handle.
W There are several of them.
M ___Is it in a case?___

2.
W Do you have any glasses?
M What do they look like?
W They have gold frames with my initials written on them.
M No, _____

3.
M I think I left my wallet in the taxi.
W Can you describe it?
M Sure. It is a brown leather wallet. It has all my cards and IDs in it.
W Is your name Michael Johnson?
M Yes.
W It's here. And _____

4.
W I'm calling about my hat.
M What does it look like?
W It is pink with a white ribbon around it.
M ___We don't have it.___

해석
1. M 우산을 잃어버렸어요. 우산 가져온 사람 없나요?
   W 어떻게 생겼나요?
   M 검은색이고 나무 손잡이가 있어요.
   W 그런 게 몇 개 있네요.
   M ___케이스 안에 들어 있나요?___

2. W 안경 가지고 있나요?
   M 어떻게 생겼나요?
   W 금테이고 제 이니셜이 새겨져 있어요.
   M 아니요, _____

3. M 지갑을 택시에 놓고 내린 것 같아요.
   W 모양을 설명해 주시겠어요?
   M 물론이죠. 갈색 가죽 지갑이에요. 제 카드와 신분증이 모두 들어 있어요.
   W 당신 이름이 Michael Johnson인가요?
   M 네.
   W 여기 있네요. 그리고 _____

4. W 내 모자 때문에 전화했어요.

M 어떻게 생겼나요?

W 하얀 리본이 둘러져 있는 분홍색이에요.

M _____ 저희한테는 없습니다. _____

Listen Again

p. 111

A. 다시 듣고 알맞은 답을 고르시오.

1. 남자가 할 말로 적절한 것은?

★a. 케이스 안에 들어 있나요?

  b. 어떤 걸 원하세요?

  c. 와서 확인해 보세요.

2. 남자가 할 말로 적절하지 <u>않은</u> 것은?

  a. 없어요.

  b. 저희가 가지고 있지 않는 것 같아요.

★c. 있습니다.

3. 여자가 할 말로 적절하지 <u>않은</u> 것은?

  a. 그리고 카드하고 신분증은 모두 그대로 있네요.

★b. 어떠세요?

  c. 오전 10시부터 오후 4시 사이에 언제든 와서 가져가세요.

B. 다시 듣고 가장 적절한 응답을 고르시오.

4. a. ☐ 케이스 안에 들어 있나요?

  b. ★ 저희한테는 없습니다.

  c. ☐ 가지고 계신가요?

스크립트

  a. Is it in a case?

  b. We don't have it.

  c. Do you have it?

Review

p. 112

1. looking, does, like, checked
2. calling, handle
3. describe, stripes, plastic
4. black, light, new, find, favorite, shoes
5. find, looking for, letters

✲ 듣고 빈칸을 채우시오.

해석

1. W 제 모자를 찾고 있어요.

M 어떻게 생겼나요?

W 체크 무늬 디자인에 갈색이에요. 약간 오래됐어요.

2. 안녕하세요, 제 우산 때문에 전화했어요.

파란색이고 나무로 된 손잡이가 있어요.

손잡이에 제 이니셜이 새겨 있어요.

3. M 당신의 가방의 모습을 설명해 주시겠어요?

W 네, 갈색 줄무늬의 회색이에요.

M 가죽으로 만들어졌나요?

W 아니요, 플라스틱 소재에요.

4. 검정색입니다. 가볍고 새것이에요. 진짜 그것을 찾아야 돼요.
제가 가장 아끼는 신발이거든요.

5. M 이런, 아무데서도 못 찾겠어.

W 뭘 찾고 있어?

M 제 운동복이요.

W 하얀색에 글자 써 있는 거?

M 맞아요.

W 빨래 바구니에 있어. 아직 안 빨았어.

On Your Own

p. 113

LISTEN & WRITE

듣고 질문을 써 보세요.

스크립트

What are you wearing today?
Can you describe your shoes?
Please describe your bag.

해석

오늘은 무엇을 입고 있습니까?

신발을 묘사해 줄 수 있습니까?

당신의 가방을 묘사해 주십시오.

PRONUNCIATION

/ k / **vs** / g /
☞ 듣고 따라해 보시오. 왔다, 모자, 카드, 오다, 추운, 게
☞ 듣고 따라해 보시오. 게임, 격차, 보호하다, 잇몸, 금, 움켜쥐다
☞ 잘 듣고 차이점을 발견해 보시오. 왔다 / 게임, 모자 / 격차, 카드 / 보호하다, 오다 / 잇몸 추운 / 금, 게 / 움켜쥐다

듣고 들리는 단어에 표시하시오.

스크립트 game, cap, card, come, gold, grab

왔다	☐	게임	★
모자	★	격차	☐
카드	★	보호하다	☐
오다	★	잇몸	☐
추운	☐	금	★
게	☐	움켜쥐다	★

| 1. 1) c | 2. 1) d 2) d | 3. 1) c 2) c |
| 4. 1) a 2) a | 5. 1) c 2) b | |

※ 듣고 알맞은 답을 고르시오.

1. 한 여자가 잃어버린 재킷을 묘사하고 있다.

스크립트

M What color is your jacket?
W It is black with brown buttons.
M What is it made of?
W It is leather, very fine leather.
M What size is it?
W It's size 6.
M Anything else?
W It is brand new. Oh, one more thing. There are two pockets on the front. Oh, it's beautiful. I must have it back.

해석

M 당신의 재킷 색깔이 무엇입니까?
W 검은색이고 갈색 단추가 있어요.
M 무엇으로 만들어 졌죠?
W 가죽이요, 매우 좋은 가죽이요.
M 사이즈가 어떻게 돼요?
W 6 사이즈예요.
M 다른 특별한 건요?
W 새로 산 거예요. 아, 한 가지 더 있어요. 앞쪽에 두 개의 주머니가 있어요. 오, 매우 멋져요. 꼭 다시 찾아야 해요.

1) 어떤 것이 그녀의 재킷인가? 맞는 그림을 고르시오.

2. 한 학생이 기숙사에서 무언가를 잃어버렸다.

스크립트

Looking for a pair of sneakers. Lost in the library. Size 8.
White with blue stripes on the side.
Leather cover. Almost new; only two weeks old.
Please call anytime at 012-675-2543.

해석

운동화 한 켤레를 찾습니다. 도서관에서 잃어버림. 사이즈는 8.
옆면에 파란 줄무늬가 있는 흰색.
가죽 커버. 거의 새것으로 겨우 2주 됐음.
언제든지 012-675-2543로 연락 주세요.

1) 무엇을 찾고 있는가?
　　a. 양말　　　b. 장갑　　　c. 바지　　★d. 운동화

2) 알림 글의 내용과 일치하는 것은?
　　a. 운동화에 흰 줄무늬가 있다.　　　b.줄무늬는 앞쪽에 있다.
　　c. 두 달밖에 안 신었다.　　　★d. 커버가 가죽이다.

3. Susan은 세탁소에 있다.

스크립트

W Excuse me. I think you gave me the wrong blouse.
M Why do you say that?
W Mine is not green. It is tan. Besides it is not striped. It is with the checked design.
M Aren't you Sarah Brown?
W No, I am Susan Brown.
M Oh, I am sorry. Here's yours.

해석

W 실례합니다만, 블라우스를 잘못 주신 것 같아요.
M 왜요?
W 제 건 녹색이 아니에요. 황갈색이에요. 그리고 제 건 줄무늬도 없어요. 체크 무늬예요.
M Sarah Brown 아니세요?
W 아뇨, 저는 Susan Brown이에요.
M 아, 죄송합니다. 손님 것은 여기 있습니다.

1) 어떤 옷에 대해서 이야기하고 있는가?
　　a. 셔츠　　　b. 재킷　　★c. 블라우스　　　d. 드레스

2) Susan의 옷은 어떻게 생겼는가?
　　a. 녹색이다.　　　b. 줄무늬이다.　　★c. 체크 무늬이다.

4. Sarah는 무엇인가를 찾고 있다.

스크립트

M May I help you?
W I'm looking for a pair of sandals.
M Okay. Can you describe them?
W Yes. They are black with high heels.
M What size?
W Six.
M Anything else?
W They look kind of old.
M Are these leather ones?
W No.
M Then I don't think we have your sandals. I'm sorry.

해석

M 무얼 도와 드릴까요?
W 샌들을 찾고 있는데요.
M 어떻게 생겼는지 말씀해 주실래요?

W 네. 검정색 하이힐이에요.

M 치수는요?

W 6이요.

M 그 밖에 다른 점은요?

W 조금 오래되어 보여요.

M 가죽 신발입니까?

W 아뇨.

M 그렇다면 찾으시는 물건이 저희한테 없는 것 같습니다. 죄송
합니다.

1) Sarah가 찾고 있는 것은 무엇인가?

2) Sarah가 찾고 있는 물건에 대해 사실이 아닌 것은?
  ★a. 가죽으로 만들어짐 b. 검정색과 흰색
  c. 오래됨   d. 치수 6

5. Paul은 야영을 위해 그가 필요한 것에 대해 묘사하고 있다.

스크립트

> It's waterproof, so you don't have to worry
> about rain. It comes in many different sizes.
> Mine is for four people but it's light and easy
> to carry. What color? It's red and I bought it
> last month so it's quite new. You need it for
> camping.

해석

방수라서, 비를 걱정할 필요가 없습니다. 다양한 크기가 있습니
다. 제 것은 4인용이지만, 가볍고 들고 다니기 편합니다. 무슨 색
이냐고요? 붉은색이며 지난달에 사서 완전히 새것입니다. 야영할
때 필요한 것입니다.

1) Paul이 묘사하는 것은 무엇인가?
  a. 침낭   b. 매트리스 ★c. 텐트   d. 파라솔

2) 이 물건에 대해 사실이 아닌 것은?
  a. 붉은색이다.   ★b. 무겁고 오래됐다.
  c. 4인용이다.   d. 야영용이다.

Dictation   p. 116

1. What color is, brown, What is it made of,
   size, Anything else, it's beautiful

2. a pair of sneakers, blue stripes, weeks old,
   2543

3. wrong, Mine is not green, checked, I am
   Susan, Here's yours

4. May I help you, Can you describe them,
   black, Six, kind of old, sandals

5. don't have to, different sizes, easy to carry,
   quite new, camping

UNIT 15
What is wrong with you?

Getting Ready   p. 117

1. 1. headache   2. cast   3. itch
   4. stomachache   5. toothache
   6. sore, runny, fever   7. watery, sneeze
2. 1. c   2. e   3. b   4. d   5. a

1. 박스 안의 단어 중 맞는 것을 골라 빈칸에 그 단어를 쓰시오.

열	아픈	콧물이 흐르는	재채기
깁스	치통	복통	가려움증
두통	눈물이 나는		

1. 머리가 아프다. 오전 내내 심한 ____두통____ 이 있다.
2. 팔이 부러졌다. 팔에 ____깁스____ 를 했다.
3. 피부에 문제가 있다. 온 몸에 심한 ____가려움증____ 이 있다.
4. 너무 많이 먹었다. ____복통____ 이 있다.
5. 치과에 가야겠다. ____치통____ 이 있다.
6. 독감에 걸렸다. 목이 ____아프고____ , 코에서 ____콧물이 흐르__ 고,
   ____열____ 이 높다.
7. 나는 봄에 알레르기가 있다. 눈에서 ____눈물이 난다____ . 내가
   ____재채기____ 를 하면 사람들이 "Bless you." 라고 말한다.

2. 질문을 답과 연결시키시오.

1. 네 다리에 무슨 문제 있니?   c. 지난달에 부러졌어요.
2. 네 눈 어떻게 된 거니?   e. 알레르기가 있어요.
3. 기분이 어때?   b. 몸이 좋지 않아요.
4. 무슨 일이야?   d. 독감에 걸린 것 같아요.
5. 의사 선생님께 가보는 게 어때?   a. 그래야겠어요.

Listening Task   p. 118~119

Listening 1	3, 4, 1, 2		
Listen Again	A 1. a	2. b	3. b
	B 4. b		
Listening 2	1, 4, 2, 3		
Listen Again	A 1. b	2. c	3. a
	B 4. b		

Listening 1   p. 118

문제점이 무엇인가? 그림에 번호를 매기시오.

1.

He can't walk. He is wearing a cast. He has sprained his ankle. He tripped when he was playing football the other day.

2.

I have a high fever. I have a headache and a sore throat. My nose is runny and I sneeze all the time. It seems like I've got a bad cold. It all started last weekend after I walked in the rain.

3.

Johnny isn't feeling well. He has a stomachache. He ate too much turkey at Thanksgiving dinner last night. He always has trouble from overeating. He can never stop himself from eating.

4.

I am itching all over my body. It's very bad. I can't sleep. I can't focus when I study. I don't know why. But it started after I came back from the woods.

해석

1. 그는 걸을 수 없어요. 그는 깁스를 하고 있어요. 그는 발목을 삐었어요. 그는 얼마 전에 축구를 하다가 발을 헛디뎠어요.

2. 나는 열이 높아요. 머리가 아프고 목도 아파요. 콧물이 나고 계속 재채기를 해요. 독한 감기에 걸린 것 같아요. 모든 것은 내가 지난 주말 빗속을 걸은 후부터 시작되었어요.

3. Johnny는 몸이 좋지 않아요. 그는 배가 아파요. 그는 어젯밤 추수 감사절 저녁 때 칠면조를 너무 많이 먹었어요. 그는 항상 과식으로 인해 고생해요. 그는 결코 먹는 것을 스스로 멈출 수 없어요.

4. 나는 온몸이 다 가려워요. 매우 심해요. 잠을 못 자요. 공부할 때 집중도 안 돼요. 왜 그런지 나도 몰라요. 그러나 이건 내가 숲에 다녀온 후부터 시작됐어요.

Listen Again   p. 118

A. 다시 듣고 알맞은 답을 고르시오.

1. 그에게 왜 이런 문제가 생겼는가?
   ★a. 축구하다가 발을 헛디뎌서
   b. 자전거 타다가 넘어져서
   c. 등산을 하다가 떨어져서

2. 그에게 왜 이런 문제가 생겼는가?
   a. 창문을 열고 자서
   ★b. 비를 맞아서
   c. 코트를 입지 않아서

3. 그에게 왜 이런 문제가 생겼는가?
   a. 초콜릿을 너무 많이 먹어서
   ★b. 칠면조를 너무 많이 먹어서
   c. 탄산음료를 너무 많이 마셔서

B. 다시 듣고 가장 적절하게 요약한 것을 고르시오.

4. a. ☐ 그녀는 온몸이 가려워서 숲에서 나는 어떤 것이 필요하다.
   b. ★ 그녀는 온몸이 가려워서 잠을 전혀 잘 수가 없다.

Listening 2   p. 119

사람들이 그들의 건강 문제에 대해 이야기하고 있다. 그림에 번호를 매기시오.

1.

W Didn't you sleep well last night? Your eyes are red.

M No, I didn't get any sleep at all. My tooth ached all night.

W Why don't you go to the dentist?

M I think I should.

2.

Mary What happened to your arm?

Jane I broke it when I fell off my bicycle the other day.

Mary That's too bad. Is it getting better?

Jane Yeah, I think so. But I have to be in the cast for one more month.

Mary Oh, I'm sorry.

3.

M Hello, is it you, Nancy? I can't hear you very well.

W I can't speak. My throat is sore. I've got the flu, and it's so bad. I think I can't see you tomorrow.

M Never mind. Are you taking any medicine?

W No. I am just drinking lots of juice.

4.

Doctor What is the problem, Mrs. Lee?

Mrs. Lee Well, doctor, my son Peter has a serious headache. He has an important test next week and he says he can't take it.

Doctor When did it start, Peter?

Peter Last Friday, when I heard about the test.

해석

1. W 지난밤에 잘 못 잤나요? 눈이 빨개요.
   M 네, 전혀 못 잤어요. 밤새 이가 아팠어요.

W 치과에 가보지 그래요?

M 그래야겠어요.

2. Mary 당신 팔 어떻게 된 거예요?

Jane 얼마 전에 자전거에서 떨어져서 부러졌어요.

Mary 안됐네요. 나아지고 있나요?

Jane 네, 그런 것 같아요. 그런데 한 달은 더 깁스를 해야 해요.

Mary 오, 안됐어요.

3. M 여보세요, 너 Nancy 맞지? 네 말이 잘 안 들려.

W 나 말을 못해. 목이 아파. 나 독감에 걸렸어. 그리고 심해. 내 생각에 내일 너를 못 볼 것 같아.

M 신경 쓰지 마. 너 약 먹고 있니?

W 아니. 그냥 주스를 많이 마시고 있어.

4. Doctor Lee 부인, 무슨 일이세요?

Mrs.Lee 글쎄요, 선생님, 우리 아들 Peter가 심한 두통이 있어요. 다음 주에 중요한 시험이 있는데 그 시험을 못 볼 것 같다고 하네요.

Doctor Peter, 머리가 언제부터 아프기 시작했니?

Peter 제가 시험에 대해 들었던 지난 금요일부터요.

Listen Again
p. 119

A. 다시 듣고 알맞은 답을 고르시오.

1. 이 사람은 이제 무엇을 할까?
   a. 안과에 간다.
   ★b. 치과에 간다.
   c. 약국에 간다.

2. 대화 내용과 일치하는 것은?
   a. 그녀는 팔을 삐었다.
   b. 점점 악화되고 있다.
   ★c. 한 달 후에 깁스를 벗을 것이다.

3. Nancy에 대한 설명과 일치하는 않는 것은?
   ★a. 약을 많이 먹고 있다.
   b. 목이 아파서 말을 잘 하지 못한다.
   c. 그녀는 친구를 만나러 갈 수가 없다.

B. 다시 듣고 맞는 문장을 고르시오.

4. a. ☐ Lee 부인의 아들은 머리가 아파서 중요한 시험을 볼 수가 없었다.
   b. ★ Lee 부인의 아들에게는 두통이 있는데 그것은 시험에 대해 들었을 때부터 시작된 것이다.

스크립트

a. Mrs. Lee's son couldn't take an important exam because he had a headache.

b. Mrs. Lee's son has a headache and it started when he heard about the test.

Review
p. 120

1. wrong, head, other, better, think
2. eyes, sneeze, medicine, take
3. hurts, Why don't, should
4. well, sore, runny, fever, doctor, cold, last night
5. flu, bad, taking

※ 듣고 빈칸을 채우시오.

해석

1. W 너 머리 왜 그러니?
   M 얼마 전 캄캄한 데서 나무에 부딪혔어.
   W 좋아지고 있니?
   M 그런 것 같아.

2. 눈이 가렵고 눈물이 납니까? 항상 재채기를 합니까? 알레르기가 있다면, 이 약은 당신을 위한 것입니다. 날마다 세 번씩 복용하기만 하면 훨씬 나아질 것입니다.

3. W 이가 너무 아파.
   M 아마 충치가 생겼나 봐. 치과에 가 보는 게 어때?
   W 그래야 할 것 같아.

4. Mary는 몸이 좋지 않다. 목이 따끔거리고, 콧물이 나고, 열이 높다. 당장 병원에 가야 한다. 내 생각에는 그녀가 어젯밤 춤추러 갔다가 감기에 걸린 것 같다.

5. M 아직도 독감에 걸려 있니?
   W 응, 너무 심해.
   M 약은 안 먹고 있어?
   W 응, 난 약이 싫어.
   M 용감하네.

On Your Own
p. 121

LISTEN & WRITE

듣고 질문을 써 보세요.

스크립트

How are you feeling today?
Did you sleep well last night?
Do you have anything to worry about?
Do you easily catch a cold?

해석

오늘 기분이 어떻습니까?
어젯밤 잘 잤습니까?
걱정되는 것이 있습니까?
쉽게 감기에 걸립니까?

PRONUNCIATION

/ p / vs / b /

☞ 듣고 따라해 보시오.

납작한 냄비, 포장하다, 파이, 돼지,
두드리다, 대걸레

☞ 듣고 따라해 보시오.

금지, 뒷면, 사다, 큰,
꼬리표, 군중

☞ 잘 듣고 차이점을 발견해 보시오.

납작한 냄비 / 금지, 포장하다 / 뒷면, 파이 / 사다,
돼지 / 큰, 두드리다 / 꼬리표, 대걸레 / 군중

단어를 듣고 들리는 단어에 표시하시오.

스크립트 pan, back, buy, pig, tap, mob

납작한 냄비	★	금지	☐
포장하다	☐	뒷면	★
파이	☐	사다	★
돼지	★	큰	☐
두드리다	★	꼬리표	☐
대걸레	☐	군중	★

Practice Test   p. 122~123

1. 1) a   2) c   2. 1) a   2) d   3. 1) c   2) d
4. 1) b   5. 1) a   2) b

✿ 듣고 알맞은 답을 고르시오.

1. Brown 씨가 그의 의사와 이야기하고 있다.

스크립트

W What's the problem, Mr. Brown?
M I am so tired these days. I am out of energy.
W Do you eat and sleep well?
M No, I don't feel like eating. And I can't sleep very well either.
W Are you worried about anything?
M No, I don't think so.
W Okay, let me check your eyes first.

해석
W Brown 씨, 무슨 일이세요?
M 요즘 너무 피곤해요. 에너지가 바닥났어요.
W 식사는 잘 하시고 잘 주무시나요?
M 아니요, 먹고 싶지 않아요. 그리고 숙면을 취할 수도 없어요.
W 무슨 고민거리가 있으세요?
M 아니요, 그렇지는 않아요.
W 좋아요, 먼저 당신의 눈을 검사해 보겠습니다.

1) Brown 씨는 _____ 문제가 있다.
★a. 수면에   b. 개인적인
   c. 말하는 것에   d. 청각적인

2) Brown 씨에 대한 설명으로 옳지 않은 것은?
   a. 힘이 별로 없다.   b. 아무런 걱정이 없다.
★c. 눈에 문제가 있다.   d. 매우 피곤하다.

2. 두 친구가 John에 대해 이야기하고 있다.

스크립트

W John is absent from school again.
M Yes, he must feel terrible now.
W What happened to him?
M He was bitten by a dog on the leg and it is not getting better.
W Oh, that is not good. When did it happen?
M Three days ago.

해석
W John이 또 결석했어.
M 어, 걔 아주 힘들 거야, 지금.
W 무슨 일이래?
M 개한테 다리를 물렸는데 나아지질 않고 있어.
W 오, 심각하네. 언제 그랬어?
M 3일 전에.

1) John은 _____ 때문에 결석했다.
★a. 다리   b. 팔
   c. 발목   d. 눈

2) 다음 중 일치하는 것은?
   a. 그는 점점 나아지고 있다.
   b. 그가 학교에 결석한 것은 이번이 처음이다.
   c. 3주일 전에 일어난 일이다.
★d. 그는 개에게 물렸다.

3. 다음은 Jeff의 일기이다.

스크립트

I feel really bad today and I've ruined my math test. The test was not hard. I knew all the answers. But I got six questions wrong. I couldn't think clearly. It's because of the flu. I keep sneezing. My eyes are watery. I have a fever and my head hurts.

해석
오늘은 몸이 너무 안 좋아서 시험을 망쳤다. 시험은 안 어려웠다. 답은 다 알았다. 그런데 6문제를 틀렸다. 제대로 생각할 수가 없었다. 독감 때문이다. 계속 재채기가 난다. 눈에서 눈물이 난다. 열이 나고 머리가 아프다.

1) Jeff는 _____ 때문에 시험을 망쳤다.
    a. 수학을 못하기   b. 시험이 어려웠기
  ★c. 독감에 걸렸기   d. 답을 몰랐기

2) 그의 몸 상태에 대해 옳지 않은 것은?
    a. 열이 난다.   b. 재채기가 많이 난다.
    c. 눈물이 나온다.   ★d. 목이 따끔거린다.

4. Tom은 Helen을 우연히 만난다.

스크립트

Tom	Hey, Helen, what's up?
Helen	I feel like crying.
Tom	Oh no, what's wrong?
Helen	I didn't pass the literacy test.
Tom	What happened to you? Didn't you study for the exam?
Helen	Yes, I did. But I had a strong headache during the exam.
Tom	Really? And how is your headache now?
Helen	It's getting better but I feel bad any way.

해석

Tom	어이, Helen, 무슨 일 있어?
Helen	울고 싶은 기분이야.
Tom	이런, 뭐가 문젠데?
Helen	문학 시험을 통과하지 못했어.
Tom	무슨 일 있었어? 시험 공부를 안 했어?
Helen	아니, 했어. 그런데 시험을 치는 동안 머리가 너무 아팠어.
Tom	정말? 지금은 머리가 좀 어때?
Helen	두통은 조금씩 나아지고 있지만 속상하긴 마찬가지야.

1) Helen의 현재 문제는 무엇인가?
    a. Tom에게 그녀의 문제를 얘기하기를 원치 않는다.
  ★b. 시험을 통과하지 못해서 기분이 좋지 않다.
    c. 울고 싶은데 울 수가 없다.
    d. 그녀는 공부를 하지 않았기 때문에 시험을 망쳤다.

5. Jenny는 엄마와 이야기를 하고 있다.

스크립트

Mom	Wake up, Jenny! You'll be late again!
Jenny	(Groan) Mom, I think I caught a cold. Can you call the school and tell them that I'm sick?
Mom	You caught a cold again?
Jenny	(Coughs) I think I have a fever and a really bad headache.
Mom	Okay. You need to rest. Go back to sleep. Do you want some tea?
Jenny	No, thanks. Do you think I need to see

| Mom | the doctor? You should take some medicine first. |

해석

Mom	일어나거라, Jenny! 또 늦겠구나!
Jenny	(끙끙거리며) 엄마, 감기 걸린 것 같아요. 학교에 전화해서 제가 아프다고 해 주실래요?
Mom	또 감기에 걸렸어?
Jenny	(기침하며) 열이 나고 두통이 심한 것 같아요.
Mom	그래. 쉬어야겠구나. 다시 자거라. 차라도 마실래?
Jenny	아뇨, 고마워요. 병원에 가야 할까요?
Mom	우선 약을 먹어야 해.

1) Jenny에 대해 사실이 아닌 것은?
  ★a. 목이 아프다.   b. 감기에 걸렸다.
    c. 열이 있다.   d. 두통이 있다.

2) Jenny의 엄마가 다음에 할 일은?
    a. 의사에게 전화할 것이다.
  ★b. 학교 출석 담당자에게 전화할 것이다.
    c. 의사에게 진찰받으러 갈 것이다.
    d. 차를 가져올 것이다.

Dictation   p. 124

1. What's the problem, eat, sleep, I don't feel, I don't think so, check
2. must feel terrible, bitten by, getting better, that is not good
3. feel, bad, couldn't, because of the flu, I have a fever
4. what's up, what's wrong, study for, strong headache, It's getting better
5. be late, I caught a cold, bad headache, Go back to sleep, to see the doctor, medicine

UNIT 16
How was the date?

1. 좋은 경험 : great, wonderful, fun, exciting, lucky
   나쁜 경험 : terrible, unhappy, sad, boring,
              disappointing

2. 1. d   2. e   3. a   4. f   5. b   6. c

1. 단어들을 알맞은 제목 아래에 나열하시오.

굉장한	끔찍한	지겨운	즐거운	흥분되는
기분 나쁜	운 좋은	슬픈	경이로운	실망스러운

2. 질문을 답과 연결시키시오.

1. 주말 어땠어?   d. 좋았어. 잘 쉬었어.
2. 영화 어땠어?   e. 재미있었어. 배우가 좋았어.
3. 파티 재미있었니?   a. 응, 재미있었어.
4. John이랑 무엇을 했니?   f. 춤을 췄어.
5. 어디에 갔었니?   b. 해변에 갔어.
6. 어디에 있었니?   c. 집에 있었어.

Listening Task   p. 126~127

Listening 1		1. b	2. a	3. a	4. b
Listen Again	A	1. b	2. c	3. c	
	B	4. b			
Listening 2		1. b	2. b	3. c	4. b
Listen Again	A	1. c	2. c	3. c	
	B	4. a			

Listening 1   p. 126

이야기와 어울리는 그림을 고르시오.

스크립트

1.
The trip? It was great. The weather was perfect, the food was delicious and the people were nice. The best part was the famous museums and all the beautiful paintings in there. I was so happy.

2.
How was my weekend? It was another long day. I cleaned the house, did the laundry and

cooked the meals. Of course I didn't do everything alone. My family helped me. But still I had so many things to do.

3.
Yesterday was a bad day, no, a terrible day. First, I overslept in the morning. My alarm clock was dead. I skipped breakfast and hurried to school. On the way to school, it began to rain. I got wet and I caught a cold.

4.
My weekend? It was wonderful. I had a date with a beautiful girl. We had so much in common and it was great talking to her. We had so much fun together and decided to meet again. I felt like I was walking on the clouds.

해석

1. 여행? 멋졌어. 날씨가 완벽했고, 음식도 맛있었어. 그리고 사람들도 좋았어. 제일 좋았던 것은 유명한 박물관과 그 안의 모든 아름다운 그림들이었어. 정말 행복했어.

2. 주말 어땠냐고? 또 다른 긴 하루였어. 나는 집을 청소하고, 빨래를 하고, 그리고 식사를 준비했어. 물론 나 혼자 다 한 건 아니야. 가족들이 나를 도와주었어. 그러나 여전히 내가 해야 할 일들이 많았어.

3. 어제는 나쁜, 아니, 끔찍한 하루였어. 우선, 나는 아침에 늦잠을 잤어. 내 자명종 시계가 멈췄던 거야. 나는 아침을 거르고 서둘러 학교에 갔어. 학교에 가는 길에 비가 오기 시작했어. 나는 젖었고 감기에 걸렸어.

4. 주말? 굉장했어. 아름다운 여자 아이와 데이트를 했어. 우리는 통하는 데가 많았고, 아주 즐거운 대화를 했어. 너무 재미있게 보내서, 다시 만나기로 결정했어. 하늘을 나는 것 같은 기분이었어.

Listen Again   p. 126

A. 다시 듣고 알맞은 답을 고르시오.

1. 여행에서 그가 가장 좋아했던 것은 무엇인가?
   a. 음식
   ★b. 박물관
   c. 사람들

2. 그녀의 주말에 대해 일치하지 않는 것은?
   a. 집안일을 많이 했다.
   b. 가족과 함께 일했다.
   ★c. 푹 쉬었다.

3. 내용과 일치하지 않는 것은?
   a. 그는 아침에 너무 늦게 일어났다.
   b. 아침밥을 못 먹었다.
   ★c. 공부를 너무 많이 해서 몸이 아프다.

4. a. ☐ 그는 여자와의 데이트가 즐거웠다. 다시 만나서 구름 위를 걷기로 했다.
   b. ★ 그는 여자와 데이트를 했는데 같이 즐겁게 보냈다. 그들을 다시 만나기로 했다.

Listening 2
p. 127

듣고 알맞은 답을 고르시오.

1. Amy는 _____.
   a. 흥분된다   ★b. 슬프다   c. 실망스럽다

2. Pat은 _____.
   a. 무섭다   ★b. 졸리다   c. 좋다

3. Jeff는 _____ 시험을 봤다.
   a. 수학   b. 영어   ★c. 과학

4. Susan은 _____ 에 시간 맞춰 갈 수가 없었다.
   a. 수업   ★b. 리허설   c. 파티

스크립트

1.
M How was the party, Amy?
W It was a farewell party, and we were all a little sad, but it was terrific. Jane cried a little. She was not ready to leave. But we had a wonderful time together.
M I am sorry I was not there.

2.
W You have sleepy eyes, Pat.
M I am sleepy. I didn't sleep very well last night.
W How come?
M I had a bad dream. Somebody chased me all night.
W Maybe you saw too many horror movies.

3.
W How was school, Jeff?
M Leave me alone. I don't want to talk about it.
W What's wrong? Did anything happen?
M I am going to fail science. I made terrible mistakes on the test.
W Oh!

4.
M You didn't show up for the rehearsal yesterday, Susan. Where were you?
W I was on the road. I got caught in a traffic jam. It was too late, and I had to return home.

M But you didn't even call me.
W I forgot my cell phone. I'm really sorry.

해석

1. M 파티 어땠어, Amy?
   W 송별 파티라서 우리 모두 조금 슬펐지만 정말 좋았어. Jane이 조금 울었어. 그녀는 떠날 준비가 안 됐어. 그러나 우리는 함께 즐거운 시간을 보냈어.
   M 내가 거기에 없던 게 유감이야.

2. W 졸린 눈이네, Pat.
   M 졸려. 지난밤에 잘 못 잤어.
   W 왜?
   M 나쁜 꿈을 꿨어. 누군가가 밤새도록 나를 쫓아왔어.
   W 네가 공포 영화를 너무 많이 봐서 그런지도 몰라.

3. W 학교 어땠어, Jeff?
   M 날 혼자 내버려 둬요. 말하고 싶지 않아요.
   W 뭐가 잘못됐어? 무슨 일이라도 있었어?
   M 전 과학에서 낙제할 거예요. 시험에서 끔찍한 실수를 해버렸어요.
   W 오!

4. M Susan, 너 어제 리허설에 안 나왔더라. 어디 있었니?
   W 나는 도로에 있었어. 길이 막히는 바람에 너무 늦어서 집에 돌아가야 했어.
   M 그렇지만 너는 전화도 하지 않았잖아.
   W 내 휴대폰을 깜빡했어. 정말 미안해.

Listen Again
p. 127

A. 다시 듣고 알맞은 답을 고르시오.

1. Jane에 대한 설명으로 옳지 않은 것은?
   a. 슬펐다.   b. 울었다.   ★c. 떠날 준비가 되어 있었다.

2. Pat에 대한 설명으로 옳은 것은?
   a. 그는 공포 영화를 좋아하지 않는다.
   b. 밤에 누군가가 그를 쫓아왔다.
   ★c. 그는 어젯밤에 제대로 못 잤다.

3. Jeff에게 무슨 일이 있었는가?
   a. 자퇴했다.   b. 친구와 싸웠다.   ★c. 시험에서 실수를 했다.

B. 다시 듣고 맞는 문장을 고르시오.

4. a. ★ Susan은 차가 막혀서 리허설에 참석하지 못했다.
   b. ☐ Susan은 휴대 전화를 잊고 와서 리허설에 참석하지 못했다.

스크립트

a. Susan didn't show up for the rehearsal because she was caught in a traffic jam.
b. Susan didn't show up for the rehearsal because she forgot her cell phone.

Review	p. 128

1. How, okay, different, again
2. date, movie, fun, seem
3. Did, have, boring, happened
4. great, way, traffic, late, tired
5. wrong, mistakes, Why, well

※ 듣고 빈칸을 채우시오.

해석

1. M 데이트 어땠어? 말해 봐.

   W 괜찮았어. 그는 잘생기고 매우 친절했어. 그러나 우리는 너무 달라. 나는 그와 다시 데이트하고 싶지 않아.

   M 오⋯⋯.

2. 어젯밤에 Brian하고 데이트를 했어. 우리는 영화를 보러 갔어. 재미있었어. 그런데 Brian은 별로인 것 같더라. 계속 하품을 하더라고.

3. W 즐거운 주말 보냈니?

   M 응, 너는 어때?

   W 내 인생에서 가장 지루한 주말을 보냈어. 나는 집에 혼자 있었고, 아무 일도 일어나지 않았어.

4. 콘서트는 훌륭했어. 굉장히 재미있었어. 그러나 집으로 오는 길에 교통 체증에 걸렸어. 집에 너무 늦게 도착해서 나는 매우 피곤했어.

5. W 수학에서 D를 받았더구나. 뭐가 잘못된 거니?

   M 시험에서 심각한 실수를 했어요.

   W 왜?

   M 몸이 안 좋았어요.

On Your Own	p. 129

LISTEN & WRITE

듣고 질문을 써 보세요.

스크립트

How was your weekend?
How was your day yesterday?
How was school today?
What did you do yesterday after school?

해석
주말은 어땠습니까?
어제 하루는 어땠습니까?
오늘 학교 생활은 어땠습니까?
어제 수업을 마치고 무엇을 했습니까?

PRONUNCIATION

/ ð / vs / θ /
☞ 듣고 따라해 보시오. 그들, 저것, 그때, 거기, 이것, 아버지
☞ 듣고 따라해 보시오. 감사, 1000, 목마른, 주제, 극장, 수학
☞ 잘 듣고 차이점을 발견해 보시오. 그들 / 감사, 저것 / 1000, 그때/목마른, 거기 / 주제, 이것 / 극장, 아버지 / 수학

잘 듣고 빈칸을 채우시오.

1. father, theater   2. There, there   3. thousand, that
4. Math   5. thirsty

해석
1. 우리 아버지는 극장에 갈 것이다.
2. 그곳에는 아무도 없다.
3. 천 명이 이미 그 영화를 봤다.
4. 수학은 내가 가장 좋아하는 과목이다.
5. 뭘 좀 마셔도 될까요? 전 정말 목이 말라요.

Practice Test	p. 130~131

1. 1) b   2) c
2. 1) b   2) baseball, window, bathroom, one
3. 1) b   2) c   4. 1) b   2) c
5. 1) 2, 3, 1   2) d

※ 듣고 알맞은 답을 고르시오.

1. 두 소년이 이야기하고 있다.

스크립트

Jason	How was your weekend, Bill?
Bill	Terrific!
Jason	How come?
Bill	I won the first place on the Internet quiz show.
Jason	Wow! What was the prize?
Bill	Three game CDs and 50 dollars.
Jason	Great! Can I play the games with you today?
Bill	Sure.

해석

Jason	주말 어떻게 지냈어, Bill?
Bill	굉장했어!
Jason	어땠는데?
Bill	인터넷 퀴즈 쇼에서 1등 했어.

Jason   와! 상이 뭐였어?

Bill   게임 CD 세 개랑 50달러.

Jason   잘 됐네! 오늘 그 게임 같이 해도 돼?

Bill   물론이지.

1) Bill의 주말은 어떠했는가?
     a. 끔찍했다.   ★b. 굉장했다.   c. 지루했다.   d. 바빴다.

2) 대화 내용과 일치하는 것은?
     a. Bill은 TV 퀴즈 쇼에서 일등을 했다.
     b. 상품은 게임 CD뿐이었다.
   ★c. 그들은 오늘 게임을 할 것이다.

2. 다음은 Jeff의 일기이다.

스크립트

Today, I was playing baseball. I hit a ball and it broke my neighbor's window. My neighbor Mr. Grumble was so angry and he called my mom. My mom told me to pay for the broken window. I said I didn't have any money. Then she said I could clean the bathroom for a week. I had no other choice.

해석

오늘 나는 야구를 하고 있었다. 내가 때린 공이 이웃집 창문을 깼다. 이웃집의 Grumble 씨는 너무 화가 나서 우리 엄마에게 전화했다. 엄마는 나한테 깨진 창문 값을 물어내라고 했다. 난 돈이 하나도 없다고 했다. 그러자 엄마는 일주일 동안 화장실 청소를 하라고 했다. 별수 없다.

1) Jeff는 지금 기분이 어떠한가?
     a. 기쁘다.   ★b. 기분 나쁘다.   c. 굉장하다.   d. 흥분된다 .

2) 알맞은 말에 동그라미 치시오.
     Jeff는 오늘 (야구 / 농구)를 하고 있었다. 이웃집 (문 / 창문)을 깼다. 이제 그는 (일 / 이)주일 동안 (차고 / 화장실) 청소를 해야 한다.

3. Amy는 친구와 이야기하고 있다.

스크립트

M   Hi, Amy! How was the camping trip?

W   It was totally sleepless.

M   You had a wonderful time all night, didn't you?

W   No. We were playing games and telling jokes. Then we heard some animal sounds. The animals howled all night. It was so scary.

해석

M   안녕, Amy! 캠프 어땠어?

W   잠을 전혀 못 잤어.

M   밤새도록 엄청 재미있었구나?

W   아니. 게임도 하고 농담도 하고 있었지. 그러다 동물 울음소리가 들렸어. 밤새 울더라. 너무 무서웠어.

1) 캠프 여행은 어땠는가?
     a. 재미있었다.   ★b. 무서웠다.
     c. 흥분됐다.   d. 굉장했다.

2) 왜 캠프에 가서 잠을 못 잤는가?
     a. 밤새 농담을 하고 놀아서
     b. 밤새 게임을 해서
   ★c. 밤새 동물 울음소리를 들어서
     d. 동물을 봐서

4. Sophie는 엄마를 만난다.

스크립트

Sophie   Hi, mom!

Mom   Hi, sweetie! Aren't you tired from your trip?

Sophie   Actually, I am. I was in the plane for 11 hours and I couldn't sleep at all.

Mom   Too bad. Did you have a good time in Mexico?

Sophie   Yeah, it was amazing. I learned so many things.

Mom   I'm glad to hear that. Let's go home.

Sophie   Yeah, I'm starving.

Mom   How was the food there?

Sophie   Spicy and hot. But I loved it.

해석

Sophie   잘 지내셨어요, 엄마!

Mom   어이구, 우리 딸! 여행에서 돌아와서 피곤하지 않니?

Sophie   사실 좀 그래요. 비행기에서 11시간을 있었는데 잠을 한숨도 못 잤어요.

Mom   저런. 멕시코에서 재미있었니?

Sophie   네, 굉장했어요. 배운 것도 많고요.

Mom   그랬다니 기쁘구나. 집에 가자.

Sophie   네, 배가 너무 고파요.

Mom   그곳 음식은 어땠니?

Sophie   자극적이고 매워요. 하지만 맛있었어요.

1) 이 대화는 어디에서 이루어지고 있는 것인가?
     a. 식당   ★b. 공항
     c. 그들의 집   d. 비행기

2) 이 상황에 대해 사실이 아닌 것은?
     a. Sophie는 방금 여행에서 돌아왔다.
     b. Sophie는 멕시코에서의 요리를 즐겼다.
   ★c. Sophie는 장거리 비행을 즐겼다.
     d. Sophie 여행을 하는 동안 좋은 경험을 했다.

5. Jim이 일기장에 쓴 글이다.

Dear Diary,
I had the most terrible day ever. I woke up from a bad dream. I missed the bus, so I was late for school. You think this sounds bad? It got even worse. I came home and realized I had forgotten my keys. I had to wait in the rain until my mom came back from her office. I'm just glad this day is over now.

해석
일기장에게,
가장 끔찍한 하루였어. 난 악몽에서 깨어났어. 버스를 놓쳐서 학교에 늦어버렸어. 이게 안 좋다고 생각하지? 더 나쁜 일이 있었어. 집에 와서 열쇠를 잊었다는 걸 알았어. 빗속에서 엄마가 사무실에서 돌아오실 때까지 기다려야 했지. 이제 오늘 하루가 끝났다니 기쁠 뿐이야.

1) Jim에게 일어난 일을 순서대로 배열하시오.

버스를 놓쳤다.	(2)
집에 들어갈 수 없었다.	(3)
악몽을 꾸었다.	(1)

2) Jim이 느낄 기분으로 가장 적절하지 <u>않은</u> 것은?
   a. 지친   b. 슬픈   c. 행복하지 않은   ★d. 굉장한

Dictation   p. 132

1. Terrific, Internet, What was, dollars, Can I play

2. I was playing baseball, window, so angry, my mom, I didn't, bathroom, other choice

3. How was the camping, a wonderful time, We were playing, animal sounds, scary

4. Aren't you tired, was in the plane, sleep, a good time, it was amazing, to hear, starving, I loved it

5. terrible day, a bad dream, school, this sounds bad, worse, keys, in the rain, came back from, this day

The best preparation for Listening

The best preparation for Listening is an integrated listening textbook series
that allows students to improve in the four-language skills.
Students will experience situations in which they can relate their understanding
of the sound-based messages to other tasks, such as speaking, summarizing,
and analyzing the text-based information.

Features

- Natural and authentic listening passages
- Full-color illustrations for better comprehension
- Listening tasks that check comprehension of listening materials
- Excellent pronunciation exercises
- Extensive recycling of dictation materials to assure retention

Components

- Student Book, Level 1-4
- Answer Key with transcripts, Level 1-4
- MP3 files, Level 1-4

www.nexusEDU.kr
넥서스 초·중·고등 사이트

www.nexusbook.com
넥서스 홈페이지